Summary of Contents

DHTML Utopia
Modern Web Design Using JavaScript & DOM

by Stuart Langridge

DHTML Utopia: Modern Web Design Using JavaScript & DOM
by Stuart Langridge

Copyright © 2005 SitePoint Pty. Ltd.

Managing Editor: Simon Mackie

Technical Director: Kevin Yank

Technical Editor: Simon Willison

Technical Editor: Nigel McFarlane

Editor: Georgina Laidlaw

Printing History:

First Edition: May 2005

Index Editor: Bill Johncocks

Cover Designer: Julian Carroll

Cover Illustrator: Lucas Licata

Latest Update: May 2005

Notice of Rights

Notice of Liability

Trademark Notice

Published by SitePoint Pty. Ltd.

424 Smith Street Collingwood
VIC Australia 3066.
Web: www.sitepoint.com
Email: business@sitepoint.com

ISBN 0–9579218–9–6
Printed and bound in the United States of America

About the Author

Stuart Langridge has been playing with the Web since 1994, and is quite possibly the only person in the world to have a BSc in Computer Science and Philosophy. He invented the term "unobtrusive DHTML," and has been a leader in the quest to popularize this new approach to scripting. When not working on the Web, he's a keen Linux user and part of the team at open-source radio show LUGRadio. He likes drinking decent beers, studying stone circles and other ancient phenomena, and trying to learn the piano. Stuart contributes to Stylish Scripting: SitePoint's DHTML and CSS Blog.

About The Technical Editors

Simon Willison is a seasoned Web developer from the UK, with a reputation for pioneering in the fields of CSS and DHTML. He specializes in both client- and server-side development, and recently became a member of the Web Standards project. Visit him at http://simon.incutio.com/, and at Stylish Scripting: SitePoint's DHTML and CSS Blog, to which he contributes.

Nigel McFarlane is the Mozilla community's regular and irregular technical commentator. He is the author of *Firefox Hacks* (O'Reilly Media) and *Rapid Application Development with Mozilla* (Prentice Hall PTR). When not working for SitePoint, Nigel writes for a number of trade publications and for the print media. He also consults to industry and government. Nigel's background is in science and technology, and in Web-enabled telecommunications software. He resides in Melbourne, Australia.

About The Technical Director

As Technical Director for SitePoint, Kevin Yank oversees all of its technical publications—books, articles, newsletters and blogs. He has written over 50 articles for SitePoint on technologies including PHP, XML, ASP.NET, Java, JavaScript and CSS, but is perhaps best known for his book, *Build Your Own Database Driven Website Using PHP & MySQL*, also from SitePoint. Kevin now lives in Melbourne, Australia. In his spare time he enjoys flying light aircraft and learning the fine art of improvised acting. Go you big red fire engine!

About SitePoint

SitePoint specializes in publishing fun, practical, and easy-to-understand content for Web professionals. Visit http://www.sitepoint.com/ to access our books, newsletters, articles and community forums.

*For Sam, who doesn't know
what all this is about, but
listens anyway.*

Table of Contents

Introduction

In a single decade, the Web has evolved from a simple method of delivering technical documents to an essential part of daily life, making and breaking relationships and fortunes along the way. "Looking something up on the Internet," by which is almost always meant the Web, is now within reach of almost anyone living in a first-world country, and the idea of conducting conversations and business (and probably orchestras) in your Web browser is no longer foreign, but part of life.

As Joe Average grows more used to the technology, he demands more: more information, more ease-of-use, more functionality, more interactivity. And here we are, ready to provide, because he (and we) wants it, and because it's fun. (One of those fortunes mentioned earlier wouldn't go amiss, either.) As the Web becomes a major (if not *the* major) application development platform, there's a greater need to give Websites the flexibility and power that client-side applications can provide. More importantly, even the simplest Website can benefit from a little interactivity here and there—making it better, more responsive, or easier to use. HTML, the workhorse, manages some of this; CSS adds a few more tricks and a breadth of possibility for the designer. For true flexibility and interactivity, though, we need scripting.

Browser scripting has a long, albeit rather undistinguished, history. From the earliest popup boxes, through rollover images, and into scrolling status bars, it has provided the means to add that touch of the dynamic—even if it wasn't used for anything very exciting. But, all the while, a quiet movement was building. The JavaScript language was refined and made more powerful; the very building blocks of the Website were made available for manipulation; the real communicative strengths of the Web were given form and the potential for use. Modern scripting—DOM scripting—is a quantum leap away from the way things were.

In this book, I'll be explaining how you can get your hands dirty with all this juicy scripting goodness, and make your sites truly come alive. From the first moment in which you use JavaScript to examine the structure of the page that contains that JavaScript, a huge vista of potential really does open up before you. The techniques described in this book will help you make your sites more dynamic and more usable. They'll assist you to overcome browser limitations and add new functions, and occasionally, to do one or two cool things.

Who Should Read This Book?

This book is aimed at people who have built Websites before. Although I'll briefly cover HTML and CSS, you should already have experience working with these technologies. Some experience with JavaScript might also be useful, but it is by no means critical: modern scripting techniques are sometimes quite different than "old-style" JavaScript.

By the time you've read the whole book, you'll have a clear understanding of how to build your sites so that you can easily hook DHTML scripts into them; you'll know how to work in a cross-browser and cross-platform way; lastly, you will understand the power and flexibility that can be brought to your sites through DOM enhancements.

What's In This Book?

The book comprises ten chapters. The chapters do build on one another, so if this is your first time working with DOM techniques, you might want to read them in order. Once you have some experience with the DOM, hopping around to refresh your memory on various points may suit you best.

Chapter 1: *DHTML Technologies*
> To successfully write DOM scripts, a few essential basics—which most readers of this book will already know—are required. In this first chapter, I'll quickly run through the essentials of HTML, CSS, and JavaScript. This chapter is worth reading, because it's critical for good scripting that your HTML and CSS are valid and well-structured; this chapter tells you what that means.

Chapter 2: *The Document Object Model*
> DOM scripting requires a deep understanding of the DOM—the Document Object Model—itself. Everything else builds on this knowledge. In this chapter, I'll explain what the DOM is, how it can be manipulated, and what such manipulations make possible.

Chapter 3: *Handling DOM Events*
> Events occur when the user does something with your HTML document: clicks a link, loads a page, or moves the mouse. In order to make your sites interactive—to react to user input—you will need to work with such events. Here, I explain what events are, show how to attach your code to them, and reveal some of the complexities inherent in DOM events.

Chapter 4: *Detecting Browser Features*
Not every Web browser supports the features required to use DOM code effectively; those that do offer various levels of DOM support. Feature sniffing is the name given to a set of techniques that have been designed to ensure that your DOM code operates only in browsers that understand it; this eradicates situations in which your sites work—but not as you expected!—and avoids the dreaded JavaScript error box.

Chapter 5: *Animation*
Animation can be a key to improving a site's usability; letting the user know when something's happening, or that something has changed, can enhance the user experience, and be of great value to your site's success. In this chapter, I describe how to add animation to your pages using DOM scripting techniques—and how to ensure that animation works across different browsers.

Chapter 6: *Forms and Validation*
Any reasonably-sized Website will contain at least a few forms to collect user input. Scripting can provide some serious improvements to these forms: the validation of user input, ease-of-use for users, the collection of better feedback, and so on. Forms are built from HTML, like everything else, but the DOM can be said to apply to them more than it does to other elements, because forms have such a wide range of actions that you can manipulate in your scripts.

Chapter 7: *Advanced Concepts and Menus*
In this chapter, we look at a more complex script: a multilevel animated dropdown menu. The chapter describes the code required to build such a script, pulling the techniques described in previous chapters together into a single, real-world example that demonstrates how much power the DOM provides, and how much easier it can be to work with than previous DHTML methods for achieving the same tasks.

Chapter 8: *Remote Scripting*
While DOM scripting alone is an extremely useful tool, it can be made more powerful still with a little assistance from the server. In this chapter, we explore how your scripts can retrieve dynamic content from the server, and integrate that content with the site, eliminating the need for constant page refreshes.

Chapter 9: *Communicating With The Server*
Communication with the server doesn't mean simply that the server hands out data. Your scripts can also pass data back, and engage in a real dialogue:

sending back a "something interesting has happened!" message can make your Websites work much more like real dynamic applications. This chapter enlarges on the previous one, describing the full power that server communication can create.

Chapter 10: *DOM Alternatives: XPath*
JavaScript offers opportunities for more advanced work through its integration with other technologies. In this final chapter, I describe two of those integrations: using XPath to work with XML, and integrating your DOM scripts with Flash.

Whither XHTML?

Some people may wonder why all the examples in this book are HTML 4.01 Strict. "Why are you using HTML?" they ask. "Why not XHTML? It's all, y'know, XML and stuff! It *must* be better."

There is a reason: using XHTML can cause a lot of upgrade issues, particularly with the DHTML that we use in this book.

If you choose XHTML, then you're placed in a "complete upgrade or do nothing" position. When XHTML is served to an ordinary browser, that browser will treat your lovely XML-compliant XHTML as perfectly ordinary HTML, unless you make a special effort to do things differently. XHTML treated as ordinary HTML removes all the supposed benefits of XHTML; it's not checked for well-formedness by the browser, for example.

The special effort that you need to make is to change the MIME type with which your Web server serves your XHTML document. By default, Web servers will serve it as `text/html`, which means that it will be treated as "tag soup" HTML, without enjoying any of the XHTML benefits, as mentioned above. Moreover, Ian "Hixie" Hickson, who's part of both the Mozilla and Opera teams as well as the CSS working group, has laid out a set of objections[1] which states that XHTML should not be served as `text/html` at all.

In order to have a browser treat your XHTML as XHTML (and thence as XML), rather than as tag soup, it must be served with MIME type `application/xhtml+xml`. Unfortunately, Internet Explorer (for one, and it's not alone) does not support XHTML documents served as `application/xhtml+xml`; it will

---

[1] http://www.hixie.ch/advocacy/xhtml

give you a "download this document" dialog rather than displaying it in the browser. That's a disaster for most Web pages.

It's possible to have the Web server detect whether the user's browser can cope with `application/xhtml+xml` and serve with an appropriate MIME type: `text/html` for those browsers that do not support `application/xhtml+xml`. (Remember that serving XHTML as `text/html` is wrong, according to Hixie's objections above.) But, even in those browsers that do support `application/xhtml+xml`, and therefore parse your XHTML document as it should be parsed, there are still other problems that take some getting around.

Here are a few examples. CSS in properly-parsed XHTML documents works differently: selectors are case-sensitive, and setting backgrounds and the like on the `body` doesn't propagate those styles up to the document as it does in HTML (the styles must be set on `html` instead).

Most importantly for *this* book, XHTML makes using DOM scripting pretty awkward. The HTML collections `document.images`, `document.forms`, `document.links`, and so on, do not exist in many browsers' implementations of the XHTML DOM. Arguably, one should avoid using these anyway in preparation for XHTML later. Instead, you must use `document.getElementsByTagName` appropriately. The element names in the DOM are also case-sensitive (and always lowercase, since XML element names are lowercase and XHTML is XML). That can be a bit of coding style trap. You also can't use `document.write` at all, although you probably should avoid it anyway, for reasons I'll explain in this book.

These are not major problems, and if you're into standards then most of these issues won't affect your code anyway, but a final issue remains: you can't use `document.createElement` to create new elements with the DOM. Instead, because XHTML is XML, and therefore supports namespaces, you must create each element specifically within the XHTML namespace. So, instead of using `document.createElement('a')`, to create a new `a` element, you must use `document.createElementNS('http://www.w3.org/1999/xhtml', 'a')`.

Of course, you must only use `document.createElementNS` when your document is being parsed as XHTML—not when it's being parsed as HTML (as in Internet Explorer)—so you'll need to detect which case you're dealing with, and change what the script does appropriately.

In short, using XHTML right now provides very little in the way of benefits, but brings with it a fair few extra complications. HTML 4.01 Strict is just as "valid" as XHTML—XHTML did not replace HTML but sits alongside it. It's just as easy to validate an HTML 4.01 page as it is to validate an XHTML page. I've used HTML 4.01 Strict for all the examples in this book, and I recommend that you use it, too.

Mark Pilgrim has written in more detail about using XHTML[2] and the problems that lie therein. For this book, we're sticking with tried-and-true HTML 4.01.

The Book's Website

Located at http://www.sitepoint.com/books/dhtml1/, the Website supporting this book will give you access to the following facilities:

The Code Archive

As you progress through the text, you'll note that most of the code listings are labelled with filenames, and a number of references are made to the code archive. This is a downloadable ZIP archive that contains complete code for all the examples presented in this book.

Updates and Errata

The Errata page on the book's Website will always have the latest information about known typographical and code errors, and necessary updates for changes to technologies.

The SitePoint Forums

While I've made every attempt to anticipate any questions you may have, and answer them in this book, there is no way that *any* book could cover everything there is to know about DHTML. If you have a question about anything in this book, the best place to go for a quick answer is http://www.sitepoint.com/forums/—SitePoint's vibrant and knowledgeable community.

The SitePoint Newsletters

In addition to books like this one, SitePoint offers free email newsletters.

---

[2] http://www.xml.com/pub/a/2003/03/19/dive-into-xml.html

The SitePoint Tech Times covers the latest news, product releases, trends, tips, and techniques for all technical aspects of Web development. The long-running *SitePoint Tribune* is a biweekly digest of the business and moneymaking aspects of the Web. Whether you're a freelance developer looking for tips to score that dream contract, or a marketing major striving to keep abreast of changes to the major search engines, this is the newsletter for you. *The SitePoint Design View* is a monthly compilation of the best in Web design. From new CSS layout methods to subtle PhotoShop techniques, SitePoint's chief designer shares his years of experience in its pages.

Browse the archives or sign up to any of SitePoint's free newsletters at http://www.sitepoint.com/newsletter/.

Your Feedback

If you can't find your answer through the forums, or you wish to contact me for any other reason, the best place to write is books@sitepoint.com. We have a well-manned email support system set up to track your inquiries, and if our support staff are unable to answer your question, they send it straight to me. Suggestions for improvement as well as notices of any mistakes you may find are especially welcome.

Acknowledgements

The two Simons, Simon Mackie, my editor, and Simon Willison, my expert reviewer, deserve quite an enormous vote of thanks. This book would not be anywhere near as good as it is without them.

I'd also like to raise a hand to the Web development community: there are people everywhere diving into these new technologies with gusto, establishing guidelines, making discoveries, and revealing hitherto unsuspected truths about how cool all this stuff is. Keep it up. We're fixing the world, and I'm proud to be a part of it.

1

DHTML Technologies

The White Rabbit put on his spectacles. 'Where shall I begin, please your Majesty?' he asked. 'Begin at the beginning,' the King said gravely, 'and go on till you come to the end: then stop.'
—Lewis Carroll, *Alice's Adventures in Wonderland*

Dynamic HTML, called DHTML for short, is the name given to a set of Web development techniques that are mostly used in Web pages that have non-trivial user-input features. DHTML means manipulating the Document Object Model of an HTML document, fiddling with CSS directives in style information, and using client-side JavaScript scripting to tie everything together.

In this introductory chapter, I'll provide a brief overview of some of the things you'll need to know about: the building blocks that make up DHTML Websites. You'll find it useful reading if you need to refresh your memory. If you already know all these details, you might want to flick through the chapter anyway; you may even be a little surprised by some of it. In the coming pages, we'll come to understand that DHTML is actually a combination of proper HTML for your content, Cascading Style Sheets for your design, and JavaScript for interactivity. Mixing these technologies together can result in a humble stew or a grandiose buffet. It's all in the art of cooking, so let's start rattling those pots and pans!

HTML Starting Points

Websites are written in HTML. If you're reading this book, you'll almost certainly know what HTML is and will probably be at least somewhat experienced with it. For a successful DHTML-enhanced Website, it's critical that your HTML is two things: valid and semantic. These needs may necessitate a shift away from your previous experiences writing HTML. They may also require a different approach than having your preferred tools write HTML for you.

Step up to Valid HTML

A specific set of rules, set out in the HTML recommendation[1], dictate how HTML should be written. HTML that complies with these rules is said to be "valid." Your HTML needs to be valid so that it can be used as a foundation on which you can build DHTML enhancements. While the set of rules is pretty complex, you can ensure that your HTML is valid by following a few simple guidelines.

Correctly Nest Tags

Don't let tags "cross over" one another. For example, don't have HTML that looks like the snippet shown below:

```
Here is some <strong>bold and <em>italic</strong> text</em>.
```

Here, the `<strong>` and `<em>` tags cross over one another; they're incorrectly nested. Nesting is extremely important for the proper use of DHTML. In later chapters of this book, we'll study the DOM tree, and the reasons why incorrect nesting causes problems will become clear. For now, simply remember that if you cross your tags, each browser will interpret your code in a different way, according to different rules (rather than according to the standard). Any hope of your being able to control the appearance and functionality of your pages across browsers goes right out the window unless you do this right.

Close Container Tags

Tags such as `<strong>` or `<p>`, which contain other items, should always be closed with `</strong>` or `</p>`, or the appropriate closing tag. It's important to know which tags contain things (e.g. text or other tags) and to make sure you close

---

[1] http://www.w3.org/TR/html4/

them. <p>, for example, doesn't mean "put a paragraph break here," but "a paragraph begins here," and should be paired with </p>, "this paragraph ends here."[1] The same logic applies to <li> tags as well.

Always Use a Document Type

A document type (or DOCTYPE) describes the dialect of HTML that's been used; there are several different options. In this book, we'll use the dialect called HTML 4.01 Strict.[2] Your DOCTYPE, which should appear at the very top of every HTML page, should look like this:

```
<!DOCTYPE HTML PUBLIC "-//W3C//DTD HTML 4.01//EN"
    "http://www.w3.org/TR/html4/strict.dtd">
```

That information can be typed on a single line, or with a line break after EN". Don't worry, for the moment, about what this means: just be sure to place it at the top of every page. The article *Fix Your Site With the Right DOCTYPE!*[2], published on A List Apart[3], lists all the DOCTYPEs you might want to use, and why you'd need to use them at all. I visit that article all the time to cut and paste the one I need!

Validate your Page

The most important page creation step is to check that your HTML is valid. There are numerous tools that you can download and run on your own computer to test your code's validity—some HTML editors even have such tools built in—or you can use one of the many online validators, the most common of which is the W3C's own validator[4]. A validator will tell you how you need to adjust your HTML in order to make it compatible with DHTML techniques. The ultimate reference for what constitutes valid HTML is the HTML recommendation[5]. It's complex and detailed, but if you have any questions about how HTML should be written, or whether a tag really exists, you'll find the answers there. As mentioned above, browsers rely on a standard that describes how validated HTML

---

[1]Those who know what they're doing with container tags will be aware that HTML 4.01 does not actually require that all container tags are closed (though XHTML still does). However, it's never invalid to close a container tag, though it is sometimes invalid to not do so. It's considerably easier to just close everything than it is to remember which tags you're allowed to leave open.

[2]If you're thinking, "but I want to use XHTML!" then I bet you already know enough about DOC-TYPEs to use them properly.

[2] http://www.alistapart.com/articles/doctype/

[3] http://www.alistapart.com/

[4] http://validator.w3.org/

[5] http://ww.w3.org/TR/html4/

should be interpreted. However, there are no standards to describe how invalid HTML should be interpreted; each browser maker has established their own rules to fill that gap. Trying to understand each of these rules would be difficult and laborious, and you have better things to do with your time. Sticking to valid HTML means that any problems you find are deemed to be bugs in that browser—bugs that you may be able to work around. Thus, using valid HTML gives you more time to spend with your family, play snooker, etc. which, if you ask me, is a good reason to do it.

Step up to Semantic HTML

In addition to its validity, your HTML should be semantic, not presentational. What this means is that you should use HTML tags to describe the nature of an element in your document, rather than the appearance of that element. So don't use a `<p>` tag if you mean, "put a blank line here." Use it to mean, "a paragraph begins here" (and place a `</p>` at the end of that paragraph). Don't use `<blockquote>` to mean, "indent this next bit of text." Use it to mean, "this block is a quotation." If you mark up your HTML in this way, you'll find it much easier to apply DHTML techniques to it further down the line. This approach is called **semantic markup**—a fancy way of saying, "uses tags to describe meaning."

Let's look at a few example snippets. First, imagine your Website has a list of links to different sections. That list should be marked up on the basis of what it is: a list. Don't make it a set of `<a>` tags separated by `<br>` tags; it's a list, so it should be marked up as such, using `<ul>` and `<li>` tags. It might look something like this:

```
<ul>
  <li><a href="index.html">Home</a></li>
  <li><a href="about.html">About this Website</a></li>
  <li><a href="email.html">Contact details</a></li>
</ul>
```

You'll find yourself using the `<ul>` tag a lot. Many of the items within a Website are really lists: a breadcrumb trail is a list of links, a menu structure is a list of lists of links, and a photo gallery is a list of images.

Similarly, if your list contains items with which comments are associated, maybe it should be marked up as a definition list:

```
<dl>
  <dt><a href="index.html">Home</a></dt>
    <dd>Back to the home page</dd>
```

```
<dt><a href="about.html">About this Website</a></dt>
  <dd>Why this site exists, how it was set up, and who did it
  </dd>
<dt><a href="email.html">Contact details</a></dt>
  <dd>Getting in contact with the Webmaster: email addresses
    and phone numbers</dd>
</dl>
```

Remember: the way your page looks isn't really relevant. The important part is that the information in the page is marked up in a way that describes what it is. There are lots of tags in HTML; don't think of them as a way to lay out information on your page, but as a means to define what that information means.

If you don't use HTML to control the presentation of your pages, how can you make them look the way you want them to? That's where Cascading Style Sheets come in.

Adding CSS

Cascading Style Sheets (CSS) is a technique that allows you to describe the presentation of your HTML. In essence, it allows you to state how you want each **element** on your page to look. An element is a piece of HTML that represents one thing: one paragraph, one heading, one image, one list. Elements usually correspond to a particular tag and its content. When CSS styles are used, DHTML pages can work on the appearance and the content of the page independently. That's a handy and clean separation. If you want to look good, you need to learn how to dress up *and* go to the gym regularly!

A Simple CSS Example

Imagine you want your main page heading (an <h1> tag) to be displayed in big, red, centered text. You should specify that in your style sheet as follows:

```
h1 {
  font-size: 300%;
  color: #FF0000;
  text-align: center;
}
```

See the section called "Further Reading" at the end of this chapter for some links to introductory tutorials on CSS, which should help if the above lines don't make a lot of sense to you.

Here's a simple HTML page before and after these styles have been applied:

Figure 1.1. That HTML's stylin'!

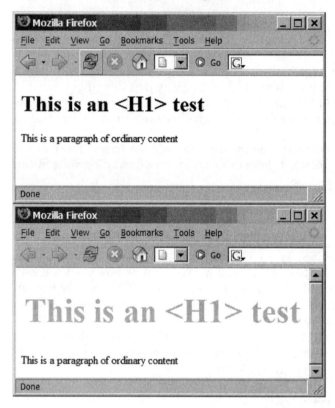

The key point here is to remove the presentation aspects from your HTML and put them into your style sheet. If , for example, you made your page heading bigger by putting `<font>` tags in your HTML, then you'd need to paste those tags into every page on which a header was used. By making your HTML semantic and moving the page's presentation into CSS, you can control the look of headings across the whole site through a single style sheet. This makes your job as Website developer much easier.

Of course, it's not quite as easy as that. Although the full definition of CSS allows you to do some fairly amazing things, and to control the presentation of your pages to a high degree, not every browser supports everything that CSS has to offer.

In order to know about the differences in browser support for CSS, you need to know what CSS can do. There are two sorts of browser incompatibilities: things that a given browser doesn't implement, and things that it implements incorrectly. Occasionally, browsers add their own "special features" as well, but we won't be worried about those in this book.

Missing implementations are relatively easy to deal with: don't rely on such rules if you want your CSS to work in browsers that have failed to implement them. This can be a pain, especially since the most commonly used browser in the world, Internet Explorer for Windows, has some serious holes in its CSS support; however, this "solution" is often a necessary compromise. Learning which rules you can and can't use is one of the steps on the path to CSS guru-hood.

Badly implemented standards are a bigger problem. In such cases, the browser gets it wrong. Another step to CSS guru-hood is understanding exactly what each browser does wrong, and how you can work around those failings. You don't need that knowledge to start with, though: you'll pick it up as you go along. Workarounds for CSS bugs in different browsers are usually achieved using CSS **hacks**. These hacks take advantage of the bugs in a browser's CSS parser to deliver it specific style sheet directives that work around its poor implementation of the standards. A huge variety of these CSS hacks is documented for each browser in various places around the Web; see the section called "Further Reading" for more.

Learning to understand and adapt to the vagaries of CSS handling in various browsers is part of the work that's required to use CSS effectively. While it can be a lot of work, many CSS bugs only become apparent with the complex use of this technology; most CSS is handled perfectly across platforms and browsers without the need for hacks or complex tests.

While CSS is powerful, it doesn't quite give us true flexibility in presentation. The capabilities of CSS increase all the time, and more "interactive" features are constantly being added to the CSS specification. However, it's not designed for building truly interactive Websites. For that, we need the final building block of DHTML: JavaScript.

Adding JavaScript

JavaScript is a simple but powerful programming language. It's used to add dynamic behavior to your Website—the D in DHTML. HTML defines the page's structure, and CSS defines how it looks, but actions, the things that happen when you interact with the page—by clicking a button, dragging an image, or moving the mouse—are defined in JavaScript. JavaScript works with the Document Object Model, described in the next chapter, to attach actions to different events (mouseovers, drags, and clicks). We're not going to describe all the gory JavaScript syntax in detail here—the section called "Further Reading" has some links to a few JavaScript tutorials if you need them.

A Simple JavaScript Example

Here's a simple piece of JavaScript that converts a text field's value to uppercase when the user tabs out of the field. First let's see the old, bad way of doing it:

File: **oldlisteners.html** (excerpt)

```
<input id="street" type="text"
    onchange="this.value = this.value.toUpperCase();">
```

In this book, we'll recommend a more modern technique. First, the HTML:

File: **newlisteners.html** (excerpt)

```
<input id="street" type="text">
```

Second, the JavaScript, which is usually located in the <head> part of the page:

File: **newlisteners.html** (excerpt)

```
<script type="text/javascript">
function uppercaseListener() {
  this.value = this.value.toUpperCase();
}

function installListeners() {
  var element = document.getElementById('street');
  element.addEventListener('change', uppercaseListener, false);
}

window.addEventListener('load', installListeners, false);
</script>
```

The first function does the work of converting the text. The second function makes sure that the first is connected to the right HTML tag. The final line performs this connection once the page has loaded in full. Although this means more code, notice how it keeps the HTML content clean and simple. In future chapters, we'll explore this kind of approach a lot. Don't worry about the mechanics too much for now—there's plenty of time for that!

Get Some Tools!

A good JavaScript development environment makes working with JavaScript far easier than it would otherwise be. Testing pages in Internet Explorer (IE) can leave something to be desired; if your page generates JavaScript errors (as it will do all the time while you're building it!), IE isn't likely to be very helpful at diagnosing where, or what, they are. The most useful, yet simple, tool for JavaScript debugging is the JavaScript Console in Mozilla or Mozilla Firefox. This console will clearly display where any JavaScript error occurs on your page, and what that error is. It's an invaluable tool when building JavaScript scripts. Mozilla Firefox works on virtually all platforms, and it's not a big download; it also offers better support for CSS than Internet Explorer, and should be part of your development toolkit. Beyond this, there's also the JavaScript debugger in Mozilla, which is named Venkman; if you're the sort of coder who has worked on large projects in other languages and are used to a debugger, Venkman can be useful, but be aware that it takes a bit of setting up. In practice, though, when you're enhancing your site with DHTML, you don't need anything as complex as a debugger; the JavaScript Console and judicious use of alert statements to identify what's going on will help you through almost every situation.

Another tool that's definitely useful is a good code editor in which to write your Website. Syntax highlighting for JavaScript is a really handy feature; it makes your code easier to read while you're writing it, and quickly alerts you when you leave out a bracket or a quote. Editors are a very personal tool, and you might have to kiss a fair few frogs before you find your prince in this regard, but a good editor will seriously speed and simplify your coding work. Plenty of powerful, customizable editors are available for free, if you don't already have a preferred program. But, if you're currently writing code in Windows Notepad, have a look at what else is available to see if any other product offers an environment that's more to your liking. You'll want syntax highlighting, as already mentioned; a way to tie in the external validation of your pages is also useful. Textpad[6] and Crimson Editor[7] are free, Windows-based editors that cover the basics if you're developing on a Windows platform; Mac users tend to swear by BBEdit[8]; Linux users have gedit or Kate or vim to do the basics, and there's always Emacs.

JavaScript is the engine on which DHTML runs. DHTML focuses on manipulating your HTML and CSS to make your page do what the user wants, and it's Java-

---

[6] http://www.textpad.com/
[7] http://www.crimsoneditor.com/
[8] http://www.barebones.com/

Script that effects that manipulation. Through the rest of this book, we'll explore that manipulation in more and more detail.

Further Reading

Try these links if you're hungry for more on CSS itself.

http://www.sitepoint.com/article/css-is-easy
SitePoint's easy introduction to the world of CSS is a great place to start.

http://www.w3schools.com/css/
W3Schools' CSS tutorials are helpful whether you're learning, or simply brushing up on your knowledge of CSS.

http://www.csszengarden.com/
The CSS Zen Garden is a marvelous demonstration of the power of Cascading Style Sheets alone. It has a real wow factor!

http://centricle.com/ref/css/filters/
This comprehensive list of CSS hacks shows you which browsers will be affected by a given hack, if you need to hide certain CSS directives (or deliver certain directives) to a particular browser.

http://www.positioniseverything.net/
This site demonstrates CSS issues in various browsers and explains how to work around them.

http://www.css-discuss.org/
The CSS-Discuss mailing list is "devoted to talking about CSS and ways to use it in the real world; in other words, practical uses and applications." The associated wiki[15] is a repository of useful tips and tricks.

http://www.sitepoint.com/books/
If you're after something more definitive, SitePoint's book, *HTML Utopia: Designing Without Tables Using CSS[17]* is a complete guide and reference for the CSS beginner. *The CSS Anthology: 101 Tips, Tricks & Hacks[18]* is a perfect choice if you prefer to learn by doing.

---

[15] http://css-discuss.incutio.com/
[17] http://www.sitepoint.com/books/css1/
[18] http://www.sitepoint.com/books/cssant1/

A lot of tutorials on the Web cover JavaScript. Some explore both DHTML and the DOM, while others do not; you should try to find the former.

http://www.sitepoint.com/article/javascript-101-1
This tutorial provides an introduction to the basics of JavaScript for the total non-programmer. Some of the techniques presented in this article aren't as modern as the alternatives presented in this book, but you'll get a good feel for the language itself.

http://www.quirksmode.org/
Peter-Paul Koch's list of JS techniques and scripts covers a considerable amount of ground in this area.

Summary

In this chapter, we've outlined the very basic building-blocks of DHTML: what HTML really is, how to arrange and display it in your documents using CSS, and how to add interactivity using JavaScript. Throughout the rest of this book, we'll look at the basic techniques you can use to start making your Websites dynamic, then move on to discuss certain advanced scripting techniques that cover specific areas. On with the show!

2

The Document Object Model

One day someone came in and observed, on the paper sticking out of one of the Teletypes, displayed in magnificent isolation, this ominous phrase:

`values of` β `will give rise to dom!`

...the phrase itself was just so striking! Utterly meaningless, but it looks like what... a warning? What is "dom?"
—Dennis M. Richie[1]

A Web page is a document. To see that document, you can either display it in the browser window, or you can look at the HTML source. It's the same document in both cases. The World Wide Web Consortium's Document Object Model (DOM) provides another way to look at that same document. It describes the document content as a set of objects that a JavaScript program can see. Naturally, this is very useful for DHTML pages on which a lot of scripting occurs. (The quote above is a pure coincidence—it's from the days before the Web!)

According to the World Wide Web Consortium[2], "the Document Object Model is a platform- and language-neutral interface that will allow programs and scripts to dynamically access and update the content, structure and style of doc-

---

[1] http://cm.bell-labs.com/cm/cs/who/dmr/odd.html
[2] http://www.w3.org/DOM/#what

uments. The document can be further processed and the results of that processing can be incorporated back into the presented page." This statement basically says that the DOM is not just a novelty—it is useful for doing things. In the coming pages, we'll take a brief look at the history of the DOM before investigating more deeply what it is and how we can use it. We'll finish up with some example scripts that demonstrate the power of this critical aspect of DHTML.

The Origins of the DOM

In Netscape Navigator 2, Netscape Communications introduced JavaScript (briefly called LiveScript), which gave Web developers scripting access to elements in their Web pages—first to forms, then, later, to images, links, and other features. Microsoft implemented JavaScript in Internet Explorer 3 (although they called it JScript) in order to keep up with Netscape.

By version 4, the two browsers had diverged significantly in terms of their respective feature sets and the access they provided to page content. Each browser manufacturer implemented its own proprietary means of providing scripting access to layers. Scripts that wanted to work in both browsers needed to contain code for each method. The ill-fated "browser wars" were all about these proprietary extensions to the Web, as each manufacturer strove to attract more developers to its platform through the lure of new features. There was little regard for cross-browser compatibility, although Microsoft copied and supported most of the early innovations made by Netscape.

While all this was taking place, the W3C developed a specification for the Document Object Model Level 1, which outlined a generic and standard method to access the various parts of an XML document using script. Since HTML can be thought of as a dialect of XML, the DOM Level 1 spec applied to HTML as well.

Both major browser manufacturers implemented the DOM Level 1 specification: in Internet Explorer 5 and in Netscape 6. The previously existing proprietary specifications were retrospectively titled; since the new standard was DOM Level 1, those old and now deprecated methods were called DOM Level 0. (Since then, the W3C has also released the DOM Level 2 and DOM Level 3 specifications, which add more features and are broken into separate modules.) There's no formal DOM Level 0 standard, though.

What is the DOM?

So, you know what the DOM *used* to be. Now let's discuss what it *is*.

Essentially, the DOM provides access to the structure of an HTML page by mapping the elements in that page to a tree of nodes. Each element becomes an element node, and each bit of text becomes a text node. Take this HTML snippet, for example:

```
<body>
  <p>
    This is a paragraph, containing
    <a href="#">
      a link
    </a>
    in the middle.
  </p>
  <ul>
    <li>
      This item has
      <em>
        some emphasized text
      </em>
      in it.
    </li>
    <li>
      This is another list item.
    </li>
  </ul>
</body>
```

I added lots of extra indenting so that you can compare this snippet with the matching DOM tree. Don't do that in real life—I'm just trying to make things clearer in this case. The matching DOM tree is shown in Figure 2.1.

As you can see, the a element, which is located inside the p element in the HTML, becomes a **child node**, or just **child**, of the p node in the DOM tree. (Symmetrically, the p node is the **parent** of the a node. The two li nodes, children of the same parent, are called **sibling nodes** or just **siblings**.)

Notice that the nesting level of each tag in the HTML markup matches the number of lines it takes to reach the same item in the DOM tree. For example, the <a> tag is nested twice inside other tags (the <p> and <body> tags), so the a node in the tree is located two lines from the top.

Figure 2.1. An example of a DOM tree.

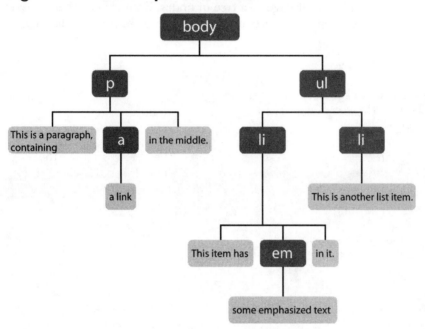

The Importance of Valid HTML

From this last example, we can see more clearly why valid HTML, including properly nested elements, is important. If elements are improperly nested, problems arise. Take the following line:

```
<strong>These <em>elements are</strong> badly nested</em>.
```

The DOM tree that results from this incorrectly nested code won't be a tree at all: it would need to be malformed in order to express the invalid element layout that this HTML requests. Each browser fixes malformed content in a different way, which can generate such horrors as an element that is its own parent node. Keeping your HTML valid avoids all these problems.

Walking DOM Trees

Trees of nodes turn up a lot in computing, because, among other things, they have a very useful property: it's easy to "walk the tree" (that is, to iterate through every one of the tree's nodes in order) with very little code. Walking a tree is easy because any element node can be considered as the top of its own little tree. Therefore, to walk through a tree, you can use a series of steps, for example:

1. Do something with the node we're looking at

2. Does this node have children? If so:

3. For each of the child nodes, go to step 1

This process is known as **recursion**, and is defined as the use of a function that calls itself. Each child is the same type of thing as the parent and can therefore be handled in the same way. We don't do much with recursion ourselves, but we rely quite heavily on the browser recursing through the page's tree. It's especially useful when it comes time to work with events, as we'll see in Chapter 3.

Finding the Top of the Tree

In order to walk the DOM tree, you need a reference to the node at its top: the root node. That "reference" will be a variable that points to the root node. The root node should be available to JavaScript as `document.documentElement`. Not all browsers support this approach, but fortunately it doesn't matter, because you'll rarely need to walk through an entire document's DOM tree starting from the root. Instead, the approach taken is to use one of the `getElementsByWhatever` methods to grab a particular part of the tree directly. Those methods start from the `window.document` object—or `document` for short.

Getting an Element from the Tree

There are two principal methods that can be used to get a particular element or set of elements. The first method, which is used all the time in DHTML programming, is `getElementById`. The second is `getElementsByTagName`. Another method, `getElementsByName`, is rarely used, so we'll look at the first two only for now.

getElementById

In HTML, any element can have a unique ID. The ID must be specified with the HTML `id` attribute:

```
<div id="codesection">
  <p id="codepara">
```

```
    </p>
    <ul>
      <li><a href="http://www.sitepoint.com/" id="splink"
          >SitePoint</a></li>
      <li><a href="http://www.yahoo.com/" id="yalink"
          >Yahoo!</a></li>
    </ul>
</div>
```

Each non-list element in that snippet has been given an ID. You should be able to spot four of them. IDs must be unique within your document—each element must have a different ID (or no ID at all)—so you can know that a specific ID identifies a given element alone. To get a reference to that element in JavaScript code, use `document.getElementById(elementId)`:

```
var sitepoint_link = document.getElementById('splink')
```

Now the variable `sitepoint_link` contains a reference to the first `<a>` tag in the above HTML snippet. We'll see a little later what you can do with that element reference. The DOM tree for this snippet of HTML is depicted in Figure 2.2.

Figure 2.2. The snippet's DOM tree.

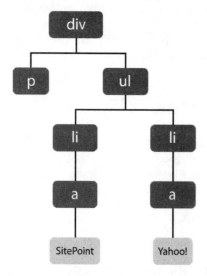

getElementsByTagName

The `document.getElementsByTagName` method is used to retrieve all elements of a particular type. The method returns an array[1] that contains all matching elements:

```
var all_links = document.getElementsByTagName('a');
var sitepoint_link = all_links[0];
```

The `all_links` variable contains an array, which contains two elements: a reference to the SitePoint link, and a reference to the Yahoo! link. The elements are returned in the order in which they are found in the HTML, so `all_links[0]` is the SitePoint link and `all_links[1]` is the Yahoo! link.

Note that `document.getElementsByTagName` always returns an array, even if only one matching element was found. Imagine we use the method as follows:

```
var body_list = document.getElementsByTagName('body');
```

To get a reference to the sole **body** element in this case, we would need to use the following:

```
var body = body_list[0];
```

We would be very surprised if `body_list.length` (the array's size) was anything other than 1, since there should be only one <body> tag! We could also shorten the process slightly by replacing the previous two lines with this one:

```
var body = document.getElementsByTagName('body')[0];
```

JavaScript allows you to collapse expressions together like this. It can make your code a lot more compact, and save you from declaring a lot of variables which aren't really used for anything.

There is another useful feature; `getElementsByTagName` is defined on any node at all, not just the document. So, to find all <a> tags in the body of the document, we could use the method like this:

```
var links_in_body = body.getElementsByTagName('a');
```

---

[1]Technically, it returns a node collection, but this works just like an array.

Note that "Element" is plural in this method's name, but singular for `getElementById`. This is a reminder that the former returns an array of elements, while the latter returns only a single element.

Walking from Parents to Children

Each node has one parent (except the root element) and may have multiple children. You can obtain a reference to a node's parent from its `parentNode` property; a node's children are found in the node's `childNodes` property, which is an array. The `childNodes` array may contain nothing if the node has no children (such nodes are called **leaf nodes**).

Suppose the variable node points to the `ul` element of the DOM tree. We can get the node's parent (the `div` element) like this:

```
parent = node.parentNode;
```

We can check if the unordered list has any list items (children) by looking at the `length` property of the `childNodes` array:

```
if (node.childNodes.length == 0) {
  alert('no list items found!');
}
```

If there are any children, their numbering starts at zero. We can obtain the second child in our example HTML (an `li` element) as follows:

```
list_item = node.childNodes[1];
```

For the special case of the first child, located here:

```
list_item = node.childNodes[0];
```

we can also use this shorthand:

```
child = node.firstChild;
```

Similarly, the last child (in this case, the second `li`) has its own special property:

```
child = node.lastChild;
```

We'll see all these properties used routinely through the rest of this book.

What to do with Elements

Now you know how to get references to elements—the nodes in your HTML page. The core of DHTML—the D-for-dynamic bit—lies in our ability to change those elements, to remove them, and to add new ones. Throughout the rest of this chapter, we'll work with the following code snippet, which we saw earlier:

```
<div id="codesection">
  <p id="codepara">
  </p>
  <ul>
    <li><a href="http://www.sitepoint.com/" id="splink"
       >SitePoint</a></li>
    <li><a href="http://www.yahoo.com/" id="yalink"
       >Yahoo!</a></li>
  </ul>
</div>
```

Changing Element Attributes

Every property of an element, and every CSS style that can be applied to it, can be set from JavaScript. The attributes that can be applied to an element in HTML—for example, the href attribute of an <a> tag—can also be set and read from your scripts, as follows:

```
// using our sitepoint_link variable from above
sitepoint_link.href = "http://www.google.com/";
```

Click on that link after the script has run, and you'll be taken to Google rather than SitePoint. The new HTML content, as it exists in the browser's imagination (the HTML file itself hasn't changed), looks like this:

```
<div id="codesection">
  <p id="codepara">
  </p>
  <ul>
    <li><a href="http://www.google.com/" id="splink"
       >SitePoint</a></li>
    <li><a href="http://www.yahoo.com/" id="yalink"
       >Yahoo!</a></li>
  </ul>
</div>
```

21

Each element has a different set of attributes that can be changed: a elements have the `href` attribute, `<img>` elements have the `src` attribute, and so on. In general, an attribute that can be applied to a tag in your HTML is also gettable and settable as a property on a node from JavaScript. So, if our code contains a reference to an `img` element, we can change the image that's displayed by altering the `img_element.src` property.[2]

The two most useful references that document elements and their supported attributes are those provided by the two major browser makers: the Microsoft DOM reference[3], and the Mozilla Foundation's DOM reference[4].

Importantly, though, when we altered our link's `href` above, all we changed was the destination for the link. The text of the link, which read "SitePoint" before, has not changed; if we need to alter that, we have to do so separately. Changing the text in a page is slightly more complex than changing an attribute; to alter text, you need to understand the concept of text nodes.

Changing Text Nodes

In Figure 2.1 above, you can see how the HTML in a document can be represented as a DOM tree. One of the important things the figure illustrates is that the text inside an element is not part of that element. In fact, the text is in a different node: a child of the element node. If you have a reference to that text node, you can change the text therein using the node's `nodeValue` property:

```
myTextNode.nodeValue = "Some text to go in the text node";
```

How can we get a reference to that text node? We need to walk the DOM tree—after all, we have to know where the text node is before we can alter it. If we consider the `sitepoint_link` node above, we can see that its `childNodes` array should contain one node: a text node with a `nodeValue` of `"SitePoint"`. We can change the value of that text node as follows:

```
sitepoint_link.childNodes[0].nodeValue = 'Google';
```

---

[2]One notable divergence from this rule is that an element's `class` attribute in HTML is available in JavaScript as `node.className`, not `node.class`. This is because "class" is a JavaScript reserved word.

[3] http://msdn.microsoft.com/workshop/author/dhtml/reference/dhtml_reference_entry.asp

[4] http://www.mozilla.org/docs/dom/domref/

Now, the text displayed on-screen for that link will read *Google*, which matches the link destination that we changed earlier. We can shorten the code slightly to the following:

```
sitepoint_link.firstChild.nodeValue = 'Google';
```

You may recall that a node's `firstChild` property, and `childNodes[0]`, both refer to the same node; in this case, you can substitute `childNodes[0]` with success. After this change, the browser will see the following document code:

```
<div id="codesection">
  <p id="codepara">
  </p>
  <ul>
    <li><a href="http://www.google.com/" id="splink"
        >Google</a></li>
    <li><a href="http://www.yahoo.com/" id="yalink"
        >Yahoo!</a></li>
  </ul>
</div>
```

Changing Style Properties

As we have seen, the attributes that are set on an HTML tag are available as properties of the corresponding DOM node. CSS style properties can also be applied to that node through the DOM, using the node's style property. Each CSS property is a property of that style property, with its name slightly transformed: a CSS property in words-and-dashes style becomes a property of style with dashes removed and all words but the first taking an initial capital letter. This is called **InterCaps format**. Here's an example. A CSS property that was named:

```
some-css-property
```

would appear to a script as the following JavaScript property:

```
someCssProperty
```

So, to set the CSS property `font-family` for our `sitepoint_link` element node, we'd use the following code:

```
sitepoint_link.style.fontFamily = 'sans-serif';
```

CSS values in JavaScript are almost always set as strings; some values, such as font-size, are strings because they must contain a dimension[3], such as "px" or "%". Only entirely numeric properties, such as z-index (which is set as node.style.zIndex, as per the above rule) may be set as a number:

```
sitepoint_link.style.zIndex = 2;
```

Many designers alter style properties to make an element appear or disappear. In CSS, the display property is used for this: if it's set to none, the element doesn't display in the browser. So, to hide an element from display, we can set its display property to none:

```
sitepoint_link.style.display = 'none';
```

To show it again, we give it another valid value:

```
sitepoint_link.style.display = 'inline';
```

For a complete reference to the available CSS style properties and what each does, see SitePoint's *HTML Utopia: Designing Without Tables Using CSS[5]*.

Bigger DOM Tree Changes

The next level of DOM manipulation, above and beyond changing the properties of elements that are already there, is to add and remove elements dynamically. Being able to change the display properties of existing elements, and to read and alter the attributes of those elements, puts a lot of power at your disposal, but the ability to dynamically create or remove parts of a page requires us to leverage a whole new set of techniques.

Moving Elements

To add an element, we must use the appendChild method of the node that will become the added node's parent. In other words, to add your new element as a child of an existing node in the document, we use that node's appendChild method:

---

[3]Internet Explorer will let you get away without using a dimension, as it assumes that a dimensionless number is actually a pixel measurement. However, do not try to take advantage of this assumption; it will break your code in other browsers, and it's in violation of the specification.
[5] http://www.sitepoint.com/books/css1/

```
// We'll add the link to the end of the paragraph
var para = document.getElementById('codepara');
para.appendChild(sitepoint_link);
```

After this, our page will look a little odd. Here's the updated HTML code:

```
<div id="codesection">
  <p id="codepara">
    <a href="http://www.google.com/" id="splink">Google</a>
  </p>
  <ul>
    <li></li>
    <li><a href="http://www.yahoo.com/" id="yalink"
        >Yahoo!</a></li>
  </ul>
</div>
```

Another useful thing to know is that, in order to move the node to its new place in the document, we don't have to *remove* it first. If you use `appendChild` to insert a node into the document, and that node already exists elsewhere in the document, the node will not be duplicated; instead, it will move from its previous location to the new location at which you've inserted it. We can do the same thing with the Yahoo! link:

```
para.appendChild(document.getElementById('yalink'));
```

After this, the page will again be rearranged to match the HTML:

```
<div id="codesection">
  <p id="codepara">
    <a href="http://www.google.com/" id="splink">Google</a>
    <a href="http://www.yahoo.com/" id="yalink">Yahoo!</a>
  </p>
  <ul>
    <li></li>
    <li></li>
  </ul>
</div>
```

Figure 2.3 shows the new DOM tree so far.

Figure 2.3. The DOM tree after changes.

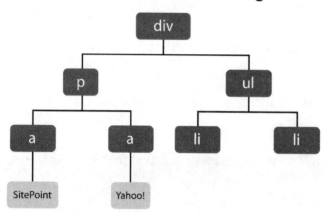

What if you didn't want to add your new (or moved) element to the end of that paragraph? In addition to `appendChild`, each node has an `insertBefore` method, which is called with two arguments: the node to insert, and the node before which it will be inserted. To move the Yahoo! link to the beginning of the paragraph, we want to insert it as a child of the paragraph that appears *before* the Google link. So, to insert the Yahoo! link (the first argument) as a child of the paragraph right before the Google link (`sitepoint_link`, the second argument), we'd use the following:

```
para.insertBefore(document.getElementById('yalink'),
    sitepoint_link);
```

Be sure that the second argument (`sitepoint_link`) really is an existing child node of `para`, or this method will fail.

Throwing Away Elements

Removing an element is very similar to the process of adding one: again, we use the `removeChild` method on the element's parent node. Remembering from earlier that we can access a given node's parent as *node*`.parentNode`, we can remove our `sitepoint_link` from the document entirely:

```
// never hurts to be paranoid: check that our node *has* a parent
if (sitepoint_link.parentNode) {
  sitepoint_link.parentNode.removeChild(sitepoint_link);
}
```

That action will change the HTML code to that shown below:

```
<div id="codesection">
  <p id="codepara">
    <a href="http://www.yahoo.com/" id="yalink">Yahoo!</a>
  </p>
  <ul>
    <li></li>
    <li></li>
  </ul>
</div>
```

 note Even after the node's removal, `sitepoint_link` still constitutes a reference to that link. It still exists, it's just not in the document any more: it's floating in limbo. We can add it back to the document somewhere else if we want to. Set the variable to `null` to make the deleted element disappear forever.

Creating Elements

Moving existing elements around within the page is a powerful and useful technique (with which you're well on the way to implementing Space Invaders or Pac Man!). But, above and beyond that, we have the ability to create brand new elements and add them to the page, providing the capacity for truly dynamic content. The point to remember is that, as before, a page's text resides in text nodes, so if we need to create an element that contains text, we must create both the new element node and a text node to contain its text. To achieve this, we need two new methods: `document.createElement` and `document.createTextNode`.

First, we create the element itself:

```
var linux_link = document.createElement('a');
```

Even though we've created the element, it's not yet part of the document. Next, we set some of its properties in the same way that we'd set properties on an existing link:

```
linux_link.href = 'http://www.linux.org/';
```

We then create the text node for the text that will appear inside the link. We pass the text for the text node as a parameter:

```
var linux_tn =
    document.createTextNode('The Linux operating system');
```

The text node is also floating around, separate from the document. We add the text node to the element's list of children, as above:

```
linux_link.appendChild(linux_tn);
```

The element and text node now form a mini-tree of two nodes (officially a **document fragment**), but they remain separate from the DOM. Finally, we insert the element into the page, which is the same as putting it into the DOM tree:

```
para.appendChild(linux_link);
```

Here's the resulting HTML:

```
<div id="codesection">
  <p id="codepara">
    <a href="http://www.yahoo.com/" id="yalink">Yahoo!</a>
    <a href="http://www.linux.org/">The Linux operating system</a>
  </p>
  <ul>
    <li></li>
    <li></li>
  </ul>
</div>
```

As you can see, to create elements, we use the same techniques and knowledge—text nodes are children of the element node, we append a child with `node.appendChild`—we use to work with nodes that are already part of the document. To the DOM, a node is a node whether it's part of the document or not: it's just a node object.

Copying Elements

Creating one element is simple, as we've seen. But what if you want to add a lot of dynamic content to a page? Having to create a whole batch of new elements and text nodes—appending the text nodes to their elements, the elements to each other, and the top element to the page—is something of a laborious process. Fortunately, if you're adding to the page a copy of something that's already there, a shortcut is available: the `cloneNode` method. This returns a *copy* of the node, including all its attributes and all its children.[4] If you have a moderately complex piece of HTML that contains many elements, `cloneNode` is a very quick way to return a copy of that block of HTML ready for insertion into the document:

---

[4]You can elect to clone the node only—not its children—by passing `false` to the `cloneNode` method.

```
var newpara = para.cloneNode(true);
document.getElementById('codesection').appendChild(newpara);
```

You can't rush ahead and just do this, though: it pays to be careful with cloneNode. This method clones all attributes of the node and all its child nodes, *including* IDs, and IDs must be unique within your document. So, if you have elements with IDs in your cloned HTML block, you need to fix those IDs before you append the cloned block to the document.

It would be nice to be able to grab the Yahoo! link in our cloned block using the following code:

```
var new_yahoo_link = newpara.getElementById('yalink');
```

But, unfortunately, we can't. The getElementById method is defined only on a document, not on any arbitrary node. The easiest way around this is to refrain from defining IDs on elements in a block that you wish to clone. Here's a line of code that will remove the Yahoo! link's id:

```
newpara.firstChild.removeAttribute('id');
```

We still have the ID on the paragraph itself, though, which means that when we append the new paragraph to the document, we'll have two paragraphs with the ID codepara. This is bad—it's not supposed to happen. We must fix it before we append the new paragraph, revising the above code as follows:

```
var newpara = para.cloneNode(true);
newpara.id = 'codepara2';
newpara.firstChild.removeAttribute('id');
document.getElementById('codesection').appendChild(newpara);
```

This code returns the following results:

```
<div id="codesection">
  <p id="codepara">
    <a href="http://www.yahoo.com/">Yahoo!</a>
    <a href="http://www.linux.org/">The Linux operating system</a>
  </p>
  <p id="codepara2">
    <a href="http://www.yahoo.com/">Yahoo!</a>
    <a href="http://www.linux.org/">The Linux operating system</a>
  </p>
  <ul>
    <li></li>
    <li></li>
```

```
    </ul>
  </div>
```

As you can see, there's a little bit of surgery involved if you choose to copy big chunks of the document. This demonstration concludes our experimentation with this particular bit of code.

Making an Expanding Form

As our first full example, we'll use the DOM's element creation methods to build a form that can grow as the user fills it. This allows users to add to the form as many entries as they like.

Let's imagine an online system through which people can sign up themselves, and any number of their friends, for free beer.[5] The users add their own names, then the names of all of the friends they wish to invite. Without the DOM, we'd require the form either to contain a large number of slots for friends' names (more than anyone would use), or to submit regularly back to the server to get a fresh (empty) list of name entry areas.

In our brave new world, we can add the extra name entry fields dynamically. We'll place a button on the form that says, Add another friend. Clicking that button will add a new field to the list, ready for submission to the server. Each newly-created field will need a different `name` attribute, so that it can be distinguished when the server eventually receives the submitted form.[6]

Our form will provide a text entry box for the user's name, a `fieldset` containing one text entry box for a friend's name, and a button to add more friends. When the button is clicked, we'll add a new text entry box for another friend's name.

File: **expandingForm.html**

```
<!DOCTYPE html PUBLIC "-//W3C//DTD HTML 4.01//EN"
    "http://www.w3.org/TR/html4/strict.dtd">
<html>
  <head>
    <title>Free beer signup form</title>

    <script type="text/javascript">
```

---

[5]Maybe there's a mad millionaire philanthropist on the loose. No, I can't give you a URL at which this system is running for real!

[6]Depending on the server-side language used to process the form, this isn't strictly necessary. Since our example form won't actually submit to anything, we'll implement it as a useful exercise.

```
      var fieldCount = 1;
      function addFriend() {
        fieldCount++;
        var newFriend = document.createElement('input');
        newFriend.type = 'text';
        newFriend.name = 'friend' + fieldCount;
        newFriend.id = 'friend' + fieldCount;
        document.getElementById('fs').appendChild(newFriend);
      }
    </script>

    <style type="text/css">
      input {
        display: block;
        margin-bottom: 2px;
      }
      button {
        float: right;
      }
      fieldset {
        border: 1px solid black;
      }
    </style>

  </head>
  <body>
    <h1>Free beer signup form</h1>
    <form>
      <label for="you">Your name</label>
      <input type="text" name="you" id="you">
      <fieldset id="fs">
        <legend>Friends you wish to invite</legend>
        <button onclick="addFriend(); return false;">
          Add another friend
        </button>
        <input type="text" name="friend1" id="friend1">
      </fieldset>
      <input type="submit" value="Save details">
    </form>
  </body>
</html>
```

Notice our `fieldCount` variable; this keeps track of how many friend fields there are.

File: **expandingForm.html (excerpt)**

```
var fieldCount = 1;
```

When the button is clicked, we run the `addFriend` function (we'll discuss handling clicks—and various other kinds of events—more in the next chapter):

```
<button onclick="addFriend(); return false;">
```

The `addFriend` function completes a number of tasks each time it's run:

1. Increments the `fieldCount`:

    File: **expandingForm.html (excerpt)**

    ```
    fieldCount++;
    ```

2. Creates a new `input` element:

    File: **expandingForm.html (excerpt)**

    ```
    var newFriend = document.createElement('input');
    ```

3. Sets its `type` to `text`—we want a text entry box, an element specified by `<input type="text">`:

    File: **expandingForm.html (excerpt)**

    ```
    newFriend.type = 'text';
    ```

4. Sets a unique `id` and `name` (because the ID must be unique, and all the entry boxes must have different names so they can be distinguished when the form's submitted):

    File: **expandingForm.html (excerpt)**

    ```
    newFriend.name = 'friend' + fieldCount;
    newFriend.id = 'friend' + fieldCount;
    ```

5. Adds this newly-created element to the document:

    File: **expandingForm.html (excerpt)**

    ```
    document.getElementById('fs').appendChild(newFriend);
    ```

Here's what the page looks like after the "add another friend" button has been clicked twice, and two friends' names have been added:

Figure 2.4. Signing up for free beer.

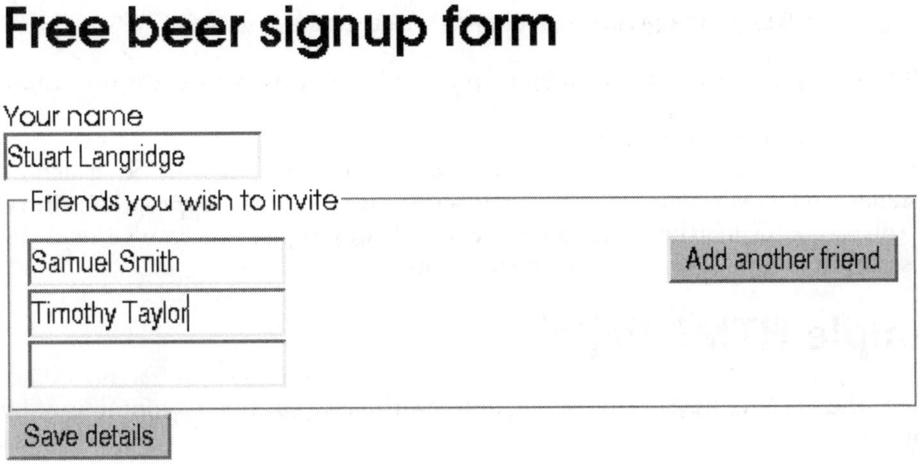

Free beer signup form

Your name

Stuart Langridge

Friends you wish to invite

Samuel Smith

Timothy Taylor

Add another friend

Save details

Free beer, thanks to the power of the DOM. We can't complain about that!

Making Modular Image Rollovers

Image rollover scripts, in which an image is used as a link, and that image changes when the user mouses over it, are a mainstay of JavaScript programming on the Web. Traditionally, they've required a lot of script, and a lot of customization, on the part of the developer. The introspective capability of the DOM—the ability of script to inspect the structure of the page in which it's running—gives us the power to detect rollover images automatically and set them up without any customization. This represents a more systematic approach than the old-fashioned use of `onmouseover` and `onmouseout` attributes, and keeps rollover code separate from other content.

We'll build our page so that the links on which we want to display rollover effects have a class of `rollover`. They'll contain one `img` element—nothing else. We'll also provide specially named rollover images: if an image within the page is called `foo.gif`, then the matching rollover image will be named `foo_over.gif`. When the page loads, we'll walk the DOM tree, identify all the appropriate links (by checking their class and whether they contain an `img` element), and set up the rollover on each. This specially-named rollover image allows us to deduce the name of any rollover image without saving that name anywhere. It reduces the amount of data we have to manage.

An alternative technique involves use of a non-HTML attribute in the image tag:

```
<img src="basic_image.gif" oversrc="roll_image.gif">
```

However, since `oversrc` isn't a standard attribute, this approach would cause your HTML to be invalid.

Some of the following script may seem a little opaque: we will be attaching listeners to DOM events to ensure that scripts are run at the appropriate times. If this is confusing, then feel free to revisit this example after you've read the discussion of DOM events in the next chapter.

A Sample HTML Page

First, the HTML: here we have our links, with class `rollover`, containing the images.

File: **rollovers.html**

```
<!DOCTYPE html PUBLIC "-//W3C//DTD HTML 4.01//EN"
    "http://www.w3.org/TR/html4/strict.dtd">
<html>
  <head>
    <title>Modular rollovers</title>
    <script type="text/javascript" src="rollovers.js"></script>
    <style type="text/css">
      /* Remove the blue border on the rollover images */
      a.rollover img {
        border-width: 0;
      }
    </style>
  </head>
  <body>
    <h1>Modular rollovers</h1>
    <p>Below we have two links, containing images that we want
      to change on mouseover.</p>
        <ul>
        <li>
          <a href="" class="rollover" alt="Roll"
              ><img src="basic_image.gif" /></a>
        </li>
```

```
      <li>
        <a href="" class="rollover" alt="Roll"
            ><img src="basic_image2.gif"></a>
      </li>
    </ul>
  </body>
</html>
```

The page also includes the JavaScript file that does all the work:

File: **rollovers.js**

```
function setupRollovers() {
  if (!document.getElementsByTagName)
    return;
  var all_links = document.getElementsByTagName('a');
  for (var i = 0; i < all_links.length; i++) {
    var link = all_links[i];
    if (link.className &&
        (' ' + link.className + ' ').indexOf(' rollover ') != -1)
    {
      if (link.childNodes &&
          link.childNodes.length == 1 &&
          link.childNodes[0].nodeName.toLowerCase() == 'img') {
        link.onmouseover = mouseover;
        link.onmouseout = mouseout;
      }
    }
  }
}

function findTarget(e)
{
  /* Begin the DOM events part, which you */
  /* can ignore for now if it's confusing */
  var target;

  if (window.event && window.event.srcElement)
    target = window.event.srcElement;
  else if (e && e.target)
    target = e.target;
  if (!target)
    return null;

  while (target != document.body &&
      target.nodeName.toLowerCase() != 'a')
    target = target.parentNode;
```

```
  if (target.nodeName.toLowerCase() != 'a')
    return null;

  return target;
}

function mouseover(e) {
  var target = findTarget(e);
  if (!target) return;

  // the only child node of the a-tag in target will be an img-tag
  var img_tag = target.childNodes[0];

  // Take the "src", which names an image called "something.ext",
  // Make it point to "something_over.ext"
  // This is done with a regular expression
  img_tag.src = img_tag.src.replace(/(\.[^.]+)$/, '_over$1');
}

function mouseout(e) {
  var target = findTarget(e);
  if (!target) return;

  // the only child node of the a-tag in target will be an img-tag
  var img_tag = target.childNodes[0];

  // Take the "src", which names an image as "something_over.ext",
  // Make it point to "something.ext"
  // This is done with a regular expression
  img_tag.src = img_tag.src.replace(/_over(\.[^.]+)$/, '$1');
}

// When the page loads, set up the rollovers
window.onload = setupRollovers;
```

The DOM-walking parts of this code are found in setupRollovers and in findTarget, which is called from the two mouseover/mouseout functions. Let's look at each of these in turn.

The setupRollovers Function

The code for the setupRollovers function starts like this:

File: **rollovers.js (excerpt)**

```
if (!document.getElementsByTagName)
  return;
```

This code confirms that we're in a DOM-supporting browser. If we're not (i.e. if
`document.getElementsByTagName`, the method, doesn't exist), we exit here and
progress no further. If the method does exist, we continue:

File: **rollovers.js (excerpt)**

```
var all_links = document.getElementsByTagName('a');
```

Here, we make `all_links` a reference to a list of all the <a> tags in the document.

File: **rollovers.js (excerpt)**

```
for (var i = 0; i < all_links.length; i++) {
  var link = all_links[i];
```

The above code iterates through the retrieved list of tags in standard JavaScript
fashion. We assign the `link` variable to each link, as a way to simplify the following code.

File: **rollovers.js (excerpt)**

```
    if (link.className &&
        (' ' + link.className + ' ').indexOf(' rollover ') != -1)
    {
```

We need to know whether each link is of class `rollover`. However, an element
may have more than one class; if this tag had two classes, `rollover` and `hotlink`,
for example, it would have `className="rollover hotlink"`. This would mean
that we could not check for an element having a specific class using the following:

```
if (element.className == "myclass")
```

If the element has multiple classes, the above condition will always evaluate to
`false`. A useful approach here is to look for the string ' *myclass* ' (the class
name with a space before and after it) in the string ' ' + *element*.className
+ ' ' (the element's `class` attribute with a space before and after it). This will
always find your class, as you're expecting. It also avoids a problem with a similar
technique, which uses `className.indexOf` to look for 'myclass'. If the element
in question is of class `myclassroom`, this technique will give a false positive.[7]

---

[7]Another option is to use a regular expression to spot the class name. In the interests of simplicity,
however, we'll stick with the method already presented.

File: **`rollovers.js` (excerpt)**

```
if (link.childNodes &&
    link.childNodes.length == 1 &&
    link.childNodes[0].nodeName.toLowerCase() == 'img') {
```

We want to confirm that this link contains nothing but an `img` element, so we make use of a very handy property of JavaScript, called **short-circuit evaluation**. In an `if` statement of the form `if (a && b && c)`, if *a* is false, then *b* and *c* are not evaluated at all. This means that *b* and *c* can be things that depend on *a*'s trueness: if *a* is not true, then they are not evaluated, so it's safe to put them into the `if` statement.

Looking at the above code may make this clearer. We need to test if the `nodeName` of the link's first child node is `img`. We might use the following code:

```
if (link.childNodes[0].nodeName.toLowerCase == 'img')
```

However, if the current link doesn't have any child nodes, this code will cause an error because there is no `link.childNodes[0]`. So, we must first check that child nodes exist; second, we confirm that there is one and only one child; third, we check whether that one-and-only first child is an image. We can safely assume in the image check that `link.childNodes[0]` exists, because we've already confirmed that that's the case: if it didn't exist, we wouldn't have got this far.

File: **`rollovers.js` (excerpt)**

```
link.onmouseover = mouseover;
```

This code attaches an event handler to the `mouseover` event on a node.

File: **`rollovers.js` (excerpt)**

```
link.onmouseout = mouseout;
```

And this line attaches an event handler to the `mouseout` event on that node. That's all!

The `findTarget` Function

This little function is called by the `mouseover` and `mouseout` functions. As we'll see, they pass event objects to `findTarget`, which, in return, passes back the link tag surrounding the image that generated the event, if any such tag is to be found.

`findTarget` starts like this:

File: **rollovers.js** (excerpt)

```
var target;

if (window.event && window.event.srcElement)
  target = window.event.srcElement;
else if (e && e.target)
  target = e.target;
if (!target)
  return null;
```

This first part is related to DOM event handling, which is explained in the next chapter. We'll ignore its workings for now, except to say that it caters for the differences between Internet Explorer and fully DOM-supporting browsers. Once this code has run, however, we should have in our variable target the element that the browser deems to be responsible for the mouseover or mouseout event—ideally the <a> tag.

File: **rollovers.js** (excerpt)

```
while (target != document.body &&
    target.nodeName.toLowerCase() != 'a')
  target = target.parentNode;

if (target.nodeName.toLowerCase() != 'a')
  return null;
```

The variable target should be a reference to the <a> tag on which the user clicked, but it may be something inside the <a> tag (as some browsers handle events this way). In such cases, the above code keeps getting the parent node of that tag until it gets to an <a> tag (which will be the one we want). If we find the document body—a <body> tag—instead, we've gone too far. We'll give up, returning null (nothing) from the function, and going no further.

If we did find an <a> tag, however, we return that:

File: **rollovers.js** (excerpt)

```
  return target;
}
```

The mouseover / mouseout Functions

These functions work in similar ways and do very similar things: mouseover is called when we move the mouse over one of our rollover links, while mouseout is called when we move the mouse out again.

The code for `mouseover` starts like this:

File: **rollovers.js (excerpt)**

```
var target = findTarget(e);
if (!target) return;
```

We call the `findTarget` function, described above, to get a reference to the link over which the mouse is located. If no element is returned, we give up, degrading gracefully. Otherwise, we have the moused-over `<a>` tag in target. Next, we dig out the image.

File: **rollovers.js (excerpt)**

```
var img_tag = target.childNodes[0];
```

We also know that the `<a>` tag has one, and only one, child node, and that's an `<img>` tag. We know this because we checked that this was the case when we set up the event handler in `setupRollovers`.

File: **rollovers.js (excerpt)**

```
img_tag.src = img_tag.src.replace(/(\.[^.]+)$/, '_over$1');
```

Images have a `src` attribute, which you can access through the DOM with the element's `src` property. In the code snippet above, we apply a regular expression substitution to that string.[8] Changing the value of an `<img>` tag's `src` attribute causes it to reload itself with the new image; thus, making this substitution (replacing `something.gif` with `something_over.gif`) causes the original image to change to the rollover image. The `mouseout` function does the exact opposite: it changes the reference to `something_over.gif` in the image's `src` attribute to `something.gif`, causing the original image to reappear.

Something for Nothing (Almost)

If you look at the code for this modular rollover, you'll see that it's divided into parts. The `setupRollovers` function does nothing but install listeners. The `findTarget` function does nothing but find the link tag for a given event. The `mouseover` and `mouseout` functions do little other than the actual image swapping work. The tasks are neatly divided.

---

[8]Although the full details of regular expressions are beyond the scope of this book, we'll look at the basics in Chapter 6. A more detailed resource is Kevin Yank's article on sitepoint.com, *Regular Expressions in JavaScript [http://www.sitepoint.com/article/expressions-javascript]*.

That means that this code is good for other applications. We can change the `mouseover` and `mouseout` functions to do something else—for example, to make popup help content appear—without needing to start from scratch to get it working. We get to reuse (or at least rip off with minimal change) the other functions in the script. This is not only convenient; it's also neat and clean. We're on the way to a better kind of scripting!

Summary

In the introduction, we referred to the DOM as a critical part of DHTML. Exploring the DOM—being able to find, change, add, and remove elements from your document—is a powerful technique all by itself, and is a fundamental aspect of modern DHTML. Once you've mastered the techniques described in this chapter, everything else will fall into place. Through the rest of the book, we'll be describing techniques and tricks with which you can do wondrous things on your sites, and in your Web applications, using DHTML. They all build upon this fundamental approach of manipulating the Document Object Model.

3

Handling DOM Events

When I can't handle events, I let them handle themselves.
—Henry Ford

An event is something that happens, be it in real life, or in DHTML programming. But to those working with DHTML, events have a very specific meaning. An event is generated, or fired, when something happens to an element: a mouse clicks on a button, for example, or a change is made to a form. DHTML programming is all about event handling; your code will run in response to the firing of this or that event.

Learning which events are available, how to hook your code up to them, and how to make best use of them is a critical part of building dynamic Web applications.[1] That's what we cover in this chapter, along with a couple of real-world examples.

About Elements and Events

We're using a modern approach to DHTML, so all our DHTML code will be set to run in response to the firing of an event. If you've done any JavaScript Web programming before, you may already be using this technique without knowing it. Let's look at the procedure by which code has traditionally been hooked up

---

[1]It does seem that there are quite a few "critical" bits, I know!

to events, learn how to do it under the DOM (and why the DOM method is better), and find out exactly what these techniques make possible.

Common Events

Every page element fires a given selection of events. Some events are common to all elements; others are more specific. For example, all visible elements will fire a mouseover event when the mouse is moved over them. A change event, however, will only be fired by elements whose contents can be changed: text boxes, text areas, and drop-down lists.

You might have noticed above that I used mouseover, rather than onmouseover, for the event name. Even though the HTML attribute for handling this event is onmouseover, the modern way to describe the event itself is simply mouseover. This allows us to talk about the *event* (mouseover) and the *event handler* (onmouseover) separately. The **event handler** is the location at which an event handler is placed. In the bad old browser days, these concepts were all mixed up, but now we can safely think of them as separate entities.

The documents that describe the events fired by a given element are the W3C DOM specifications and HTML recommendations, which were mentioned in the last chapter, as well as the W3C DOM 2 Events specification[1]. There's also some extra information on key events in the DOM 3 Events specification[2].

A summary of the events that you're likely to find useful, and that have cross-browser support, is given in Table 3.1. Note that this isn't an exhaustive survey: it's a listing of events that you're likely to use often, rather than everything under the sun.

---

[1] http://www.w3.org/TR/DOM-Level-2-Events/Overview.html
[2] http://www.w3.org/TR/2003/NOTE-DOM-Level-3-Events-20031107/events.html

Table 3.1. Useful Events.

Event(s)	Fired by Element(s)	Fired when
`load`	`window`	The page finishes loading.
`unload`	`window`	The page is unloaded (i.e. the user closes the browser, or clicks a link, and a new page loads).
`change`	`input`, `select`, `textarea`	The element loses focus (the user clicks outside it or tabs away from it), and the content has been changed (note: the event does not fire immediately when the change is made!).
`focus`	`label`, `input`, `select`, `textarea`, `button`	The element gets the focus (it is tabbed to, or clicked upon).
`blur`	`label`, `input`, `select`, `textarea`, `button`	The element loses the focus.
`resize`	`window`	The user resizes the window.
`scroll`	`window`	The user scrolls the window.
`submit`	`form`	The user submits the form by clicking the submit button or hitting **Enter** in a text field.
`mouseover`	any visible	The user moves the mouse onto an element.
`mouseout`	any visible	The user moves the mouse off an element.
`mousedown`	any visible	The user presses any mouse button while on the element.
`mouseup`	any visible	The user releases the mouse button while on the element.
`mousemove`	any visible	The user moves the mouse anywhere on the element.
`click`	any	The user clicks any mouse button while on the element (this is the same as a `mousedown` followed by a `mouseup`).
`keypress`	any element that can be focused	A key is pressed while the element has focus.

Hooking Code to Events

So, now you know some common events, and when they fire. But how do you make your code run in response to those events?

Hooking up the Old Way

If you've done any JavaScript coding before, you'll probably have written something like this:

```
<a href="somewhere.html"
    onclick="myJavaScriptFunction(); return false;"
    >click me!</a>
```

That `onclick` attribute connects some JavaScript code to that link's `click` event. When the link is clicked, it will fire a click event, and that code will run. No problem! Notice, though, that the code never actually mentions "click," which is the actual name of the event.

What if we wanted to detect a keypress? Here's the equivalent script:

```
function aKeyWasPressed() {
  // put event handler code here ...
}
```

And here's the matching snippet of HTML:

```
<textarea id="myta" onkeypress="aKeyWasPressed()"></textarea>
```

In this case, how does our `aKeyWasPressed` function know which key was pressed? Well, it doesn't. That's a major limitation of the old-fashioned approach. But we can improve on that!

Hooking up the DOM Way

The DOM specifications enlarge the idea of event handlers by providing **event targets** and **event listeners**. An event target is the thing at which an event is aimed—an element, essentially. An event listener is the thing that grabs the event when it appears, and responds to it. Where do events come from in the first place? They come from the user. The browser software captures the user action and sends the event to the right event target.

A given event source can be relevant to more than one event listener. Using the old-fashioned method above, only one piece of code could be run in response to any event. For example, an element could have only one `onclick` attribute.[2] Using the modern method, you can run as many pieces of code as you want upon the firing of an event or events. Listeners get to share events, and events get to share listeners. To facilitate this, we must move our "hookup" code from the HTML to a separate script section: as noted above, no element can have more than one `onclick` attribute.

Event handling works in different ways, depending on the browser. We'll examine the W3C-approved way first, before we look at event handling in Internet Explorer. Here's the W3C approach.

File: **keycodedetect.html** (excerpt)

```
function aKeyWasPressed(e) {
  // put event listener code here...
}

var textarea = document.getElementById('myta');
textarea.addEventListener('keyup', aKeyWasPressed, false);
```

And here's the matching bit of HTML:

File: **keycodedetect.html** (excerpt)

```
<textarea id="myta"></textarea>
```

IMPORTANT

HTML Before Script... for Now

If you're working through this example in your HTML editor of choice, be sure to place the JavaScript code after the HTML in this and the next few examples in this chapter. The `textarea` must exist before the JavaScript code can assign an event listener to it.

If you're used to placing JavaScript at the top of your HTML files, don't fret. We'll discuss an elegant way around this restriction at the end of the section.

Those few lines of code contain a number of complex concepts. Consider this snippet:

---

[2]Actually, you could have as many as you liked, but each one would overwrite the one before it, so, effectively, you have only one. Alternatively, you could string JavaScript statements together, using semicolons in the attribute, but this makes the HTML code even more cluttered.

File: **keycodedetect.html (excerpt)**

```
var textarea = document.getElementById('myta');
```

Here, we see a familiar reference to the `<textarea>`. Next, there's something new:

File: **keycodedetect.html (excerpt)**

```
textarea.addEventListener('keyup', aKeyWasPressed, false);
```

This is the crucial line that sets everything up. Each element has an `addEventListener` method, which allows you to hook a function to any event[3] that the element receives. The method takes three arguments: the event, the function that should be called, and a true-or-false value for *useCapture*. This last item relates to a rarely-used feature of DOM events called **event capture**. For the moment, we'll just set it to `false`, to indicate that we don't want to use event capture. If you'd like to get the full story, see the DOM Level 3 Events specification[3] (not for the faint of heart!).

The event is specified as a string, which is the (modern) name of the event (i.e. without the "on" prefix). The function is specified using only the name of the function; do not place brackets after it, as in `aKeyWasPressed()`, as this would call the function. We don't want to call it now; we want to call it later, when the event is fired.[4]

Now, when a key is pressed in our `<textarea>`, our `aKeyWasPressed` function will be called. Note that JavaScript no longer clutters up our HTML; much like the separation of design and content facilitated by CSS, *we've separated our page content (HTML) from our page behavior (JavaScript)*. This is an important benefit of the new technique: we can switch new event listeners in and out without altering the HTML in our page. It's the modern way!

We still haven't addressed the question we posed earlier, though: how does the `aKeyWasPressed` function know which key was pressed?

---

[3]We've used the `keyup` event here, rather than the more commonly expected `keypress`, because, at the time of writing, Safari on Macintosh does not support the assigning of `keypress` events using `addEventListener`. Perhaps more importantly, the DOM3 recommendation does not mention a `keypress` event.

[3] http://www.w3.org/TR/DOM-Level-3-Events/events.html#Events-flow

[4]If you have worked in other languages, you may recognize that this means that functions are first-class objects in JavaScript; we can pass around references to a function using its name, but without calling it. This procedure doesn't work in all languages, but it's a very useful feature of JavaScript.

Getting Event Information

A subtle change that we made in the above code was to give the `aKeyWasPressed` function an argument, `e`.

File: **keycodedetect.html** (excerpt)

```
function aKeyWasPressed(e) {
  ...
```

When a function is called as an event listener, it is passed, in the case of a W3C events-compliant browser, to an **event object**, which holds details of the event. This object has a number of properties containing useful information, such as target, and a reference to the element that fired the event. The precise properties that are available will depend on the type of event in question, but the most useful properties are listed in Table 3.2.

Table 3.2. Useful Properties.

Event object property	Meaning
`target`	The element that fired the event.
`type`	The event that was fired (e.g. `keyup`).
`button`	The mouse button that was pressed (if this is a mouse event): 0 for the left button, 1 for middle, 2 for right.
`keyCode`	The character code of the key that was pressed[5]
`shiftKey`	Whether the **Shift** key was pressed (`true` or `false`).

[5]Don't use `charCode` here, even though some Websites tell you to. `keyCode` has good cross-browser support, and `charCode` does not. Key codes in the DOM are a standards mess! There are three ways to get the code: `keyCode` (IE), `charCode` (Mozilla/Netscape) and `data` (the official DOM 3 Events way). Fortunately, all major browsers support the nonstandard `keyCode`. So always use this, at least until the `data` property is widespread (in about 2010!).

Code that identifies which key was pressed would look like this:

File: **keycodedetect.html** (excerpt)

```
function aKeyWasPressed(e) {
  var key = e.keyCode;
  alert('You pressed the key: ' + String.fromCharCode(key));
}
```

```
var textarea = document.getElementById('myta');
textarea.addEventListener('keyup', aKeyWasPressed, false);
```

When a key is pressed, our function will pop up a dialog box to tell us so.[6]

Re-using Listeners Across Targets

The target attribute might not seem very useful; after all, we know that it will be a reference to the `<textarea>`. But we can hook up the same function as an event listener on more than one element. We can, for example, attach one single function as an event listener for click events to every link in our page. When any link is clicked, our function will be called; we can then tell which link was clicked by examining the function's `e.target`. We'll come back to this in later examples in this chapter.

For now, all we need to know is that we don't have to write a separate event listener for every single tag in which we're interested.

What Happens After an Event Fires?

Events have two further important properties: **bubbling** and **default actions**. Think about an HTML document. It's hierarchical: elements are contained by other elements. Consider this HTML snippet:

```
<div>
  <p>
    <a href="">a link</a>
  </p>
</div>
```

Clicking on the link will cause that link to fire a click event. But the link is contained within the paragraph, and the paragraph is contained within the `<div>`. So clicking the link will also cause both the paragraph and the `<div>` to see the click event. This is called **event bubbling**; an event "bubbles" up through the DOM tree, starting with the target element, until it reaches the top. Not all events bubble; for example, `focus` and `blur` events do not. Bubbling can often be ignored,[7] but there are times when you'll want to prevent a specific event from bubbling.

---

[6]Note that we use the `String.fromCharCode` method to convert the keyboard code provided by `keyCode` to a human-readable string.

[7]There are a lot of complex rules about event bubbling and event capturing, the phase of event propagation that occurs before event bubbling. In practice, we don't need to know much beyond how to stop it happening, but a complete write-up is available at

Once you've got an event, the DOM Events specification says that you can stop any further bubbling like this:

```
function aKeyWasPressed(e) {
  var key = e.keyCode;
  e.stopPropagation();
  ...
}
```

Once the call to stopPropagation is in place, the event will occur on the <a> tag only: any listeners on the <p> or <div> tags will miss out. If there are no listeners on those other tags, there's no need to stop bubbling. In this case, the event silently passes through the parent tags, having no extra effect.

Some events have a default action. The most obvious example is clicking a link: the default action for this event is to navigate the current window or frame to the link's destination. If we wanted to handle clicks on a link entirely within our JavaScript code, we might want to prevent that default action from being taken.

In our examples so far, we have handled the keyup event, which is fired when a key is released. As it turns out, this event has no default action. A closely-related event that does have a default action is keypress, which occurs whenever a character is typed using the combination of keydown and keyup. The keypress event is nonstandard (i.e. it is not described by the W3C DOM standard), which is why I have avoided mentioning it until now, but it is well supported by the major browsers.

Let's say we want to prevent keypress events from inputting text into our textarea. We could do this by setting up an event listener that cancelled the default action of that type of event. The DOM standard specifies a method, named preventDefault, that achieves this, but again, Internet Explorer implements its own proprietary technique. Here's the DOM approach:

```
function aKeyWasPressed(e) {
  e.preventDefault();
}
var textarea = document.getElementById('myta');
textarea.addEventListener('keypress', aKeyWasPressed, false);
```

---

http://www.quirksmode.org/js/events_order.html for those who would like to know more of the theory underlying this aspect of the DOM.

Assigning Event Listeners on Page Load

In all of the examples we've seen so far in this chapter, the JavaScript code has had to follow the HTML code to which it assigns event listeners. If the JavaScript code were to come first, it would be unable to find the HTML elements in question, as they would not yet exist.

A solution to this problem is to assign event listeners for specific document elements in a listener assigned to the window's `load` event. As a result, event listeners will only be assigned once the document has finished loading, and all elements are available.

Here's the complete listing for our keystroke detection example, restructured in this way:

File: **keycodedetect.html**

```
<!DOCTYPE html PUBLIC "-//W3C//DTD HTML 4.01//EN"
    "http://www.w3.org/TR/html4/strict.dtd">
<html>
  <head>
    <title>Detect keystrokes</title>
    <script type="text/javascript">
      function aKeyWasPressed(e) {
        var key = e.keyCode;
        alert('You pressed the key: ' + String.fromCharCode(key));
      }

      function addListeners(e) {
        var textarea = document.getElementById('myta');
        textarea.addEventListener('keyup', aKeyWasPressed, false);
      }

      window.addEventListener('load', addListeners, false);
    </script>
  </head>
  <body>
    <form>
      <textarea id="myta"></textarea>
    </form>
  </body>
</html>
```

Our main event listener, aKeyWasPressed, has not been changed. What has changed is the way in which this listener is assigned. The code that assigns it has been placed inside a new function, addListeners:

File: **keycodedetect.html (excerpt)**

```
function addListeners(e) {
   var textarea = document.getElementById('myta');
   textarea.addEventListener('keyup', aKeyWasPressed, false);
}
```

This function is itself an event listener, which we assign to the window object's load event:

File: **keycodedetect.html (excerpt)**

```
window.addEventListener('load', addListeners, false);
```

This event is fired once the document has finished loading, to signal that all HTML elements are now available. The addListeners function takes this opportunity to assign listeners to elements as required.

We'll continue to use this structure as we move forward through this chapter, and the rest of the book.

Making Events Work Cross-Browser

Naturally, making events work cross-browser is not as easy as just following the DOM standard. Internet Explorer doesn't implement the DOM Events model very well. Instead, it offers a proprietary and different way to hook up event listeners and gain access to event data.

Adding Event Listeners Portably

Instead of using an addEventListener method on an element, IE has an attachEvent method, and instead of passing an event object to each event listener, it has a global event object in window.event. This is inconvenient but not catastrophic; it just means that you have to take different actions for different browsers. In practice, what this means is that you have a small number of standard functions and techniques that you use to carry out event handling actions. One of these is the addEvent function, created by Scott Andrew:

File: **portabledetect.php** (excerpt)

```
function addEvent(elm, evType, fn, useCapture)
// cross-browser event handling for IE5+, NS6+ and Mozilla/Gecko
// By Scott Andrew
{
  if (elm.addEventListener) {
    elm.addEventListener(evType, fn, useCapture);
    return true;
  } else if (elm.attachEvent) {
    var r = elm.attachEvent('on' + evType, fn);
    return r;
  } else {
    elm['on' + evType] = fn;
  }
}
```

IE's `attachEvent` method is called, with an event name and a function to be the listener, but the event name should have "on" at the beginning. The `addEvent` function above takes care of the cross-browser differences;[8] simply include it in your code, then use it to attach events. As such, the code above becomes:

```
function aKeyWasPressed(e) {
  var key = e.keyCode;
  alert('You pressed the key: ' + String.fromCharCode(key));
}

function addListeners(e) {
  var textarea = document.getElementById('myta');
  addEvent(textarea, 'keyup', aKeyWasPressed, false);
}

addEvent(window, 'load', addListeners, false);

function addEvent(elm, evType, fn, useCapture)
// cross-browser event handling for IE5+, NS6+ and Mozilla/Gecko
// By Scott Andrew
{
  if (elm.addEventListener) {
```

---

[8]Note that if the browser doesn't support either **addEventListener** or **attachEvent**, which is the case for IE5 for Macintosh, the code assigns the event listener directly to the element as an event handler using its **onevent** property. This will overwrite any previous event handler that was attached to that event, which isn't good, but it's an interim solution (and better than it not working at all). There is a way around this issue, which, though it makes the code significantly more complex, does avoid this problem; details can be found in Simon Willison's Stylish Scripting blog post at http://www.sitepoint.com/blog-post-view.php?id=171578.

```
    elm.addEventListener(evType, fn, useCapture);
    return true;
  } else if (elm.attachEvent) {
    var r = elm.attachEvent('on' + evType, fn);
    return r;
  } else {
    elm['on' + evType] = fn;
  }
}
```

We're now using the addEvent function to make aKeyWasPressed listen for keyup events on the textarea.

Inspecting Event Objects Portably

This is not the only change that's required; we also have to take into account the fact that IE doesn't pass an event object to our event listener, but instead stores the event object in the window object. Just to make our lives as DHTML developers a little more complex, it also uses slightly different properties on the event object that it creates. These are shown in Table 3.3.

Table 3.3. W3C Event Object Properties.

W3C Event Object Property	IE window.event Property
target	srcElement
type	type
button[9]	button[10]
data[11]	keyCode
shiftKey	shiftKey

[9]0 = left button; 2 = right button; 1 = middle button.

[10]1 = left button; 2 = right button; 4 = middle button. For combinations, add numbers: 7 means all three buttons pressed.

[11]As previously noted, the standard data property is not well supported.

Taking all this into consideration, our portable code becomes:

File: **portabledetect.html** (excerpt)

```
function aKeyWasPressed(e) {
  if (window.event) {
    var key = window.event.keyCode;
```

```
    } else {
      var key = e.keyCode;
    }
    alert('You pressed the key: ' + String.fromCharCode(key));
}

function addListeners(e) {
  var textarea = document.getElementById('myta');
  addEvent(textarea, 'keyup', aKeyWasPressed, false);
}

addEvent(window, 'load', addListeners, false);

function addEvent(elm, evType, fn, useCapture)
// cross-browser event handling for IE5+, NS6+ and Mozilla/Gecko
// By Scott Andrew
{
  if (elm.addEventListener) {
    elm.addEventListener(evType, fn, useCapture);
    return true;
  } else if (elm.attachEvent) {
    var r = elm.attachEvent('on' + evType, fn);
    return r;
  } else {
    elm['on' + evType] = fn;
  }
}
```

This updated version of aKeyWasPressed first checks whether a window.event object exists:

<hr>

File: **portabledetect.html (excerpt)**

```
  if (window.event) {
```

If it does, then it and its corresponding window.event.keyCode[12] property, are used to obtain the code of the pressed key. If not, the event object passed to the function (as e), which also has a keyCode property, is used.

Stopping Propagation and Default Actions Portably

Halting bubbling can be done in two ways, as is the case with much event handling: via the DOM approach and the Internet Explorer approach. In DOM-com-

<hr>

[12]This technique for checking that something exists is called **feature sniffing**, and will be explained in more detail in the next chapter.

pliant browsers, we can prevent an event from bubbling by calling the event object's `stopPropagation` method inside the event listener.

In Internet Explorer (where there is a global `window.event` object), we set `window.event.cancelBubble` to `true` inside the event listener. In practice, the usual technique is to use feature sniffing to Do The Right Thing:

```
if (window.event && window.event.cancelBubble) {
  window.event.cancelBubble = true;
}
if (e && e.stopPropagation) {
  // e is the event object passed to this listener
  e.stopPropagation();
}
```

Unfortunately, even this doesn't cover all the major browsers. Arguably a worse offender even than Internet Explorer, Apple's Safari browser provides the `stopPropagation` method, but doesn't actually do anything when it is called. There is no easy way around this, but since event bubbling will not significantly affect any of the examples in this book, we'll just ignore this problem for now.

We also need to feature-sniff to stop default actions. With the DOM, we use the passed event object's `preventDefault` method; with Internet Explorer, we set the global `event` object's `returnValue` property to `false`.

```
if (window.event && window.event.returnValue) {
  window.event.returnValue = false;
}
if (e && e.preventDefault) {
  e.preventDefault();
}
```

Again, Safari appears to support `preventDefault`, but doesn't actually do anything when it is called. Unfortunately, preventing the default action associated with an event is a rather vital feature for many of the examples we'll look at in this book. The only way to do it in Safari (at least until Apple fixes its DOM standard event support) is to use an old-style event handler that returns `false`.

For example, to prevent the `click` event of a link from navigating to the target of the link, we would normally just use an event listener that prevented the default action of the link:

```
function cancelClick(e) {
  if (window.event && window.event.returnValue) {
    window.event.returnValue = false;
```

```
    }
    if (e && e.preventDefault) {
      e.preventDefault();
    }
  }
addEvent(myLink, 'click', cancelClick, false);
```

To make this work in Safari, we need a second function, which will return `false` to cancel the event, and which we will assign as the `onclick` event handler of the link:

```
function cancelClick(e) {
    if (window.event && window.event.returnValue) {
      window.event.returnValue = false;
    }
    if (e && e.preventDefault) {
      e.preventDefault();
    }
  }
function cancelClickSafari() {
  return false;
}
addEvent(myLink, 'click', cancelClick, false);
myLink.onclick = cancelClickSafari;
```

This is actually quite an ugly solution, as it will overwrite any `onclick` event handler that another script may have installed. This kind of inter-script conflict is what modern event listeners are designed to avoid. Unfortunately, there is simply no better way around the problem in Safari. We'll see an example of this solution in practice later in this chapter.

This sort of cross-browser coding is obviated to a large extent by browser manufacturers coming together to implement the W3C DOM, but for event handling it's still required.

Smart Uses of Events

That's enough about how events work. Let's see a couple of practical examples. You should also know enough now to fully understand the image rollover code we saw in Chapter 2.

Creating Smarter Links

Some Websites open all clicked links in a new window. Often, they do this with the intention that the user will return to their site more readily if it's still open in another browser window. Some users find this useful; others find it heartily annoying. It would be possible, given our event-handling techniques above, to give them the choice.

Imagine we placed a checkbox on the page, which, initially unchecked, was accompanied by the label Open links in new window. Clicking any link will open that link in a new window if the box is checked.

We could implement this functionality using a combination of event listeners: we attach to each link on the page a click listener, which investigates the checkbox and opens the corresponding link in a new window if the box is checked. We also need a listener to run upon page load, to actually attach the listener to each link.

First, here's the HTML page we'll work on:

File: **smartlinks.html**

```
<!DOCTYPE html PUBLIC "-//W3C//DTD HTML 4.01//EN"
    "http://www.w3.org/TR/html4/strict.dtd">
<html>
  <head>
    <title>Smart Links</title>
    <script type="text/javascript" src="smartlink.js"></script>
    <style type="text/css">
      form {
          float: right;
          width: 25em;
          height: 5em;
          border: 1px solid blue;
          padding: 1em;
      }
    </style>
  </head>
  <body>
    <h1>Smart Links</h1>
    <form action=""><p>
      <label for="newwin">Open links in new window?
        <input type="checkbox" id="newwin">
      </label>
    </p></form>
```

```
    <p>This page contains several links, such as
      <a href="http://www.sitepoint.com/">SitePoint</a>,
      <a href="http://www.yahoo.com/">Yahoo!</a>, and
      <a href="http://www.google.com/">Google</a>.
      These links should ordinarily open in the same window when
      clicked, unless the checkbox is checked; this will make them
      open in a new window.
    </p>
  </body>
</html>
```

As you can see, this page is quite simple, and contains no JavaScript except for the file that the `<script>` tag brings in. Figure 3.1 shows how the code displays:

Figure 3.1. The example "smart links" Web page.

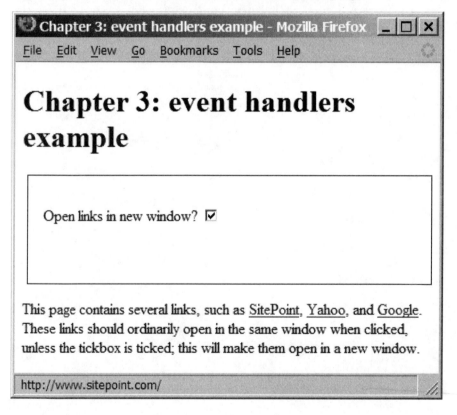

Next, let's look at the content of `smartlink.js`. This code has been assembled from our earlier discussions, although it contains some extra code for this particular page. First, here's an outline of what the script holds:

File: **smartlink.js (excerpt)**

```
function addEvent(elm, evType, fn, useCapture) { ... }
function handleLink(e) { ... }
function cancelClick() { ... }
function addListeners(e) { ... }

addEvent(window, 'load', addListeners, false);
```

And here are those four items in detail:

File: **smartlink.js**

```
function addEvent(elm, evType, fn, useCapture) {
  // cross-browser event handling for IE5+, NS6+ and Mozilla/Gecko
  // By Scott Andrew
  if (elm.addEventListener) {
    elm.addEventListener(evType, fn, useCapture);
    return true;
  } else if (elm.attachEvent) {
    var r = elm.attachEvent('on' + evType, fn);
    return r;
  } else {
    elm['on' + evType] = fn;
  }
}

function handleLink(e) {
  var el;
  if (window.event && window.event.srcElement)
    el = window.event.srcElement;
  if (e && e.target)
    el = e.target;
  if (!el)
    return;

  while (el.nodeName.toLowerCase() != 'a' &&
      el.nodeName.toLowerCase() != 'body')
    el = el.parentNode;

  if (document.getElementById('newwin') &&
      document.getElementById('newwin').checked) {
    window.open(el.href);
```

```
    if (window.event) {
      window.event.cancelBubble = true;
      window.event.returnValue = false;
    }
    if (e && e.stopPropagation && e.preventDefault) {
      e.stopPropagation();
      e.preventDefault();
    }
  }
}

function cancelClick() {
  if (document.getElementById('newwin') &&
      document.getElementById('newwin').checked) {
    return false;
  }
  return true;
}

function addListeners() {
  if (!document.getElementById)
    return;

  var all_links = document.getElementsByTagName('a');
  for (var i = 0; i < all_links.length; i++) {
    addEvent(all_links[i], 'click', handleLink, false);
    all_links[i].onclick = cancelClick;
  }
}

addEvent(window, 'load', addListeners, false);
```

Our code includes the now-familiar addEvent function to carry out cross-browser event hookups. We use it to call the addListeners function once the page has loaded.

The addListeners function uses another familiar technique; it iterates through all the links on the page and does something to them. In this case, it attaches the handleLink function as a click event listener for each link, so that when a link is clicked, that function will be called. It also attaches the cancelClick function as the old-style click event listener for each link—this will permit us to cancel the default action of each link in Safari.

When we click a link, that link fires a click event, and handleLink is run. The function does the following:

File: **smartlink.js** (excerpt)

```
if (window.event && window.event.srcElement)
  el = window.event.srcElement;
if (e && e.target)
  el = e.target;
if (!el)
  return;
```

This is the cross-browser approach to identifying which link was clicked; we check for a window.event object and, if it exists, use it to get window.event.srcElement, the clicked link. Alternatively, if e, the passed-in parameter, exists, and e.target exists, then we use that as the clicked link. If we've checked for both e and e.target, but neither exists, we give up and exit the function (with return).

Next up, we want to make sure that we have a reference to our link element:

File: **smartlink.js** (excerpt)

```
while (el.nodeName.toLowerCase() != 'a' &&
    el.nodeName.toLowerCase() != 'body')
  el = el.parentNode;
if (el.nodeName.toLowerCase() == 'body')
  return;
```

Some browsers may pass the text node inside a link as the clicked-on node, instead of the link itself. If the clicked element is not an <a> tag, we ascend the DOM tree, getting its parent (and that node's parent, and so on) until we get to the a element. (We also check for body, to prevent an infinite loop; if we get as far up the tree as the document body, we give up.)

Note that we also use toLowerCase on the nodeName of the element. This is the easiest way to ensure that a browser that returns a nodeName of A, and one that returns a nodeName of a, will both be handled correctly by the function.

Next, we check our checkbox:

File: **smartlink.js** (excerpt)

```
if (document.getElementById('newwin') &&
    document.getElementById('newwin').checked) {
```

We first confirm (for paranoia's sake) that there *is* an element with id newwin (which is the checkbox). Then, if that checkbox is checked, we open the link in a new window:

File: **smartlink.js (excerpt)**

```
window.open(el.href);
```

We know that `el`, the clicked link, is a link object, and that link objects have an `href` property. The `window.open` method creates a new window and navigates it to the specified URL.

Finally, we take care of what happens afterward:

File: **smartlink.js (excerpt)**

```
if (window.event) {
  window.event.cancelBubble = true;
  window.event.returnValue = false;
}
if (e && e.stopPropagation && e.preventDefault) {
  e.stopPropagation();
  e.preventDefault();
}
}
```

We don't want the link to have its normal effect of navigating the current window to the link's destination. So, in a cross-browser fashion, we stop the link's normal action from taking place.

As previously mentioned, Safari doesn't support the standard method of cancelling the link's default action, so we have an old-style event listener, `cancelClick`, that will cancel the event in that browser:

File: **smartlink.js (excerpt)**

```
function cancelClick() {
  if (document.getElementById('newwin') &&
      document.getElementById('newwin').checked) {
    return false;
  }
  return true;
}
```

You can see that some of this code is likely to appear in every project we attempt, particularly those parts that have to do with listener installation.

Making Tables More Readable

A handy trick that many applications use to display tables of data is to highlight the individual row and column that the viewer is looking at; paper-based tables often shade table rows and columns alternately to provide a similar (although non-dynamic[13]) effect.

Here's a screenshot of this effect in action. Note the location of the cursor. If we had another cursor, you could see that the second table is highlighted differently. But we don't, so you'll just have to try the example code for yourself…

Figure 3.2. Example of table highlighting in a Web page.

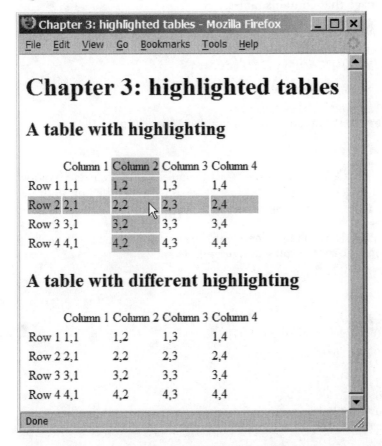

We can apply this effect to tables in an HTML document using event listeners. We'll attach a `mouseover` listener to each cell in a table, and have that listener highlight all the other cells located in that cell's row and column. We'll also attach a `mouseout` listener that turns the highlight off again.

---

[13] …until paper technology gets a lot cooler than it is now, at any rate!

The techniques we have explored in this chapter are at their most powerful when we combine the dynamic capabilities of DHTML with the page styling of CSS. Instead of specifically applying a highlight to each cell we wish to illuminate, we'll just apply a new class, hi, to those cells; our CSS will define exactly how table cells with class hi should be displayed. To change the highlight, simply change the CSS. For a more powerful effect still, use CSS's selectors to apply different styles to highlighted cells depending on the table in which they appear.

Here's an example page that contains tables:

File: **tableHighlight.html**

```
<!DOCTYPE html PUBLIC "-//W3C//DTD HTML 4.01//EN"
    "http://www.w3.org/TR/html4/strict.dtd">
<html>
  <head>
    <title>Highlighted Tables</title>
    <script type="text/javascript" src="tableHighlight.js">
    </script>
    <style type="text/css">
      tr.hi td, td.hi {
        background-color: #ccc;
      }
      table.extra tr.hi td, table.extra td.hi {
        color: red;
        text-decoration: underline overline;
        background-color: transparent;
      }
    </style>
  </head>
  <body>
    <h1>Highlighted Tables</h1>

    <h2>A table with highlighting</h2>
    <table>
      <tr>
        <td></td>
        <td>Column 1</td>
        <td>Column 2</td>
        <td>Column 3</td>
        <td>Column 4</td>
      </tr>
      <tr>
        <td>Row 1</td>
        <td>1,1</td><td>1,2</td><td>1,3</td><td>1,4</td>
      </tr>
```

```
    <tr>
       <td>Row 2</td>
       <td>2,1</td><td>2,2</td><td>2,3</td><td>2,4</td>
    </tr>
    <tr>
      <td>Row 3</td>
      <td>3,1</td><td>3,2</td><td>3,3</td><td>3,4</td>
    </tr>
    <tr>
       <td>Row 4</td>
       <td>4,1</td><td>4,2</td><td>4,3</td><td>4,4</td>
    </tr>
  </table>

  <h2>A table with different highlighting</h2>
  <table class="extra">
    <tr>
       <td></td>
       <td>Column 1</td>
       <td>Column 2</td>
       <td>Column 3</td>
       <td>Column 4</td>
    </tr>
    <tr>
       <td>Row 1</td>
       <td>1,1</td><td>1,2</td><td>1,3</td><td>1,4</td>
    </tr>
    <tr>
       <td>Row 2</td>
       <td>2,1</td><td>2,2</td><td>2,3</td><td>2,4</td>
    </tr>
    <tr>
       <td>Row 3</td>
       <td>3,1</td><td>3,2</td><td>3,3</td><td>3,4</td>
    </tr>
    <tr>
       <td>Row 4</td>
       <td>4,1</td><td>4,2</td><td>4,3</td><td>4,4</td>
    </tr>
  </table>
 </body>
</html>
```

That code creates two four-by-four tables, each with column and row headings (so each table contains five rows and five columns in total). Notice that none of the styles have any effect because, as yet, there are no elements with class="hi".

Let's look at the matching `tableHighlight.js` script. Its structure reflects our earlier discussions, but it contains some additional code for this particular technique. Here's an outline of the script:

File: **tableHighlight.js (excerpt)**

```
function addEvent(elm, evType, fn, useCapture) { ... }
function ascendDOM(e, target) { ... }
function hi_cell(e) { ... }
function lo_cell(e) { ... }
function addListeners() { ... }

addEvent(window, 'load', addListeners, false);
```

Notice how similar the function outline is to the smart links example. Here are the six items in all their detail.

File: **tableHighlight.js**

```
function addEvent(elm, evType, fn, useCapture)
// cross-browser event handling for IE5+, NS6+ and Mozilla/Gecko
// By Scott Andrew
{
  if (elm.addEventListener) {
    elm.addEventListener(evType, fn, useCapture);
    return true;
  } else if (elm.attachEvent) {
    var r = elm.attachEvent('on' + evType, fn);
    return r;
  } else {
    elm['on' + evType] = fn;
  }
}

// climb up the tree to the supplied tag.
function ascendDOM(e, target) {
  while (e.nodeName.toLowerCase() != target &&
      e.nodeName.toLowerCase() != 'html')
    e = e.parentNode;

  return (e.nodeName.toLowerCase() == 'html') ? null : e;
}

// turn on highlighting
function hi_cell(e) {
  var el;
  if (window.event && window.event.srcElement)
```

```
   el = window.event.srcElement;
 if (e && e.target)
   el = e.target;
 if (!el) return;

 el = ascendDOM(el, 'td');
 if (el == null) return;

 var parent_row = ascendDOM(el, 'tr');
 if (parent_row == null) return;

 var parent_table = ascendDOM(parent_row, 'table');
 if (parent_table == null) return;

 // row styling
 parent_row.className += ' hi';

 // column styling
 var ci = -1;
 for (var i = 0; i < parent_row.cells.length; i++) {
   if (el === parent_row.cells[i]) {
     ci = i;
   }
 }
 if (ci == -1) return; // this should never happen

 for (var i = 0; i < parent_table.rows.length; i++) {
   var cell = parent_table.rows[i].cells[ci];
   cell.className += ' hi';
 }
}

// turn off highlighting
function lo_cell(e) {
 var el;
 if (window.event && window.event.srcElement)
   el = window.event.srcElement;
 if (e && e.target)
   el = e.target;
 if (!el) return;

 el = ascendDOM(el, 'td');
 if (el == null) return;

 var parent_row = ascendDOM(el, 'tr');
 if (parent_row == null) return;
```

```
    var parent_table = ascendDOM(parent_row, 'table');
    if (parent_table == null) return;

    // row de-styling
    parent_row.className =
        parent_row.className.replace(/\b ?hi\b/, '');

    // column de-styling
    var ci = el.cellIndex;
    for (var i = 0; i < parent_table.rows.length; i++) {
      var cell = parent_table.rows[i].cells[ci];
      cell.className = cell.className.replace(/\b ?hi\b/, '');
    }
}

function addListeners() {
  if (!document.getElementsByTagName) return;

  var all_cells = document.getElementsByTagName('td');
  for (var i = 0; i < all_cells.length; i++) {
    addEvent(all_cells[i], 'mouseover', hi_cell, false);
    addEvent(all_cells[i], 'mouseout', lo_cell, false);
  }
}

addEvent(window, 'load', addListeners, false);
```

We add our mouseover and mouseout event listeners using the standard approach. The addListeners function sets up our hi_cell and lo_cell functions as mouseover and mouseout event listeners, respectively.

To minimize duplicate code, we've added a handy little utility function called ascendDOM. This marches up the tree from the element supplied in the first argument to find the first enclosing tag whose name matches the second argument.

Processing happens as follows. Mousing over a table cell triggers the hi_cell function. This finds the moused-over cell, then calculates the row and the table in which that cell appears. The ascendDOM function is called quite often in the code, so you can see the benefit of putting that code into a function. In hi_cell, the lines that actually do the styling work are these:

File: **tableHighlight.js (excerpt)**

```
    parent_row.className += ' hi';
```

File: **tableHighlight.js** (excerpt)

```
cell.className += ' hi';
```

The rest of the code is simply concerned with picking out the right elements for these lines to work on.

Our intention here is to apply the class hi to the other cells in the row that contains the moused-over cell, and its column. The first line above executes the first task. The second line applies the class to a given cell, but our script needs to find the appropriate cells first.

This is where things get a little complicated. The row is a simple <tr> tag, whereas the column is a list of cells scattered across all the rows in the table. According to the DOM Level 2 specification, table cell elements have a cellIndex property, which indicates the cell's index in the row. To find the other cells in this column, we could iterate through all the rows in the table and find within each row the cell that has the same cellIndex.

Sadly, Safari doesn't properly support cellIndex—it is always set to 0, no matter what the actual index should be. If Safari supported cellIndex, the process could have been simple:

```
var ci = el.cellIndex;
```

In fact, this concise snippet must be replaced with the much longer section below:

File: **tableHighlight.js** (excerpt)

```
var ci = -1;
for (var i = 0; i < parent_row.cells.length; i++) {
  if (el === parent_row.cells[i]) {
    ci = i;
  }
}
if (ci == -1) return; // this should never happen
```

ci is the cellIndex, and can be used to highlight other cells with the same cellIndex in the other rows in the table:

File: **tableHighlight.js** (excerpt)

```
for (var i = 0; i < parent_table.rows.length; i++) {
  var cell = parent_table.rows[i].cells[ci];
  cell.className += ' hi';
}
```

All the table's rows are held in the table's `rows` array. We walk through that array, applying the `hi` class to the cell in each row that has the same index as the moused-over cell.

The upshot of this exercise is that all the cells in the same column as the moused-over cell will have class `hi`; the table row containing the cell will also have class `hi`.

Our CSS code takes care of the appearance of these cells:

File: **tableHighlight.html** (excerpt)

```
tr.hi td, td.hi {
   background-color: #ccc;
}
```

We've applied a background color of class `hi` to both `tds`, and `tds` in a `tr` of class `hi`; thus, these cells will be highlighted. The `lo_cell` function works similarly, except that it removes the class `hi` from the row and column rather than applying it. The removal is done with the following lines:

File: **tableHighlight.js** (excerpt)

```
parent_row.className =
   parent_row.className.replace(/\b ?hi\b/, '');
```

File: **tableHighlight.js** (excerpt)

```
cell.className = cell.className.replace(/\b ?hi\b/, '');
```

Since a `className` is a string, it has all the methods of a string, one of which is `replace`; we can call the `replace` method with a regular expression (first parameter) and a substitute string (second parameter). If a match for the regular expression is found in the string, it is replaced by the substitute string. In our example, we look for matches to the expression \b ?hi\b (note that regular expressions are delimited by slashes, not quotes)—that is, a word boundary followed by an optional space, the word 'hi', and another word boundary—and replace it with a blank string, thus removing it from the `className`.

An added bonus of using CSS to provide the style information is that we can apply different highlighting to different tables on the page without changing the script. For example, the HTML of the page contains two tables, one with a class of `extra`. We apply some CSS specifically to tables with class `extra`:

File: **tableHighlight.html** (excerpt)

```
table.extra tr.hi td, table.extra td.hi {
  color: red;
  text-decoration: underline overline;
  background-color: transparent;
}
```

As a result, the highlighted cells in that particular table will be highlighted differently. CSS makes achieving this kind of effect very easy.

Summary

Understanding the processes by which events are fired, and by which code is hooked to those events, is vital to DHTML programming. Almost everything you do in DHTML will involve attaching code to events, as described in this chapter. We've examined some common events and the two browser models for listening to them. We have also covered what happens when an event fires, and how you can interrupt or alter that process. Finally, we looked at a few events in detail, and saw some simple examples of how code can attach to those events and improve the user experience on sites that employ these techniques.

Detecting Browser Features

You just listed all my best features.
—The Cat, *Red Dwarf*, Series 3, Episode *DNA*

An important design constraint when adding DHTML to your Websites is that it should be unobtrusive. By "unobtrusive," I mean that if a given Web browser doesn't support the DHTML features you're using, that absence should affect the user experience as little as possible. Errors should not be shown to the user: the site should be perfectly usable without the DHTML enhancements. The browsers that render your site will fall into the following broad categories:

1. Offer no JavaScript support at all, or have JavaScript turned off.

2. Provide some JavaScript support, but modern features are missing.

3. Have full JavaScript support, but offer no W3C DOM support at all.

4. Provide incomplete DOM support, but some DOM features are missing or buggy.

5. Offer complete DOM support without bugs.

The first and the last categories hold no concerns for you as a DHTML developer. A browser that does not run JavaScript at all will simply work without calling any of your DHTML code, so you can ignore it for the purposes of this discussion.

You just need to make sure that your page displays correctly when JavaScript is turned off.[1] Similarly, a browser that implements the DOM completely and without bugs would make life very easy. It's a shame that such browsers do not exist.

The three categories in the middle of the list are of concern to us in this chapter. Here, we'll explore how to identify which DHTML features are supported by a given browser before we try to utilize those features in running our code.

There are basically two ways[2] to working out whether the browser that's being used supports a given feature. The first approach is to work out which browser is being used, then have a list within your code that states which browser supports which features. The second way is to test for the existence of a required feature directly. In the following discussion, we'll see that classifying browsers by type isn't as good as detecting features on a case-by-case basis.

Old-Fashioned Browser Sniffing

In the bad old days, before browser manufacturers standardized on the DOM, JavaScript developers relied on detection of the browser's brand and version via a process known as browser sniffing. Each browser provides a `window.navigator` object, containing details about the browser, which can be checked from JavaScript. We can, for example, find the name of the browser (the "user agent string") as follows:

```
var browserName = navigator.userAgent;
var isIE = browserName.match(/MSIE/); // find IE and look-alikes
```

Don't do this any more! This technique, like many other relics from the Dark Ages of JavaScript coding (before the W3C DOM specifications appeared), *should not be used*. Browser sniffing is flaky and prone to error, and should be avoided like the black plague. *Really*: I'm not kidding here.

Why am I so unenthusiastic about browser sniffing? There are lots of reasons. Some browsers lie about, or attempt to disguise, their true details; some, such as Opera, can be configured to deliver a user agent string of the user's choice. It's pretty much impossible to stay up-to-date with every version of every browser,

---

[1] For example, if your DHTML shows and hides some areas of the page, those areas should show initially, then be hidden with DHTML, so that they are available to non-DHTML browsers.
[2] Actually, there's a third way to identify browser support. The DOM standards specify a `document.implementation.hasFeature` method that you can use to detect DOM support. It's rarely used, though.

and it's definitely impossible to know which features each version supported upon its release. Moreover, if your site is required to last for any reasonable period of time, new browser versions will be released after your site, and your browser-sniffing code will be unable to account for them. Browser sniffing—what little of it remains—should be confined to the dustbin of history. Put it in the "we didn't know any better" category. There is a significantly better method available: feature sniffing.

Modern DOM Feature Sniffing

Instead of detecting the user's browser, then working out for yourself whether it supports a given feature, simply ask the browser directly whether it supports the feature. For example, a high proportion of DHTML scripts use the DOM method `getElementById`. To work out whether a particular visitor's browser supports this method, you can use:

```
if (document.getElementById) {
  // and here you know it is supported
}
```

If the `if` statement test passes, we know that the browser supports the feature in question. It is important to note that `getElementById` is not followed by brackets! We do not say:

```
if (document.getElementById())
```

If we include the brackets, we call the method `getElementById`. If we do not include the brackets, we're referring to the JavaScript `Function` object that underlies the method. This is a very important distinction. Including the brackets would mean that we were testing the return value of the method call, which we do not want to do. For a start, this would cause an error in a non-DOM browser, because we can't call the `getElementById` method there at all—it doesn't exist! When we test the `Function` object instead, we're assessing it for existence. Browsers that don't support the method will fail the test. Therefore, they will not run the code enclosed by the `if` statement; nor will they display an error.

This feature of JavaScript—the ability to test whether a method exists—has been part of the language since its inception; thus, it is safe to use it on even the oldest JavaScript-supporting browsers. You may recall from the previous chapter the technique of referring to a `Function` object without calling it. In Chapter 3, we used it to assign a function as an event listener without actually calling it. In

JavaScript, everything can be treated as an object if you try hard enough; methods are no exception!

Which DOM Features Should We Test?

The easiest approach is to test for every DOM method you intend to use. If your code uses `getElementById` and `createElement`, test for the existence of both methods. This will cover browsers in the fourth category above: the ones that implement some—but not all—of the DOM.

It is not reasonable to assume that a browser that supports `getElementById` also supports `getElementsByTagName`. You must explicitly test for each feature.

Where Should We Test for DOM Features?

An easy way to handle these tests is to execute them before your DHTML sets up any event listeners. A large subset of DHTML scripts work by setting on page load some event listeners that will be called as various elements in the browser fire events. If, before setting up the event listeners, you check that the browser supplies all the DOM features required by the code, event listeners will not be set up for browsers that do not support those features. You can therefore reasonably assume in setting up your event listeners that all the features you require are available; this assumption can simplify your code immensely. Here's an example:

```
function myScriptInit() {
  if (!document.getElementById ||
      !document.getElementsByTagName ||
      !document.createElement) {
    return;
  }
  // set up the event listeners here
}

function myScriptEventListener() {
  var foo = document.getElementById('foo');  // safe to use
}

addEvent(window, 'load', myScriptInit, false);
```

This script contains a `myScriptInit` function, which sets up `myScriptEventListener` as an event listener. But, before we set up that listener, we check for the existence of the DOM methods `getElementById`, `getElementsByTagName`, and `createElement`.

The `if` statement says: "if the JavaScript `Function` object `document.getElementById` does not exist, or if the `Function` object `document.getElementsByTagName` does not exist, or if the `Function` object `document.createElement` does not exist, exit the `myScriptInit` function." This means that, should any of those objects not be supported, the `myScriptInit` function will exit at that point: it will not even get as far as setting up the event listeners. Our code will set up listeners only on browsers that do support those methods. Therefore, as above, the listener function `myScriptEventListener` can feel safe in using `document.getElementById` without first checking to ensure that it is supported. If it wasn't supported, the listener function would not have been set up.

All this sniffing relies on JavaScript's runtime behavior. Even though the scripts are read by the browser at load time, no checks are done on the objects stated in the scripts until the code is run. This allows us to put browser objects in all scripts, and use them only when our detection code gets around to it: an arrangement called **late binding**.

Testing Non-DOM Features

Feature sniffing can be used on any JavaScript object: not just methods, and not just those methods that are part of the DOM. Commonly used examples are the offset properties (`offsetWidth`, `offsetHeight`, `offsetLeft` and `offsetTop`) of an element. These JavaScript properties are an extension to the DOM provided by all the major browsers. They return information on the size and position of an element in pixels. We can test whether those properties are defined on a given element's object as follows:

```
var foo = document.getElementById('foo');

if (typeof foo.offsetHeight != 'undefined') {
  var fooHeight = foo.offsetHeight;
}
```

Here, we set `fooHeight` if, and only if, `offsetHeight` is supported on `foo`. This is a different type of check from the method we used before, though: isn't it possible simply to say, `if (foo.offsetHeight)`? This isn't a good approach to use. If `foo.offsetHeight` is not defined, `if (foo.offsetHeight)` will not be true, just as we expect. However, the `if` statement will also fail if `foo.offsetHeight` does exist, but is equal to `0` (zero). This is possible because JavaScript treats zero as meaning `false`. Testing whether a given item is defined just got a little more complex (but only a little!).

If you are testing for the existence of function `functionName`, or method `methodName` (on an object `obj`), use the function/method name without the brackets to do so:

```
if (functionName) { ... }
if (obj.methodName) { ... }
```

Likewise, if you're testing for a variable `v`, or for a DOM property `prop` of an object, you can often use the variable or the DOM attribute's property name directly:

```
if (v) { ... }
if (obj.prop) { ... }
```

But, watch out! If the variable or property contains numbers or strings (as does `offsetHeight`, for example) then use `typeof`, because a number might be `0` (zero), and a string might be the empty string `""`, both which also evaluate to `false`:

```
if (typeof v != 'undefined') { ... }
if (typeof obj.prop != 'undefined') { ... }
```

Sniffing at Work: `scrollImage`

Lots of Websites contain photo galleries: pages listing thumbnails of photographs that, when clicked on, display the photos at full size. An interesting enhancement to such a site might be to let the user see the full-size photo without having to click to load it. When the user mouses over the thumbnail, that thumbnail could become a "viewing area" in which a snippet of the full-sized image is shown. This technique is useful if your thumbnails aren't detailed enough to enable users to tell the difference between superficially similar images. It's especially handy if your thumbnails display something like a document, rather than a photo. Figure 4.1 shows the final effect:

Figure 4.1. The thumbnail display implemented by the `scrollImage` example.

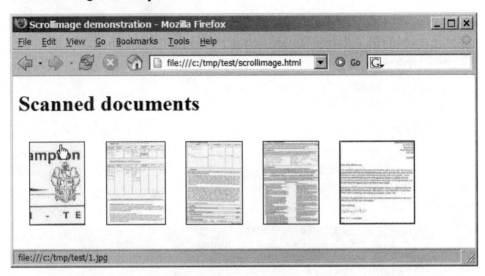

We'll describe what's going on here in a moment. We'll review the code first, then see a demonstration before we get to the explanation.

Setting Up the Page

The HTML file for this technique is straightforward:

File: **scrollImage.html**

```
<!DOCTYPE HTML PUBLIC "-//W3C//DTD HTML 4.01//EN"
    "http://www.w3.org/TR/html4/strict.dtd">
<html>
  <head>
    <title>ScrollImage demonstration</title>
    <script src="scrollImage.js" type="text/javascript"></script>
    <style type="text/css">
      .scrollimage {
        display: block;
        float: left;
        border: 1px solid black;
        margin: 1em;
        padding: 0;
      }
```

```
    .scrollimage:hover {
      position: relative;
    }

    .scrollimage img {
      border: none;
    }

    .scrollimage:hover img {
      display: none;
    }
  </style>
</head>
<body>

  <h1>Scanned documents</h1>

  <p>
    <a href="1.jpg" class="scrollimage"
       mainx="563" mainy="823" thumbx="82" thumby="120"
       style="background: url(1.jpg); width: 82px;
       height: 120px;"
    ><img src="1-thumb.jpg"></a>

    <a href="2.jpg" class="scrollimage"
       mainx="563" mainy="777" thumbx="87" thumby="120"
       style="background: url(2.jpg); width: 87px;
       height: 120px;"
    ><img src="2-thumb.jpg"></a>

    <a href="3.jpg" class="scrollimage"
       mainx="567" mainy="823" thumbx="83" thumby="120"
       style="background: url(3.jpg); width: 83px;
       height: 120px;"
    ><img src="3-thumb.jpg"></a>

    <a href="4.jpg" class="scrollimage"
       mainx="558" mainy="806" thumbx="83" thumby="120"
       style="background: url(4.jpg); width: 83px;
       height: 120px;"
    ><img src="4-thumb.jpg"></a>

    <a href="5.jpg" class="scrollimage"
       mainx="434" mainy="467" thumbx="112" thumby="120"
       style="background: url(5.jpg); width: 112px;
       height: 120px;"
```

```
      ><img src="5-thumb.jpg"></a>
    </p>

  </body>
</html>
```

The content of this page is fairly obvious. Notice how the image elements are hidden by CSS styles when the mouse moves over them. This page also includes—with the `<script src="scrollImage.js" type="text/javascript"></script>` line—this JavaScript file:

File: **scrollImage.js**

```
// Based on findPos*, by ppk
// (http://www.quirksmode.org/js/findpos.html)
function findPosX(obj) {
  var curLeft = 0;
  if (obj.offsetParent) {
    do {
      curLeft += obj.offsetLeft;
    } while (obj = obj.offsetParent);
  }
  else if (obj.x) {
    curLeft += obj.x;
  }
  return curLeft;
}

function findPosY(obj) {
  var curTop = 0;
  if (obj.offsetParent) {
    do {
      curTop += obj.offsetTop;
    } while (obj = obj.offsetParent);
  }
  else if (obj.y) {
    curTop += obj.y;
  }
  return curTop;
}

// cross-browser event handling for IE5+, NS6+ and Mozilla/Gecko
// By Scott Andrew
function addEvent(obj, evType, fn, useCapture) {
  if (obj.addEventListener) {
    obj.addEventListener(evType, fn, useCapture);
    return true;
```

```
  } else if (obj.attachEvent) {
    var r = obj.attachEvent('on' + evType, fn);
    return r;
  } else {
    obj['on' + evType] = fn;
  }
}

addEvent(window, 'load', scrollInit, false);

function scrollInit() {
  if (!document.getElementsByTagName)
    return;
  var allLinks = document.getElementsByTagName('a');
  for (var i = 0; i < allLinks.length; i++) {
    var link = allLinks[i];
    if ((' ' + link . className + ' ').indexOf(' scrollimage ') !=
        -1) {
      addEvent(link, 'mousemove', moveListener, false);
    }
  }
}

function attVal(element, attName) {
  return parseInt(element.getAttribute(attName));
}

function moveListener(ev) {
  var e = window.event ? window.event : ev;
  var t = e.target ? e.target : e.srcElement;

  var xPos = e.clientX - findPosX(t);
  var yPos = e.clientY - findPosY(t);

  if (t.nodeName.toLowerCase() == 'img')
    t = t.parentNode;
  if (t.nodeName.toLowerCase() == 'a') {

    // scaleFactorY = (width(big) - width(small)) / width(small)
    var scaleFactorY =
        (attVal(t, 'mainy') - attVal(t, 'thumby')) / attVal(t,
        'thumby');
    var scaleFactorX =
        (attVal(t, 'mainx') - attVal(t, 'thumbx')) / attVal(t,
        'thumbx');
```

```
    t.style.backgroundPosition =
        (-parseInt(xPos * scaleFactorX)) + 'px ' +
        (-parseInt(yPos * scaleFactorY)) + 'px';
  }
}
```

We'll explore (and fix!) this code shortly. Finally, the page also contains images: five at full-size, and five thumbnails. You can find them in the code archive for this book.

Demonstrating the DHTML Effect

Let's see how the page works. The HTML document shows five images as thumbnails; in this example, they're thumbnails of individual pages of a scanned-in document. Figure 4.2 shows the page content under normal circumstances.

Figure 4.2. Thumbnails of a document.

Scanned documents

When we mouse-over a thumbnail image, though, the display of that thumbnail changes to show the actual image to which it's linked, as shown in Figure 4.3.

The thumbnail becomes a viewing area in which we can see a snippet of the full-size image. As the cursor moves over the third image, we see the content of the third image at full size through the viewing area. For a document thumbnail such as this, we can use the cursor to move around the document within the viewing area, so that we can read the content and see if it's the document we want. This technique can also be useful, as mentioned, in photo galleries containing images that look similar when displayed at thumbnail size.

Figure 4.3. Mousing over a thumbnail.

Scanned documents

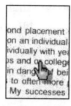

How the Code Works

Conceptually, the code works as follows: we set up the page so that every "scrollable" image is made up of an `<a>` tag of class `scrollimage`, which contains an `<img>` tag displaying the thumbnail. We apply the full-size image as the CSS background image of the `<a>` tag. Then, when the user mouses over the a element, we hide the `img` element entirely, allowing the a element's background image to show through. We then manipulate the position of that background image so that it moves in accordance with the cursor.[3]

This is all fairly advanced stuff, so we need to confirm that the running browser supports all the features we need in order to make it work. We start by making the script initialize on page load with the line:

File: **scrollImage.js (excerpt)**

```
addEvent(window, 'load', scrollInit, false);
```

We saw the `addEvent` method in Chapter 3, but, with what we've learned about feature detection, its workings should now be much clearer to you. First, we check for the existence of an `addEventListener` method on the passed object, to see if the user's browser supports the DOM Events model correctly:

---

[3]We're storing the dimensions of the larger image in custom attributes on the a element: `mainx`, `mainy`, `thumbx`, and `thumby`. This is a slightly suspect technique: it will prevent the HTML from validating, and should therefore be approached with caution. In this case, however, it is the easiest way to tie the required values to each of the a elements.

```
function addEvent(obj, evType, fn, useCapture) {
  if (obj.addEventListener) {
    obj.addEventListener(evType, fn, useCapture);
    return true;
```

Failing that, we look for Internet Explorer's proprietary `attachEvent` method on the object.

```
  } else if (obj.attachEvent) {
    var r = obj.attachEvent('on' + evType, fn);
    return r;
```

Failing *that*, we attach the event listener directly to the element, as an event handler; this is required for IE5 on Macintosh.

```
  } else {
    obj['on' + evType] = fn;
  }
```

This procedure caters for all the ways by which we might attach an event listener, using feature sniffing to see which option is available.

The initialization function that sets up the scrolling effect, `scrollInit`, uses `document.getElementsByTagName` to find all the a elements in the document. Therefore, `scrollInit` checks for this method's existence before proceeding:

```
function scrollInit() {
  if (!document.getElementsByTagName)
    return;
```

If the user's browser doesn't support `document.getElementsByTagName`, then we return from the `scrollInit` function and don't progress any further.

One extra trick in the feature sniffing code, as described in Chapter 3, addresses the way in which we find the event object when we're inside the `moveListener` event listener. As we know, the DOM Events specification mandates that an event object is passed to the event listener as an argument, whereas Internet Explorer makes the event object available as the global `window.event`. So, our code checks for the existence of `window.event`, and uses it as the event object if it exists; the code falls back to the passed-in argument if `window.event` is not present:

File: **scrollImage.js (excerpt)**

```
function moveListener(ev) {
  var e = window.event ? window.event : ev;
```

Next, we need to get the event's target from that event object; the DOM specifies `e.target`, and Internet Explorer provides `e.srcElement`. Another feature-sniff gives us the appropriate value:

File: **scrollImage.js (excerpt)**

```
var t = e.target ? e.target : e.srcElement;
```

This is a compressed, shorthand version of the code we saw in Chapter 3.

The next step is for the code to get the position of the mouse inside the thumbnail image area. This is the code from the full listing above that is supposed to do this:

```
var xPos = e.clientX - findPosX(t);
var yPos = e.clientY - findPosY(t);
```

In theory, `e.clientX` and `e.clientY` give the x- and y-coordinates of the mouse within the browser window, respectively. By subtracting from these the x- and y-coordinates of the target element, we obtain the mouse's position within that element.

Depending on your browser of choice, this might seem to work just fine at first glance. Peter-Paul Koch's `findPosX` and `findPosY` functions make short work of getting the target element's position.[4] Unfortunately, the `clientX` and `clientY` properties of the event object are nowhere near as reliable.

clientX and clientY Problems

The code above is flawed: the event listener uses `e.clientX` and `e.clientY` to ascertain the position of the mouse.

But that's not a flaw, is it? After all, it's in the DOM specifications!

---

[4]For a complete description of how `findPosX` and `findPosY` work, visit Peter-Paul Koch's page on the subject at http://www.quirksmode.org/js/findpos.html.

Well, it's *sort of* a flaw—a flaw in the way browser manufacturers interpret the specification. Peter-Paul Koch studies this problem in great detail in his comprehensive article, *Mission Impossible—Mouse Position*[2]. The problem occurs only when the page is scrolled (which was not the case with the above page). When a page is scrolled, the specification is rather vague on whether clientX and clientY are returned relative to the whole document, or to the window (the part of the document that is visible). Internet Explorer returns them relative to the window, as does Mozilla, but all of Opera, Konqueror, and iCab return them relative to the document. Netscape also provides pageX and pageY, which are mouse coordinates relative to the document. (Ironically enough, Internet Explorer may be the only browser which is fully compliant with the standard; the best reading of the specification is that clientX and clientY should be relative to the window.)

So, we need to use pageX and pageY if they exist, and clientX and clientY if they do not; if we're in Internet Explorer, however, we have to add to clientX and clientY the amounts by which the page has been scrolled. But how do we know if we're in Internet Explorer? We use browser detection.

Browser Detection You Can't Avoid

That spluttering noise you can hear in the background is the crowd rightly pointing out that we consigned browser detection to the dustbin of history only a few pages back, and they're not wrong. However, there are occasions when different browsers implement the same properties (in this case, clientX and clientY) in different ways *and* when there are no other objects available for sniffing that can us tell which of the different implementations is in use.

On such occasions, there is no alternative but to use the dreaded browser sniffing to work out what to do. The mouse position issue described here is almost the only such situation. The very thought that it might be necessary to use browser detection should make all right-thinking DHTML developers shudder with guilt, but, sadly, there's nothing for it! We add the browser detection script to the code just before we call addEvent to set up our window load listener:

File: **scrollImage.js (excerpt)**

```
var isIE = !window.opera && navigator.userAgent.indexOf('MSIE') !=
    -1;
```

Note that, first, we check that window.opera is false or non-existent; Opera sets this variable to make it easy for scripts to detect that it is the browser in use

---

[2] http://evolt.org/article/Mission_Impossible_mouse_position/17/23335/

(Opera also implements user-agent switching, so that, from a `navigator.userAgent` perspective, it can appear to be Internet Explorer). Once we've established that we're *not* using Opera, we go on to look for "MSIE" in the user agent string; if this is present, Internet Explorer is the browser in use.

Our updated `moveListener` event listener now looks like this:

File: **scrollImage.js (excerpt)**

```
function moveListener(ev) {
  var e = window.event ? window.event : ev;
  var t = e.target ? e.target : e.srcElement;

  var mX, mY;
  if (e.pageX && e.pageY) {
    mX = e.pageX;
    my = e.pageY;
  } else if (e.clientX && e.clientY) {
    mX = e.clientX;
    mY = e.clientY;
    if (isIE) {
      mX += document.body.scrollLeft;
      mY += document.body.scrollTop;
    }
  }

  var xPos = mX - findPosX(t);
  var yPos = mY - findPosY(t);

// ... the rest as before ...
```

Note that we check first for `pageX` and `pageY` (for Mozilla), then fall through to `clientX` and `clientY`. We handle Internet Explorer by checking the `isIE` variable; if it's `true`, we add the document's scroll amounts as required. We're using the browser detect as little as possible; specifically, Netscape/Mozilla provide the `pageX` and `pageY` properties, and we look for them through feature sniffing, *not* by performing browser detection for Mozilla.

Calculating Screen Positions

The last section of our code has little to do with browser detects, but, having spent all this time to get the right X and Y coordinates, it makes sense to understand how to use them.

The last part of the moveListener function starts with a couple of ifs, which ensure that we have in hand a reference to the <a> tag surrounding the thumbnail <img> of interest. No surprises there, so we grab the required DOM element:

File: **scrollImage.js (excerpt)**

```
if (t.nodeName.toLowerCase() == 'img')
  t = t.parentNode;
if (t.nodeName.toLowerCase() == 'a') {
```

Next, we have the first of two sets of calculations:

File: **scrollImage.js (excerpt)**

```
// scaleFactorY = (width(big) - width(small)) / width(small)
var scaleFactorY =
    (attVal(t, 'mainy') - attVal(t, 'thumby')) / attVal(t,
    'thumby');
var scaleFactorX =
    (attVal(t, 'mainx') - attVal(t, 'thumbx')) / attVal(t,
    'thumbx');
```

Code like this is liable to be specific to each DHTML effect you undertake, but the mind-bending you have to do to come up with the code is similar in all cases. Take a deep breath: here we go!

With the large background image showing through the viewing area, what should appear when the cursor is in the top-left corner of that viewing area? The top-left corner of the big image should be in the top-left corner of the viewing area: that's straightforward. Now, what should appear when the cursor is located at the bottom-right corner of the viewing area? Should the bottom-right corner of the full-sized image be in the top-left corner of the viewing area? That's what would happen if the big image were moved by its full size across the viewing area as the cursor was moved the full distance across the viewing area. Think about it carefully; you might like to try experimenting with two pieces of paper, one of which has a rectangular hole in it. The big image would eventually disappear off the top-left corner of the viewing area! If the background image were tiled (the default), additional copies of the image would be visible at this bottom-right corner—a very odd result.

We don't want the image to move that far. If we move the cursor to the extreme bottom-right of the viewing area, we want the big image to move by almost its entire size—but not quite! We want the bottom-right corner of the big image to move only as far as the bottom-right corner of the viewing area, and not move any further towards the top-left.

Now, to make the big image move, we have to calculate a distance by which to move it. Take some example figures: suppose the big image is ten times the size of the thumbnail. Let's suppose the image is 500 pixels on each side, and the thumbnail's 50 pixels on each side. For every pixel by which the cursor moves, the big image should move 500/50: ten times as fast. So the "scale factor" is ten. But, wait a minute! If the cursor moves 50 pixels left, the big image will move 500 pixels left: right off the left edge of the viewing area. That's too far. We want it to move at most 500 *minus* 50 pixels, so that it's always "inside" the viewing area. Therefore, the real scale factor is (500 – 50) / 50 = 9. The full-sized image should move nine times as fast as the cursor. That's what the first set of calculations does, except that it calculates scale factors in both dimensions, since most images are rectangles, not squares.

Next, we want to move the big image. Here's the second set of calculations:

File: **scrollImage.js** (excerpt)

```
t.style.backgroundPosition =
    (-parseInt(xPos * scaleFactorX)) + 'px ' +
    (-parseInt(yPos * scaleFactorY)) + 'px';
```

Now, if (for example) we move the mouse from the top-left towards the bottom-right, we're scanning diagonally across the viewing area. As we move, we want new areas of the big image to come into view. So the big image had better slide in the opposite direction to the mouse: up towards, and beyond, the top left. It's like using a negative margin to bleed text to the left and top of a page. And that's what we do by calculating negative pixel amounts.

This idea may seem back-to-front initially. Think of it as though you were shooting a scene for a movie. The camera (the thumbnail viewing area) is fixed into place, so it must be the scene at which the camera points that moves if there's to be any panning effect. Alternately, imagine yourself looking out of the window of a moving train without turning your head. It's the same effect again, provided the train goes backwards!

Summary

In this chapter, we've learned that browsers don't always support all the DOM features we'd like, and discussed how feature sniffing helps us as DHTML developers to code defensively around this issue. Browser sniffing allows us to deliver dynamic features to browsers that can handle them and, at the same time, to avoid crashing or throwing errors in browsers that can't. We looked at the old method, browser sniffing, and explained why it shouldn't be used if at all possible.

We then explored one occasion on which feature sniffing can't provide everything we need, leaving us the old method as a last resort.

5

Animation

Anyone can now enter the lucrative field of animated cartoons with the new Tom and Jerry Cartoon Kit. This kit contains everything needed for quiet, sophisticated humor—one mean, stupid cat; one sweet, lovable mouse; and assorted deadly weapons. The coffee and cigarettes are for the cartoonists.
—The Tom and Jerry Cartoon Kit, 1962

Adding animation to your DHTML pages can really boost usability. Animation lets the user know that something is happening (think of a progress bar, or an hourglass), it can provide context for something that's happening (think of a drop-down menu; you know that the contents of the menu are related to the header of the menu), and it does look pretty cool when it's used correctly. Here, we'll consider the principles of the appropriate use of animation, then we'll see how to use it smoothly and well. Animation is fun! It's the cherry on the top of the Web development pie, so grab the opportunity to use it when an decent excuse comes along.

Tastefulness and Usability

Animated elements of a page draw the user's eye like nothing else. This is an important thing to know; if you want to draw the user's eye to an element, animating it is a good way to do so. But it is vital to remember that an animated element will draw attention away from everything else on the page. Frivolous animations will divert your users' focus from valuable content. When implemented subtly and tastefully, though, animation can tie the disparate parts of your page together very neatly. It is therefore very important not to overuse animation techniques. Apply animation with a light hand.

Animation Basics

Animation in DHTML falls into two categories: causing an element to change its appearance while remaining still, and causing an element to move. Both of these approaches rely on having the transition occur in numerous little steps (small movements, or small changes of appearance), which occur in quick succession. Each step builds on the previous step until, at the end of the animation, the item has fully changed or moved to its final position. So, to make a block of text change color, from black to white, each little step would make the text a slightly lighter shade of grey than the previous step, until the text reaches white and the animation stops. This effect is shown in Figure 5.1 below.

Figure 5.1. The text fades in steps.

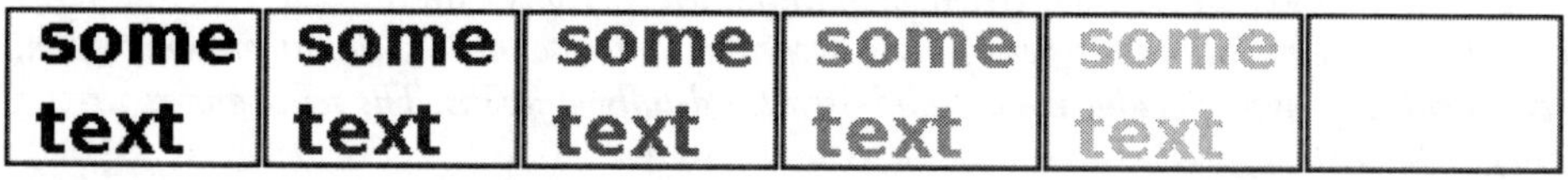

Each step takes place without any prompting from users; they are not required to do anything to make the steps execute. Let's see how we can make these steps occur one after the other.

I'll provide a full working example in this chapter, but if you're impatient, you can check out the effect in action[1]. This project management site lets you experiment with its services for free. Enroll, create a test project, go to the project home page, and click the Messages tab (or click "All Messages"). The first time you add a message, the effect might occur too quickly for you to spot, but add a second message, and you'll see how the fading effect provides an excellent reminder of the content that was just added.

The setTimeout Function

Almost all timed activity in JavaScript takes place through the use of the setTimeout function (this is actually a method, which belongs to the window

---

[1] http://www.basecamphq.com/

object). We pass a string containing JavaScript code and a number of milliseconds (one millisecond being one thousandth of a second), and that code will be run once the specified number of milliseconds has elapsed. So, to pop up an alert two seconds from now, we could use the following:

```
setTimeout('alert("Hello, world!")', 2000);
```

The first argument is a string that contains code; it's not the code stated literally. If we leave out the single quotes in the above, the code will be run immediately and its return value will be used as the code that's run in two seconds' time. Since executing the JavaScript expression 2 (if that happens to be the return value) doesn't do much (it evaluates 2 to mean 2, then throws it away!), this is probably not what you want. You must be careful to remember to pass the code in correctly as a string.[1] Since it is a string, you must also be careful about quoting: quotes inside the string might need to be escaped:

```
setTimeout('alert("Why oh why didn\'t I take the blue pill?")',
    2000);
```

Note that the apostrophe in "didn't" is escaped, to prevent it from ending the entire string early. It's a good idea use one type of quote mark (say, single quotes) for the whole string, then use the other kind of quote mark (double quotes) wherever they're needed inside the string. The example above does that, but we're also stuck with an extra single quote that's literally required for "didn't", so it needs to be escaped with a backslash.

This extra quoting may be quite a difficult concept to get your head around, but it's vital that you understand it: we pass a string containing code, not the code itself. We put quotes around the whole code, even if it contains quotes already.

Because the timed code is stated outside the normal flow of code, and because it's executed later, it's best to try to keep the timed code simple. Make timed code short; make it do its job, then finish up quickly. Complex timed code just leads to a big, tangled mess. Vote against JavaScript spaghetti code by using short timed code!

Passing in a Function

Using a string that contains JavaScript code does create a fairly serious problem, though: how do you use an existing object or a variable in that string? For example, imagine this code:

---

[1] Of course, this can be useful; you could call a function directly, which returns some code to be run.

```
function testSetTimeout() {
  var myVariable = 'A string';
  setTimeout('alert(myVariable)', 1000);
}

testSetTimeout();
```

What will that do?

What it *won't* do is present a dialog box containing the words, "A string." Instead, we get a JavaScript error: "myVariable is not defined." Why is this?

The string passed to `setTimeout` is evaluated in the context of the `window` object. It is not evaluated in the context of the function or method from which it was called. What this means is that, although our `myVariable` exists inside the `testSetTimeout` function, it doesn't exist as a global variable, but that's what the `window` object contains: global variables. If you use a variable in code passed to `setTimeout`, it has to be a global variable. If it isn't, when the code runs, it won't be able to find the variable.

Fortunately, there is a better solution. Instead of a string, we can pass a function to `setTimeout`, and that function will be executed when the timeout occurs (but beware of really old browsers, in which this won't work). If this function is defined within another function, it will be able to access the variables inside that outer function. In other words, the context (or home) of our timed function is its parent function, so the parent function's variables are available in the timed code. That's what we want!

As with event listeners, we pass a function to `setTimeout` by supplying its name:

```
function testSetTimeout() {
  var privateVar = 'A string';
  function bar() { alert(privateVar); }
  window.setTimeout(bar, 1000);
}
testSetTimeout();
```

This will display the text "A string" in a dialog box, as expected. Both `bar` and `privateVar` have the same context—the function `testSetTimeout`. In fact, we need not even assign the function a name: we can define the function inline as an **anonymous function**:

```
function testSetTimeout() {
  var privateVar = 'A string';
```

```
  window.setTimeout(function() { alert(privateVar); }, 1000);
}
testSetTimeout();
```

Surrounding the actual code with `function() { ... }` is a quick hack that gives us access to the variables we need. It also allows us to put our timer setup in a custom function, which can be called after the page is loaded.

setTimeout Runs Later On

An animation would not be a useful enhancement if the rest of the browser locked up while the animation was running. To avoid this problem, `setTimeout` itself is asynchronous: when you call it, it returns immediately. That means the browser continues to respond immediately to user input. Nothing is "stopped" while waiting for the timed event to occur. After the defined period, the browser runs the timed code as soon as it isn't busy doing something else. You may call `setTimeout` as many times as you wish, and each scheduled piece of code will run in turn after the allotted time without further prompting.

Some programming languages offer sleep, select or wait functions that pause everything for the specified amount of time. Such functionality is impossible in a Web page. All you can do is schedule pieces of code to run at some time in the future, then finish up what you were doing. The scheduled piece of code will come back at the right time, like a boomerang. So, learn to duck!

Canceling Timed Code

A call to `setTimeout` returns a value. If you want the option to cancel the scheduled code before it runs, you can store this value and pass it to the `clearTimeout` function.

Here's an example of a simple cancelled timing system at work. It provides a tooltip, otherwise known as flyover help. First, here's the HTML:

File: **cancelTips.html**

```
<!DOCTYPE HTML PUBLIC "-//W3C//DTD HTML 4.01//EN"
    "http://www.w3.org/TR/html4/strict.dtd">
<html>
  <head>
    <script type="text/javascript" src="cancelTips.js"></script>
    <style type="text/css">
      #explain {
        float: right;
```

```
        width: 20em;
        height: 6em;
        border: 3px solid red;
        padding: 0.5em;
        margin: 1em;
      }
    </style>
  </head>
  <body>
    <a href="" id="mylink">Home</a>
    <p id="explain"> </p>
  </body>
</html>
```

This page is a single link with a carefully styled paragraph that contains nothing. Here's the matching script:

File: **cancelTips.js**

```
function addEvent(elm, evType, fn, useCapture) {
  if (elm.addEventListener) {
    elm.addEventListener(evType, fn, useCapture);
    return true;
  } else if (elm.attachEvent) {
    var r = elm.attachEvent('on' + evType, fn);
    return r;
  } else {
    elm['on' + evType] = fn;
  }
}

function init() {
  if (!document.getElementById) return;
  var mylink = document.getElementById('mylink');
  addEvent(mylink, 'mouseover', mover, false);
  addEvent(mylink, 'mouseout', mout, false);
}

function mover() {
  TIMEOUT_ID = setTimeout(
    'document.getElementById("explain").innerHTML' +
    ' = "Return to the homepage"',
    2000);
}

function mout() {
  // put in an   placeholder to clear the current content
```

```
  document.getElementById('explain').innerHTML =
    ' ';
  clearTimeout(TIMEOUT_ID);
}

var TIMEOUT_ID;
addEvent(window, 'load', init, false);
```

We've got the now-familiar `addEvent` code, a listener initialization function, and some listeners. It's all stuff we've discussed before. Let's see what's new.

We want a link that displays descriptive text if we hover over it for a little while. We've chosen 2000 (2 seconds) to exaggerate the effect—normally you'd use a number like 500 (half a second). However, if we mouse away from the link before the descriptive text is displayed, we don't want it to appear later. First, we attach `mouseover` and `mouseout` listeners to the link in the standard way. Here's the `mouseover` listener:

File: **cancelTips.js** (excerpt)

```
function mover() {
  TIMEOUT_ID = setTimeout(
    'document.getElementById("explain").innerHTML' +
    ' = "Return to the homepage"',
    2000);
}
```

The `mouseover` listener controls the display of the descriptive text; when we hover over the link, we start a timeout counter by passing a string to `setTimeout`. That string is code that will display the descriptive text, and that code will run 2000ms after we hover over the link. In the listing, we've chopped the string into two sections, so that it's easy to read on the page.

Next, here's the `mouseout` listener.

File: **cancelTips.js** (excerpt)

```
function mout() {
  // put in an   placeholder to clear the current content
  document.getElementById('explain').innerHTML =
    ' ';
  clearTimeout(TIMEOUT_ID);
}
```

If we move the mouse off the link before the 2000ms is up, we want to cancel that timeout so that the text doesn't show. The `mouseout` listener cancels the timeout by calling `clearTimeout` with the value returned from the original `setTimeout` call. Note that the `TIMEOUT_ID` variable is a global variable and is declared (with `var TIMEOUT_ID`) outside any functions. It's declared globally like this because each function (`mover` and `mout`) needs access to the variable.

The `setInterval` Function

An alternative to `setTimeout` is `setInterval`. Calling `setTimeout` runs the code you supply once and once only; to create animation with `setTimeout`, the code you call should, in turn, call `setTimeout` again, in order to execute the next step of the animation.

By contrast, `setInterval` calls the code every given number of milliseconds, forever. This is useful for a constantly-running animation, but, as I said above, animation should be used to spruce up or improve the usability of an action; an animation which really does run all the time is ultimately distracting. However, as with `setTimeout`, it is also possible to cancel an interval timer using `clearInterval`. So an alternative to running code that calls `setTimeout` repeatedly is to call `setInterval` once to execute the same code repeatedly, store the return value, and then use that return value to cancel the interval timer once the animation is finished.

Implementing a Clock

Here's a simple application of a timer: displaying a constantly updating digital clock on a Web page. The clock displays the time in the format: HH:MM:SS. Here's a quick example HTML page for this effect:

File: **clock.html**

```
<!DOCTYPE HTML PUBLIC "-//W3C//DTD HTML 4.01//EN"
    "http://www.w3.org/TR/html4/strict.dtd">
<html>
  <head>
    <script type="text/javascript" src="clock.js"></script>
    <style type="text/css">
      #clock {
        color: white;
        background-color: black;
      }
    </style>
  </head>
  <body>
    <span id="clock"> </span>
```

```
    </body>
</html>
```

That's about as simple as a test page can be. Here's the script:

File: **clock.js**

```
function addEvent(elm, evType, fn, useCapture) {
  if (elm.addEventListener) {
    elm.addEventListener(evType, fn, useCapture);
    return true;
  } else if (elm.attachEvent) {
    var r = elm.attachEvent('on' + evType, fn);
    return r;
  } else {
    elm['on' + evType] = fn;
  }
}

function init() {
  if (!document.getElementById)
    return;
  var clock = document.getElementById('clock');
  if (!clock.innerHTML)
    return;
  setInterval(function() { update(clock); }, 1000);
}

function update(clock) {
  var ua = navigator.userAgent.toLowerCase();
  var d = new Date();
  var digits, readout = '';

  digits = d.getHours();
  readout += (digits > 9 ? '' : '0') + digits + ':';

  digits = d.getMinutes();
  readout += (digits > 9 ? '' : '0') + digits + ':';

  digits = d.getSeconds();
  readout += (digits > 9 ? '' : '0') + digits;

  clock.innerHTML = readout;
}

addEvent(window, 'load', init, false);
```

As ever, our `init` function sets up the effect on page load; in this case, it checks that we have the requisite DOM support (`document.getElementById`) and also that this browser implements `innerHTML` on HTML elements. The bit that sets the clock going is as follows:

File: **clock.js** (excerpt)

```
setInterval(function() { update(clock); }, 1000);
```

This code sets the `update` function to be called every second. Note that this time we're using an anonymous function, so that we can pass it `clock`, the reference to the `span` element in which we'll display the time. Here's `update`:

File: **clock.js** (excerpt)

```
function update(clock) {
  var d = new Date();
  var digits, readout = '';

  digits = d.getHours();
  readout += (digits > 9 ? '' : '0') + digits + ':';

  digits = d.getMinutes();
  readout += (digits > 9 ? '' : '0') + digits + ':';

  digits = d.getSeconds();
  readout += (digits > 9 ? '' : '0') + digits;

  clock.innerHTML = readout;
}
```

The `update` function simply sets the HTML inside the `clock` element (which is passed as a parameter) to reflect the current time.

It would have been better not to use `innerHTML`—not only is it not an official DOM property, but it can cause the clock to visibly flicker in Mozilla/Firefox if a `position: fixed` style is added. Alas, the standards-endorsed alternative isn't portable enough: Safari doesn't handle the proper DOM method of doing this (i.e. assigning the time value to `clock.firstChild.nodeValue`) properly. Such is the nature of cross-browser compromise.

Handling Errors

Handling errors during normal DHTML manipulations is obviously vital in order to avoid the dreaded "JavaScript Error" dialog box appearing. It is even more vital during DHTML-controlled animations, because an error in code that's called every second will produce a lot of dialog boxes. It is therefore very important that your code protects against errors by using object detection to ensure that you're not referencing objects that don't exist in the browser viewing the page.

When to use `try` and `catch`

If you happen to know about JavaScript's `try...catch` feature, you might be thinking that it will be useful here. Briefly, browsers provide a `try` statement that can be used to wrap JavaScript code; if an error (a JavaScript exception) occurs when running code in a `try` block, control is transferred to the `try`'s matching `catch` block. Here's an example:

File: **trycatch.html** (excerpt)

```
try {
  // here goes some JavaScript code
  alert('hello');
  alert(thisVarDoesntExist);
} catch(e) {
  // handle your error here
  alert('An error occurred!');
}
```

If an error occurs in the `try` block—in the above code, we have erroneously referenced a nonexistent variable—control is transferred to the `catch` block and, in this example, "An error occurred" is displayed.

This technique would provide a useful way to handle errors in animation code, but for the fact that the `try...catch` statement doesn't exist at all in older browsers. Therefore, the above code will cause an error in browsers that do not support `try...catch`—an error that cannot be trapped. As such, the syntax is not recommended because it is not unobtrusive; DHTML techniques should work in supporting browsers and fail silently and without problems in non-supporting browsers. Browsers that do not offer support include IE 4.x and Netscape versions below 4.5.

The good news is that modern DOM-enabled browsers support `try...catch` rather well. While you can't use object detection to test for a browser supporting `try...catch`, it is possible to use this (useful) technique in a restricted environment (such as in an intranet).

The body onerror Handler

A similar technique to try...catch is to use an onerror handler on the document body; this can be used to set up an event handler that's fired whenever an error occurs:

```
<script type='text/javascript'>
function init() {
  window.onerror = myErrorHandler;
}
addEvent(window, 'load', init, false);

function myErrorHandler() {
  // here we handle the error, or do nothing
  // Doing nothing will suppress the error message dialog
}
</script>
```

This technique would run without error in older browsers, because it does not use an unknown statement like try; however, it is not supported by Safari 1.2 on Mac. It will, however, fail silently on that browser, so this approach is a convenient one to take.

Scriptless Animation with GIFs

If you're looking for an easy way to highlight something as it happens—a mouseover effect on a link, for example—and you're thinking of using animation for this, it's entirely possible that you may not need DHTML at all. Our old friend the animated GIF can still have a role to play. Animated GIFs are somewhat frowned upon because they've been over-used for winking yellow smiley faces and spinning envelopes next to the word "email." That, however, is not the fault of the technology; it's just poor design. An animated GIF can be used to show that something's happening without flashing bright yellow text at the user. In Figure 5.2, we see an HTML page in which external links are highlighted with a grey globe; when the link is moused over, the globe switches to full-color. The colored globe is also an animated GIF, so when the link is moused over, the globe rotates.

Figure 5.2. Using an animated GIF to highlight a hovered link.

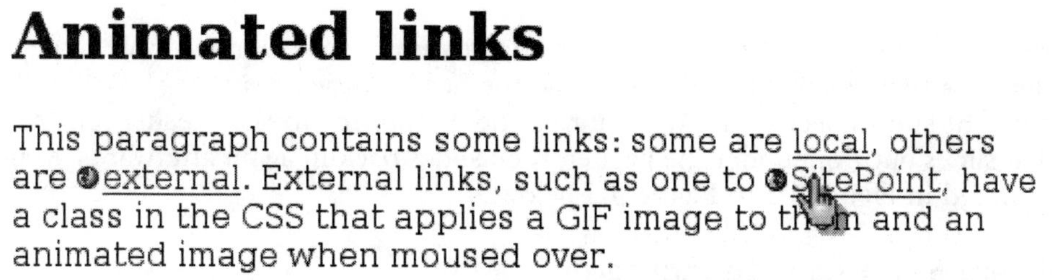

Animated links

This paragraph contains some links: some are local, others are ●external. External links, such as one to ●SitePoint, have a class in the CSS that applies a GIF image to them and an animated image when moused over.

This effect is accomplished with some simple CSS (no JavaScript at all). First, we give each external link a class of external in the HTML:

File: **animated_links.html** (excerpt)

```
<p>
  This paragraph contains some links: some are
  <a href="somewhere">local</a>, others are
  <a class="external" href="http://www.google.com/">external</a>.
  External links, such as one to
  <a class="external" href="http://www.sitepoint.com">SitePoint</a
  >, have a class in the CSS that applies a GIF image to them and
  an animated image when moused over.
</p>
```

Next, we display the globe on external links via our CSS:

File: **animated_links.html** (excerpt)

```
a.external {
  padding-left: 13px;
  background: url(remote.gif) center left no-repeat;
}
a.external:hover {
  background-image: url(remote_a.gif);
}
```

The padding-left property value provides some space for the globe to display; the grey globe (remote.gif) is set as a background image on each of these links. When the link is moused over—the a:hover selector means "links that are being moused over," so a.external:hover means "links of class external that are being moused over"—we change its background image to remote_a.gif, which is the animated GIF of the spinning, colored globe.

Movement Example: Rising Tooltips

We've considered on-the-spot animation; let's now look at an example of page elements that change position. Imagine the header of your site has links to the different site subject areas. We want to add a "tooltip" to that header, but one that slides out from under the header, then slides back in again afterwards, as illustrated in Figure 5.3 to Figure 5.5 below.

Figure 5.3. Ready to mouse-over a link.

Figure 5.4. The tooltip starts to emerge on mouseover

Figure 5.5. The tooltip is fully displayed

Creating Special Tooltip Content

Our header is simply built as an unordered list,[2] and the rising tooltip text is contained in `<span>` tags. Here's the HTML we'll use as an example:

---

[2]Obviously, in a real site, the links would point somewhere useful.

File: **risingTooltips.html**

```
<!DOCTYPE HTML PUBLIC "-//W3C//DTD HTML 4.01//EN"
    "http://www.w3.org/TR/html4/strict.dtd">
<html>
  <head>
    <script type="text/javascript" src="risingTooltips.js"
        ></script>
    <link type="text/css" rel="stylesheet"
        href="risingTooltips.css">
  </head>
  <body>
    <ul id="nav">
      <li id="home"><a href="#home">home</a>
        <span>back to the home page</span></li>
      <li id="beer"><a href="#beer">free beer</a>
        <span>we all love beer</span></li>
      <li id="software"><a href="#soft">free software</a>
        <span>free as in speech</span></li>
      <li id="willy"><a href="#willy">free willy</a>
        <span>the films section</span></li>
    </ul>
    <div id="extra"></div>
  </body>
</html>
```

This is a backwards-compatible strategy. If both JavaScript and CSS are absent, the header will still display well, with some helpful text next to each link. That's good for accessibility. Notice also the empty div at the end of the page. We'll explain this shortly.

Styling the Tooltips

Our header uses some fairly simple styling to make the list display in a single line on a colored background:

File: **risingTooltips.css (excerpt)**

```
ul {
  display: block;
  background-color: blue;
  position: absolute;
  top: 30px;
  left: 0;
  width: 100%;
  height: 2em;
  padding: 0;
```

```
    margin: 0;
}
li {
  display: inline;
  font-weight: bold;
  padding: 0;
  margin: 0;
}
li a {
  color: white;
  background-color: blue;
}
span {
  position: absolute;
  top: 0;
  background: yellow;
  border: 1px solid blue;
  border-width: 1px 1px 0 1px;
  display: none;
}
```

We want to hide the span elements beneath the ul so that they can scroll into view from behind it. This is normally handled with the CSS z-index property; if the display of two elements overlaps in an HTML document, the element with the higher z-index appears on top. However, we can't simply set the span elements to have a lower z-index than the ul element, because no element may have a lower z-index than an element in which it is contained.[3] For now, we've hidden the tooltip text so that we can see that the header displays with the layout we want.

Stacking the Tooltips

To resolve this z-index problem, we've added another element—a div—to our document.

File: **risingTooltips.html** (excerpt)

```
<div id="extra"></div>
```

We'll position that div in the same place as the ul, but behind it, then we'll move the spans into the div when the page loads. This means that the HTML

---

[3]The CSS2 specification explains this, in a roundabout way, at http://www.w3.org/TR/REC-CSS2/visuren.html#z-index. Each positioned element creates a "local stacking context," and elements inside it have their z-indices resolved relative to that local stacking context. Thus, an element can't appear below its container.

of the page will still be intuitive and easy to work with, but the span elements will be moved to beneath the ul and can, therefore, scroll up from behind it.

Here's the modified CSS that will ensure that the div is positioned to appear at the same coordinates as the ul, but behind it:

File: **risingTooltips.css** (excerpt)

```
ul, div#extra {
  display: block;
  background-color: blue;
  position: absolute;
  width: 100%;
  top: 30px;
  left: 0;
  height: 2em;
  padding: 0;
  margin: 0;
  z-index: 20;
}
div#extra {
  z-index: 10;
}
```

Note that we've given the ul a z-index of 20, and the div a z-index of 10, to ensure that the div displays beneath the ul. We'll move the spans into this new div later, using JavaScript. Since this is a more complicated example, we'll first do some groundwork to keep our scripts tidy. Once we've done that, we'll come back to the task of content manipulation.

Designing the DHTML Library

To keep all our DHTML code nicely encapsulated, so that it doesn't interfere with any other scripts on the page, we'll wrap it up in one big JavaScript object. JavaScript allows us to create new objects with a unique syntax called an object literal. Such objects may have methods and properties, just like other JavaScript objects. For example, consider the code below:

```
var myNewObject = {
  firstProperty: 'a string',
  secondProperty: 6,
  listProperty: [1, 2, 3, 4],
  firstMethod: function() { alert('This is a method'); }
}
```

This code creates an object with three properties—one contains a string, one an integer, and one a list or array—and one method. We can pass this object around as a single entity. We can use its properties and call its methods wherever we have a reference to it. Take a look at this example:

```
alert(myNewObject.secondProperty);
myNewObject.firstMethod();
```

First, this code will show a dialog containing the numeral 6; then it will display a second dialog containing the words, "This is a method."

This technique is a useful way to keep the code that handles the tooltip animation from clashing with any other code on the page (which will cause problems that are difficult to debug). We'll use our own variable and function names as properties and methods in the object, where they'll be separate from those on the rest of the page. You can see why we call it a library object: it stores all the bits and pieces in one tidy place.

Identifying the Library Object Signature

Since the tooltips rise up from behind the header, we'll track the library object with a variable named rH, to denote "riser handler." That's not a perfect name (it's too cryptic), but you'll soon see that we use the object a lot, so a shorthand name is, in this case, too convenient to pass up.

Here's what the object eventually will look like:

File: **risingTooltips.js (excerpt)**

```
var rH = {
  addEvent: function(elm, evType, fn, useCapture) { … },
  init: function() { … },
  mOver: function(e) { … },
  mOut: function(e) { … },
  moveLinks: function() { … },
  links: []
};
```

First, there's our handy addEvent method, which we've used in previous chapters. This time, we'll specify it as a method of the rH object, rather than as a global function. Then there's an initialization method, init. After that, we see three event listener methods. Although they're specified as part of our object, we'll attach them to page elements as before. Finally, there's an array. In that links array, we'll store all the header elements (hyperlinks) that should have a rising tooltip.

We'll also use this array to mark each of those elements with the current status of its rising tooltip.

Placing Event Listeners

Our system will, in essence, be quite simple. When we mouse-over a link, that link's corresponding tooltip should start to rise up from behind the ul. When we move the mouse off a link, the tooltip should fall down again behind the ul. For this, we'll need to attach two event listeners: one to each link's mouseover event, and one to each link's mouseout event. When we attach these listeners, we'll also move the corresponding tooltips into the extra div, so that they may be displayed behind the list items in which they're contained. Having done this, we'll need to have some way of associating each link with its tooltip: to do so, we can make use of the handy JavaScript feature that allows us to add arbitrary properties to any object. So, to each link, we'll add a tipSpan property that holds a reference to that link's tooltip.

All of that work will enhance and reorganize the existing page content in preparation for our effect. We'll also have to record in our rH object all of the links, so that we can keep track of what's going on. Here's the init method that does all the setup:

File: **risingTooltips.js (excerpt)**

```
init: function() {

  // get the header links
  if (!document.getElementsByTagName ||
      !document.getElementById)
    return;
  var navList = document.getElementById('nav');
  rH.links = navList.getElementsByTagName('a');

  var extra = document.getElementById('extra');

  for (var i = 0; i < rH.links.length; i++) {

    // install event listeners
    rH.addEvent(rH.links[i], 'mouseover', rH.mOver, false);
    rH.addEvent(rH.links[i], 'mouseout', rH.mOut, false);

    // move the corresponding span into the extra div
    var theLi = rH.links[i].parentNode;
    var theSpan = theLi.getElementsByTagName('span')[0];
    extra.appendChild(theSpan);
```

```
      theSpan.style.display = 'block';

      // remember where the span is, and what's happening
      rH.links[i].tipSpan = theSpan;
      rH.links[i].tipState = 'none';

    }
    setInterval(rH.moveLinks, 50); // test with 500
  },
```

Notice the comma at the end of the method! It says: "that's the end of this property/method for the surrounding object." Putting in a semi-colon by accident is a common mistake and leads directly to error messages in the JavaScript console. Watch out for that.

As always, we first check for the methods we need, in this case getElementsByTagName and getElementById, and exit early if they don't exist. With the necessary tools in place, we can obtain a list of all the links within our navigation list:

File: **risingTooltips.js (excerpt)**

```
var navList = document.getElementById('nav');
rH.links = navList.getElementsByTagName('a');
```

We then walk through this list of links, and for each link carry out a few tasks. First, we attach a **mouseover** listener and a **mouseout** listener:

File: **risingTooltips.js (excerpt)**

```
rH.addEvent(rH.links[i], 'mouseover', rH.mOver, false);
rH.addEvent(rH.links[i], 'mouseout', rH.mOut, false);
```

Next, we identify the link's corresponding tooltip. The tooltip for a link is the first (and only) **span** in the same **li** as the link itself; that **li** is the link's **parentNode**. We get to the tooltip **span** that corresponds to each link like this:

File: **risingTooltips.js (excerpt)**

```
var theLi = rH.links[i].parentNode;
var theSpan = theLi.getElementsByTagName('span')[0];
```

The code would be shorter if we used the **nextSibling** DOM property, but that's too fragile an approach. When you're editing your HTML, it's easy to introduce extra whitespace by accident, and this would change the number of sibling nodes that an element has. It's better to ask for the element needed by name.

Having found the tooltip, let's move it into the special `div`, ready for use. Remember that if we use `appendChild` to add one element to another, and the child element is already in the document, then the child element is moved to its new location.

```
extra.appendChild(theSpan);
theSpan.style.display = 'block';
```

We also ensure that the `span` is displayed with this last line. It is initially hidden (with `display: none` in the CSS) and revealed here (once it has been moved to the extra `div` and is thus hidden from view behind the `ul`) to ensure that the user doesn't see it in its initial position before the move.

Modeling Animation States

Next, we add to the link a reference to its tooltip, so that we can keep track of it among the other tooltips that have been moved into the `div` along with it:

```
rH.links[i].tipSpan = theSpan;
```

Finally, we set a special `state` property on each link. We'll use this to track what the tooltip for that link is currently doing. We'll allow the following possible states:

none   This means the rising tooltip is hidden and doing nothing. This state can change to rising if the tooltip is made to appear.

rising   The rising tooltip is appearing. This state can change to `full` if it finishes appearing, or to `falling` if the user changes his mind and moves the cursor away.

full   The rising tooltip is fully exposed and not moving. This state can change to `falling` if the user moves his cursor away.

falling   The rising tooltip is being hidden. This state can change to `rising` if the user changes his mind and returns to the link, or to `none` if the tooltip becomes fully hidden.

The starting state is, of course, `none`:

File: **risingTooltips.js** (excerpt)

```
rH.links[i].tipState = 'none';
```

Finally, we use `setInterval` to call `moveLinks` every 50 milliseconds, in order to update the positions of the tooltips based on their states. Use a bigger number during testing, like 500, if you want to see the effect occur at a slower pace:

File: **risingTooltips.js** (excerpt)

```
setInterval(rH.moveLinks, 50); // test with 500
```

Animating the Content

Now that we've got the content set up, all that remains is to fill out the library object with the snippets of code that create the actual animation. We want to start the animation when the user does something, and we want to keep it going even when the user does nothing.

Starting Movement

Our two event listeners, `rH.mOver` and `rH.mOut`, are what start the tooltips moving (either up or down). The way we'll do this is to make everything depend on the `state` property. The listeners inspect the current state of the link's tooltip and, if it makes sense to do so, alter the state to match the user action. So the `mouseover` listener `mOver` should change the state to `rising`, unless the rising tooltip is already fully exposed. The `mouseout` listener `mOut` will do the opposite, changing the state to `falling`, unless the tooltip is already hidden. Here's the `mOver` listener first:

File: **risingTooltips.js** (excerpt)

```
mOver: function(e) {
  var link;
  if (e && e.target)
    link = e.target;
  if (window.event && window.event.srcElement)
    link = window.event.srcElement;
  if (!link)
    return;

  if (link.nodeType == 3) {
    link = link.parentNode; // Fix for Safari
  }

  if (link.tipState != 'full') {
```

```
        link.tipState = 'rising';
    }
},
```

We start by grabbing the moused-over link in the standard way (that's the first cluster of lines), but this time there is an extra wrinkle: in Safari, the event object doesn't fire on the link itself. Rather, it fires on the text node contained within the link. So, check to see if `link` has a `nodeType` of `3` (meaning that it is a text node, and thus meaning that we're running in Safari),[4] and, if it does, set `link` to be that text node's `parentNode` (the link itself).

Now that the correct link has been obtained, check to see what state it's in. We want the rising tooltip to rise, so, as long as the state's not `full`, set it to `rising`. If the rising tooltip is already fully exposed, we don't want it to rise further.

There's something unusual going on here! The listener didn't actually do any DHTML animation! All it did was record the new state of the rising tooltip in response to the user event. On the one hand, this seems quite odd (aren't we here to do animation?), but on the other hand, it's a very tidy approach. We make the listeners concentrate on responding to the events only. That keeps them simple.

The `mOut` listener's code is near-identical to `mOver`. Only the states under consideration are different:

*File: **risingTooltips.js** (excerpt)*

```
    if (link.tipState != 'none') {
        link.tipState = 'falling';
    }
```

In this case, we want the rising tooltip to fall in all cases, except when it's already fully hidden.

Executing Movement

Finally, after all that preparation, we can think about actually animating the tooltips. Given the way we've built the script, that isn't too difficult: the `moveLinks` method, which does the animation, will be called repeatedly thanks to `setInterval`. That method will examine the current state of every link's

---

[4]The DOM Recommendation defines `Node.TEXT_NODE` as a constant to be used for this purpose, but not all browsers define it, so we must use its raw value, `3`, instead.

tooltip, perform any animation required, review the results, then update the state if required. Here's the code:

File: **risingTooltips.js (excerpt)**

```
moveLinks: function() {
  for (var i = 0; i < rH.links.length; i++) {
    var link = rH.links[i];
    if (link.tipState == 'none' ||
        link.tipState == 'full') {
      continue;
    }
    var theSpan = link.tipSpan;
    var height = parseInt(theSpan.style.top);
    if (isNaN(height)) {
      height = 0;
    }
    if (link.tipState == 'rising') {
      height -= 2;
      if (height <= -theSpan.offsetHeight) {
        link.tipState = 'full';
      }
    } else {
      height += 2;
      if (height >= 0) {
        link.tipState = 'none';
      }
    }
    theSpan.style.top = height + 'px';
  }
},
```

We scheduled this moveLinks method, which is just a big for loop, to run every 50 milliseconds in our init function above, using setInterval:

File: **risingTooltips.js (excerpt)**

```
setInterval(rH.moveLinks, 50);
```

Let's see how the code works. For each link, we first check the state. If the tooltip is not moving (none or full), we do nothing. Otherwise, we get the location of the top edge of the tooltip (which we call height). That's a measurement relative to the top of the div that's directly behind the navigation links, so by adjusting it, we can make the tooltip stick up.

We adjust the height up or down two pixels, depending on whether the state is rising or falling, and we write it back to the tooltip's style.

After we calculate the new height, we use it to update the state. Since the Y-co-ordinate goes down the screen, `height` will be negative when the tooltip is rising. If it hits zero, it's time to stop falling. If it hits an offset equal to the element's vertical size, it's time to stop rising.

Activating the DHTML Effect

The only task that remains is to start the process when the page first loads:

File: **risingTooltips.js** (excerpt)

```
rH.addEvent(window, 'load', rH.init, false);
```

Our tooltips are now nicely animated, rising and falling as we move the mouse into and out of the links in the header. Yay!

Full Rising Tooltips Example Listing

Here's the complete code, shown as a whole for easy study. First, here's the HTML:

File: **risingTooltips.html**

```
<!DOCTYPE HTML PUBLIC "-//W3C//DTD HTML 4.01//EN"
    "http://www.w3.org/TR/html4/strict.dtd">
<html>
  <head>
    <script type="text/javascript" src="risingTooltips.js"
        ></script>
    <link type="text/css" rel="stylesheet"
        href="risingTooltips.css">
  </head>
  <body>
    <ul id="nav">
      <li id="home"><a href="#home">home</a>
        <span>back to the home page</span></li>
      <li id="beer"><a href="#beer">free beer</a>
        <span>we all love beer</span></li>
      <li id="software"><a href="#soft">free software</a>
        <span>free as in speech</span></li>
      <li id="willy"><a href="#willy">free willy</a>
        <span>the films section</span></li>
    </ul>
    <div id="extra"></div>
  </body>
</html>
```

Here's the style sheet:

File: **risingTooltips.css**

```css
ul, div#extra {
  display: block;
  background-color:blue;
  position: absolute;
  top: 30px;
  left: 0;
  width: 100%;
  height: 2em;
  padding: 0;
  margin: 0;
  z-index: 20;
}

div#extra {
  z-index: 10;
}

li {
  display: inline;
  font-weight: bold;
  padding: 0; margin: 0;
}

li a {
  color: white;
  background-color: blue;
}

span {
  position: absolute;
  top: 0;
  background: yellow;
  border: 1px solid blue;
  border-width: 1px 1px 0 1px;
  display: none;
}
```

Finally, here's the script:

File: **risingTooltips.js**

```javascript
var rH = {
  addEvent: function(elm, evType, fn, useCapture) {
    // addEvent cross-browser event handling for IE5+ NS6/Mozilla
```

```javascript
    // By Scott Andrew
    if (elm.addEventListener) {
      elm.addEventListener(evType, fn, useCapture);
      return true;
    } else if (elm.attachEvent) {
      var r = elm.attachEvent('on' + evType, fn);
      return r;
    } else {
      elm['on' + evType] = fn;
    }
  },

  init: function() {

    // get the header links
    if (!document.getElementsByTagName ||
        !document.getElementById)
      return;
    var navList = document.getElementById('nav');
    rH.links = navList.getElementById('extra');

    var extra = document.getElementById('extra');

    for (var i = 0; i < rH.links.length; i++) {

      // install event listeners
      rH.addEvent(rH.links[i], 'mouseover', rH.mOver, false);
      rH.addEvent(rH.links[i], 'mouseout', rH.mOut, false);

      // move the corresponding span into the extra div
      var theLi = rH.links[i].parentNode;
      var theSpan = theLi.getElementsByTagName('span')[0];
      extra.appendChild(theSpan);
      theSpan.style.display = 'block';

      // remember where the span is, and what's happening
      rH.links[i].tipSpan = theSpan;
      rH.links[i].tipState = 'none';

    }
    setInterval(rH.moveLinks, 50); // test with 500
  },

  mOver: function(e) {
    var link;
    if (e && e.target)
```

```
      link = e.target;
    if (window.event && window.event.srcElement)
      link = window.event.srcElement;
    if (!link)
      return;

    if (link.nodeType == 3) {
      link = link.parentNode; // Fix for Safari
    }

    if (link.tipState != 'full') {
      link.tipState = 'rising';
    }
  },

  mOut: function(e) {
    var link;
    if (e && e.target)
      link = e.target;
    if (window.event && window.event.srcElement)
      link = window.event.srcElement;
    if (!link)
      return;

    if (link.nodeType == 3) {
      link = link.parentNode; // Fix for Safari
    }

    if (link.tipState != 'none') {
      link.tipState = 'falling';
    }

  },

  moveLinks: function() {

    for (var i = 0; i < rH.links.length; i++) {
      var link = rH.links[i];
      if (link.tipState == 'none' ||
          link.tipState == 'full') {
        continue;
      }
      var theSpan = link.tipSpan;
      var height = parseInt(theSpan.style.top);
      if (isNaN(height)) {
        height = 0;
```

```
    }
    if (link.tipState == 'rising') {
      height -= 2;
      if (height <= -theSpan.offsetHeight) {
        link.tipState = 'full';
      }
    } else {
      height += 2;
      if (height >= 0) {
        link.tipState = 'none';
      }
    }
    theSpan.style.top = height + 'px';
  }
},

links: []
}

rH.addEvent(window, 'load', rH.init, false);
```

That's it!

Summary

Animation can be a real enhancement to your sites and Web applications, provided it's used tastefully. It's possible to use animated GIFs to add a touch of eye-candy to your pages, but JavaScript's `setTimeout` and `setInterval` functions are a handy tool for even basic animation effects. We've looked at how to use these methods, calling them with strings containing JavaScript code or with other functions, and we've seen how they can be used in a longer example of animated tooltips. We've also explored more advanced function usage in JavaScript, both by specifying anonymous functions and by wrapping a script inside a larger object to avoid it clashing with other included functionality.

6

Forms and Validation

Ancient spirits of evil, transform this decayed form ... to Mumm-Ra, the Ever Living!
—Mumm-Ra (the Ever Living)

Getting user input into your applications through forms is a major part of any Web application or reasonably-sized site. That user input, however, needs to be checked to ensure that it's correct, both to keep your data clean and to avoid security breaches. In this chapter, we'll learn how to build forms that use JavaScript to validate user input before it's sent to the server, how to tie together server-side and client-side validation methods, and learn some DHTML techniques to improve the usability or convenience of your form pages.

Ultimately, the information that's submitted to your Web server is entirely under the control of the end user, no matter how many client-side safeguards you put in place. Any improvement in the user experience must always rest atop a secure foundation on the server. Client-side validation can only ever be an enhancement to an already secure system. Your server-side code must always check the user's input, no matter how sophisticated the page's client-side processing is.

With that dire warning out of the way, let's see how DHTML can bring benefits to forms.

Reasons for Form Validation

The whole purpose of computer-based data management systems is to store user data more reliably than a paper-based system. That's why HTML forms exist. HTML forms alone are not enough, however. Generally speaking, form elements need to be wrapped in extra processing. Here are some basic reasons why form validation is a good idea.

Storing Clean Data

When the back end of your Web application receives user input through a form, it's vital to check that the data arrives in a proper format, and reject it if it does not. For example, if you need to capture an email address from the user, you need to check that the entered address matches the format: `someone@somewhere.something`. Addresses entered incorrectly, whether through mistyping on the part of the user, or as a deliberate attempt to hide the address, will pollute your database and are not worth capturing.[1] A polluted or corrupt database is a data administration nightmare, and can ruin the performance of reports, Web pages, screens and other applications that exist miles away from your own code. You don't want that.

Defending Against Security Exploits

Unknown and unchecked data can cause security breaches when its processed on the server. There are many well-publicized attacks on Websites that involve techniques such as **SQL injection** and **cross-site scripting**.[2] You can't resist all security attacks just by validating incoming data, but making sure that submitted data matches expected formats is a big step in the right direction.

In the trivial case, in which data is not submitted to a complex interpreted system like a database, simple formatting checks might suffice for validation. For example, a phone number shouldn't ever contain a left-angle-bracket or an apostrophe. Usually, though, when data is submitted to a database (or to any interpreted language, such as SQL, PHP, Perl, or Python), you should make use of any features

---

[1] Note that, if you're getting a lot of invalid data, it's important to think about why that's happening. If many users don't want to supply an email address, maybe that field should be optional rather than compulsory.

[2] Descriptions of vulnerabilities and the methods that you can use to avoid them are beyond the scope of this book: the whitepapers at http://www.spidynamics.com/support/whitepapers/ provide a useful grounding. Web application developers must be aware of these problems.

that language makes available to safely handle unexpected input (e.g. character escaping). Again, these procedures must be handled on the server, as any measures that utilize JavaScript on the client side may be disabled with little effort on the part of an attacker.

Improving User Interactivity

Finally, form validation can improve the user's data entry experience. If some of the user's input errors can be caught using JavaScript validation on the client-side, then the need for a round trip to the server is avoided, and the user receives feedback faster. That's good for the user's workflow, and good for reducing server load. If the client-side validation includes useful visual hints, then the user's life can be made easier again. With the right hints in place, the user will be led helpfully through the form and will make fewer data entry mistakes in the first place.

Simple Client-Side Validation

Let's look at the building blocks we'll use to implement DHTML form validation. These two object signatures should give you a taste of where we're headed:

```
var validationSet = {
  'field1': { … },
  'field2': { … },
  …
};

var fV = {
  addEvent: function(elm, evType, fn, useCapture) { … },
  init: function() { … },

  checkValidSubmit: function(e) { … },
  checkSubmit: function() { … },
  checkValid: function(e) { … },
  handleValidity: function(t) { … }
}
```

The first of these objects will hold validation data for a specific page. The second object is a library object that holds all the DHTML processing code. It's always the same, no matter what form fields are on the page.

Using Regular Expressions

The simplest way to express validation requirements such as "this phone number field can only contain digits, parentheses, spaces, and hyphens" is to use regular expressions. Although they're sometimes difficult to compose, regular expressions are generally a better choice that trying to construct validation code that analyses submissions with string operations. The problem with string analysis is that every case requires different logic, whereas with regular expressions, at least you know that there will be exactly one per form field. That's a bit more, well, regular!

A regular expression that matched our phone number requirement above might be:

```
^[- ()0-9]+$
```

This regular expression makes the field compulsory: the [- 0-9] section means "match any single character that's a hyphen, a parenthesis, a space, or a digit." The trailing + means "match the longest available string consisting of one or more of the preceding characters." Finally, the two anchors ^ (match the start of the string) and $ (match the end of the string) ensure that the whole typed-in value—not just some part of it—must match. Put together, these restrictions mean that not only is a phone number required to match this regular expression, but an empty string will not match it: the field is compulsory. If the field was optional, we could use this alternate regular expression:

```
^[- ()0-9]*$
```

Here, the * means "match *zero or more* of the preceding characters." Since an empty-string is indeed zero or more characters, it will match, so the field can be left empty in this case.

We can apply validation checks to fields by specifying a regular expression for each field we wish to validate. The contents of the field must match the regular expression, or we will refuse to submit the form. Note, however, that a simple way around this is to turn JavaScript off in the Web browser and reload the page. Again: this solution is good for usability, not security.

Regular expressions are powerful, but represent quite a complex subject. Fortunately, there are a lot of resources designed to help the newcomer. SitePoint's own guide[2] is a good primer.

---

[2] http://www.sitepoint.com/article/expressions-javascript

You can never be too careful with regular expressions. The expression we saw above allows these (correct) phone numbers:

```
(03) 9415 5200
911
(916) 657-9900
```

However, it also allows this messy possibility:

```
00034 5(--(1)(4    2-2-(2(
```

Clearly, in a real application, you need to do your best to craft a regular expression that's bulletproof. The simple one we picked earlier is suitable for this discussion, though.

Connecting Regular Expressions to Fields

The best time to check whether a field's contents are valid is when the user moves away from the field, either by pressing **Tab**, by hitting **Enter**, or by clicking elsewhere in the document. Sometimes, you might validate a second time just before the form is submitted. This is also a good point at which to check that any dependencies between fields are correct. Finally, if you want, you can validate on every letter that's typed; such measures are usually used only for special effects, since it's harder to provide non-disruptive feedback. It's best to wait until each field has been exited before you perform your checks.

Here's how you can do just that. Each form element fires a `blur` event when the user moves away from it, so that's where we should attach an event listener. That listener will examine the content of the field and warn the user if it's not valid. We will also need a set of regular expressions—one for each field that needs validating—against which to check the field contents. The easiest way to maintain this set will be to record the regular expression against the name of the matching field. On loading the page, we'll walk through the set of field names and regular expressions and attach one event listener to each element named in the list.

An example may clarify this slightly: imagine that we have a page with two text elements, one with the name `phone`, for entry of a phone number, and one with the name `email`, for entry of an email address.

JavaScript has a variable type that's ideal for storing a set of named items: the `Object` type. We saw in Chapter 5 how an object literal can be used to store a set of methods. It's just as easy to store plain data. In this case, we'll use **nested**

literal objects (objects inside objects). We do that because we might (eventually) want to store more than one piece of information against each form field. So, each field name will have its own object. Here's the result:

```
var validationSet = {
  'phone': {
    'regexp': /^[- ()0-9]+$/
  },
  'email': {
    'regexp': /^.+?@.+?\..+?$/
  }
};
```

Notice that the object property *names* are strings (`'foo'`), rather than variable names (`foo`). JavaScript allows this, provided you're careful when accessing the properties. Effectively, the result is a set of fields indexed by strings. In other languages, this type of set (which associates a key, in this case a string like `'phone'`, with a value like `'^[- ()0-9]+$'`) is variously called a **dictionary**, a **hash**, an **associative array**, or a **map**. One difference between JavaScript and such other languages is that, in JavaScript, all these things are one: an object. Only JavaScript arrays (which we're not using here) have the extra feature of a `length` property that makes them stand slightly apart from other objects like the one we're using here.

Another new piece of syntactic sugar in this example is the use of slashes (*/.../*) to delimit regular expressions, thereby distinguishing them from normal strings, which use quotes.

When the page loads, we can then iterate through the set, look up the fields that have names recorded in the set (**phone** and **email**), and add a single listener, `checkValid`, to each one:

File: **genericValidation.js** (excerpt)

```
for (var i in validationSet) {
  if (document.getElementsByName(i)) {
    var formField = document.getElementsByName(i)[0];
    fV.addEvent(formField, 'blur', fV.checkValid, false);
  }
}
```

The idiom `for (var i in validationSet)` iterates through each key (property name) in a dictionary (a JavaScript object), and is very useful when using dictionaries to hold data. For each key in the dictionary, we then check that there is an element with that name,[3] and, if so, we attach an event listener (the checkValid method) to that element's blur event. We expect every name to match a page element; if it doesn't, then we've accidentally deleted something from the page. We don't bother to enforce that, though.

We'll see shortly how checkValid connects the validationSet object's regular expressions to the form fields. Before we do that, however, we'll fill out the validationSet object a little more.

Preparing Quality Error Messages

Sometimes, the user will enter invalid data. Rather than just throw any old error at them, it's important to think about how errors should be phrased. No validation code should display a generic error message ("This field is not valid") for invalid input. Generic errors are lazy on the part of the developer and bad (very bad) for usability. If the users' input is invalid, they should be told not just that it is invalid, but why it is invalid, so they can take steps to correct it. Each field should have its own specific "this is not valid" message, which describes what a correct input would be.

Since there's one error message per form field, we can enlarge the object that holds our set of regular expressions to contain these messages as well:

File: **exampleValidation.js**

```
var validationSet = {
  'email': {
    'regexp': /^.+?@.+?\..+$/,
    'error': 'This email address is invalid. ' +
        'It should be of the form someone@example.com.'
  },
  'phone': {
    'regexp': /^[- ()0-9]+$/,
    'error': 'A phone number must be digits only.'
  },
  'country': {
    'regexp': /^[a-zA-Z][a-zA-Z]$/,
    'error': 'Country codes are two letters only. ' +
            'Examples are US, UK or FR.'
  }
};
```

---

[3]This is an example in which document.getElementsByName can be useful.

Note that the phone error message doesn't describe the whole truth: a phone number, according to the regular expression, can actually be composed of digits, parentheses, hyphens, and spaces. The error message, however, implies that the field is more restrictive; this keeps the message short and to the point. It also keeps the user focused on the simplest possible thing that they can type.

You might have noticed that each of these error messages is presented in English. That won't do if your site has a variety of non-English-speaking users. Fortunately, it's easy to extend this system to contain messages in each of several languages if you don't have the luxury of serving separate pages for each language. We won't do that extra work here, though.

Validation Processing

When the checkValid method is called, establishing whether the data in the form field is valid or not is a simple matter of testing it against the appropriate regular expression. Here's the first part of the checkValid method, plus the helper method handleValidity:

File: **genericValidation.js (excerpt)**

```
checkValid: function(e) {
  var target = window.event ? window.event.srcElement : e ?
      e.target : null;
  if (!target) return;

  var failedE = fV.handleValidity(target);
  if (failedE)
    // code to display the error message goes here
},

handleValidity: function(field) {
  if (!field.value) {
    return = null;
  }
  var re = validationSet[field.name]['regexp'];
  if (!field.value.match(re)) {
    return field;
  } else {
    return null;
  }
}
```

Let's examine this code more closely. The `checkValid` function first establishes which element fired the event, using a new shortcut technique. This is a further reduction of the standard target element detection code from previous chapters:

File: **genericValidation.js** (excerpt)

```
var target = window.event ? window.event.srcElement : e ?
    e.target : null;
if (!target) return;
```

JavaScript's **ternary** operator (`?:`) is at work here. Using `?` and `:` together is shorthand for an `if...then` statement, plus a variable assignment. Consider this example:

```
x = a ? b : c
```

This code will set x to b if a is `true`, and x to c if a is `false`. Here's another example:

```
x = (a1 == true && a2 == false) ? b + 1 : c + 2;
```

This code is equivalent to the following:

```
if (a1 == true && a2 == false) {
  x = b + 1;
} else {
  x = c + 2;
}
```

You can see that the `?:` operator is a very useful way of compressing this sort of `if` statement. In our code we use two `?:` operators nested together:

File: **genericValidation.js** (excerpt)

```
var target = window.event ? window.event.srcElement : e ?
    e.target : null;
```

That code is short for the more familiar, but also more long-winded:

```
if (window.event) {
  var target = window.event.srcElement;
} else {
  if (e) {
    var target = e.target;
  } else {
    var target = null;
  }
}
```

After finding and using the event object to identify the target element (the field), checkValid calls handleValidity to check that field against the supplied regular expression. It returns the field's element if validation fails, or null if it succeeds. The method merely checks the field to see that there's something in it, extracts the appropriate regular expression from the supplied set, and compares it against the contents of the field. Any text field's contents are kept in *field*.value. That's a string, so we use the string's match method to perform the regular expression match.

Back in checkValid, we test the return value of handleValidity; if it is not null (i.e. the field was returned), we'll go on to display an error message. That will need more code.

Displaying an Error

There are two main techniques that we can use to display an error message to users: we can put the message text inline in the page, or display it in a dialog box. The inline method is better from a usability perspective, because users can refer to the error as they correct the field input, but it requires some collusion on the part of the page designer: a place must be allocated for display of the error message.

In this example, we'll require that if the code finds an error in a field named foo, it should look for a span element that has id="error_foo". If it finds one, it should display the error there; if it doesn't, it should pop up a dialog box. If we add that code, then checkValid will comprise the following:

File: **genericValidation.js (excerpt)**

```
checkValid: function(e) {
  var target = window.event ? window.event.srcElement : e ?
      e.target : null;
  if (!target) return;

  var failedE = fV.handleValidity(target);

  var errDisplay = document.getElementById('error_' +
      target.name);
  if (errDisplay && !errDisplay.hasChildNodes()) {
    errDisplay.appendChild(document.createTextNode(''));
  }

  if (failedE && errDisplay) {
    errDisplay.firstChild.nodeValue =
```

```
        validationSet[failedE.name]['error'];
    failedE.focus();
  }
  if (failedE && !errDisplay) {
    alert(validationSet[failedE.name]['error']);
  }
  if (!failedE && errDisplay) {
    errDisplay.firstChild.nodeValue = '';
  }
},
```

Let's step through this method. After the initial check for the event's target, there's the call to handleValidity, which we discussed earlier. We need to work with two elements, not one. First, we have the form field element that failed; second, we have the page element in which an error message might go. Let's get that second element next:

File: **genericValidation.js** (excerpt)

```
var errDisplay = document.getElementById('error_' +
    target.name);
```

For each form field, an inline error span may or may not be present in the document. Our code must handle these uncertainties to ensure flexibility. In total, there are two elements that might or might not be present, so we have four (2x2) cases to deal with.

File: **genericValidation.js** (excerpt)

```
if (failedE && errDisplay) {
  errDisplay.innerHTML =
      validationSet[failedE.name]['error'];
  failedE.focus();
}
```

In this first test, there's an invalid field and an in-page element into which we can write the error. We dig the error text out of the set of validation data, write it to the page,[4] then move the input focus to the offending field so that the user can correct it.

---

[4]Once again, we use the nonstandard but widely supported innerHTML property to write to the page, since Safari doesn't support the standard method of setting the nodeValue of a text node in the document.

File: **genericValidation.js** (excerpt)

```
if (failedE && !errDisplay) {
  alert(validationSet[failedE.name]['error']);
}
```

In this second test, there's an invalid element, but there's no in-page location at which we can put a message. Instead, we use an alert.

File: **genericValidation.js** (excerpt)

```
if (!failedE && errDisplay) {
  errDisplay.innerHTML = '';
}
```

In this third test, there's no invalid element, but there is an in-page place for error messages. We empty that element in case an old error is lingering in it. The fourth case occurs when validation passes, and there's no message field. There's nothing to do in that case.

An extra usability improvement might involve adding a class to the invalid form element itself, or, better still, to an element (p or div or similar) containing both the invalid form element and its associated label. CSS could then be used to add style to the invalid element—a red border or a "warning" icon are common approaches here.

Checking on Submission

When the form is submitted, all the validated fields should be checked again. Required fields, for example, won't be validated by the blur event listener if the user never clicks into them. This pre-submit check is especially useful if dependencies exist between the fields.

It would be useful if you could display in a dialog a summary of all the errors detected before submission, as well as updating any error_foo span elements that exist. There is, however, complexity here: when users are editing only one field, a dialog box that pops up as they tab out of it is obviously attached to that field. But, when we display a list of errors on the page, it can be difficult for users to tell which error applies to which field. Carefully written error messages can help with this (a message saying "Phone numbers may contain only digits" clearly applies only to a phone number field). They aren't, however, the whole answer: what if there is more than one phone number field on the page?

Label Field Enhancements

An underused HTML element is `label`: it supplies a label for a form element. This tag is your friend, and can be used to improve both user interaction and error processing.

Most forms will display form elements alongside descriptive text (e.g. "Phone number" etc.). Wrapping that descriptive text in `<label for="`*`form_element_id`*`">…</label>` makes the text smarter. The `<label>` tag builds a semantic relationship between the label and its form field, and usually means that, if the user clicks the label text, the focus will change to that form element. This second point is a usability benefit, especially for checkboxes and radio buttons, because it vastly improves their "active" clickable area.

A form with `<label>` tags (and `error_foo` `<span>` tags) might look like this:

File: **exampleValidation.html (excerpt)**

```
<form action="">
  <p><label for="email">Email address</label>
    <input type="text" name="email" id="email">
    <span id="error_email" class="errormessage"></span></p>

  <p><label for="phone">Phone number</label>
    <input type="text" name="phone" id="phone"></p>

  <p><label for="country">Country code</label>
    <input type="text" name="country" id="country" size="2"
        maxlength="2"></p>

  <p><input type="submit" value="submit"></p>

</form>
```

This suggests a solution to the problem of displaying multiple errors at once: an error in a field can be displayed alongside the text of the label for that field. This approach gives users a clear indication of which field is problematic.

Attaching Validation to Form Submission

The form that contains these elements should have an event listener attached to its `submit` event. We can alter the code from above that attaches the `blur` event listeners to also attach a `submit` listener to the form. This new code is shown in bold below:

File: **genericValidation.js** (excerpt)

```
for (var i in validationSet) {
  if (document.getElementsByName(i)) {
    var formField = document.getElementsByName(i)[0];
    fV.addEvent(formField, 'blur', fV.checkValid, false);

    if (!formField.form.validateSubmit) {
      fV.addEvent(formField.form, 'submit',
        fV.checkValidSubmit, false);
      formField.form.onsubmit = fV.checkSubmit; // Safari
      formField.form.validateSubmit = true;
    }
  }
}
```

Each form field element has a `form` property: a reference to its containing `form`, which we use to assign the event listener.

Obviously, we need to be able to cancel the `submit` event if a validation error is detected. As I explained in Chapter 3, Safari's support for cancelling events in event listeners is broken, so we must also attach an old-style `onsubmit` event handler to the form.

We must be careful to set only one event listener on the form's `submit` event; if we set it once for each of the form elements that require validation, our form's `submit` listener will run more than once, which would almost certainly break something. So, in addition to setting a `submit` listener on the form, we set the form's `validateSubmit` property to `true`: we check this variable before setting the `submit` listener, to confirm that it has not already been set. In this way, we can ensure that we set the `submit` listener only once per form.

Validation Tasks at Submit Time

The `checkValidSubmit` method, called on form submission, is a little more complex than `checkValid`, although it's similar in essence:

File: **genericValidation.js** (excerpt)

```
checkValidSubmit: function(e) {
  var frm = window.event ? window.event.srcElement : e ?
      e.target : null;
  if (!frm) return;
  var errText = [];

  for (var i = 0; i < frm.elements.length; i++) {
```

```
      if (frm.elements[i].name &&
         validationSet[frm.elements[i].name]) {

      var failedE = fV.handleValidity(frm.elements[i]);

      var errDisplay = document.getElementById('error_' +
         frm.elements[i].name);
      if (failedE && errDisplay) {
        errDisplay.innerHTML =
           validationSet[failedE.name]['error'];
      }
      if (!failedE && errDisplay) {
        errDisplay.innerHTML = '';
      }

      if (failedE) {
        var labels = document.getElementsByTagName('label');
        errText[errText.length] =
           validationSet[failedE.name]['error'];
        for (var j = 0; j < labels.length; j++) {
          if (labels[j].htmlFor == failedE.id) {
            errText[errText.length - 1] +=
               ' (field \'' + labels[j].firstChild.nodeValue +
               '\')';
          }
        }
      }
    }   /* end 'if' */
} /* end 'for' */

if (errText.length > 0) {
  alert('Please fix the following errors and resubmit:\n' +
     errText.join('\n'));
  frm.submitAllowed = false;
  if (e && e.stopPropagation && e.preventDefault) {
    e.stopPropagation();
    e.preventDefault();
  }
  if (window.event) {
    window.event.cancelBubble = true;
    window.event.returnValue = false;
    return false;
  }
} else {
  frm.submitAllowed = true;
```

```
      }
   },
```

This code contains several small but critical differences from the single field validation case. Let's look at each of these variances in turn.

We put error messages for all the fields that fail validation into an array:

File: **genericValidation.js** (excerpt)

```
   var errText = [];
```

We're going to step through all the form elements and check only the ones our validation set has regular expressions for:

File: **genericValidation.js** (excerpt)

```
   for (var i = 0; i < frm.elements.length; i++) {
      if (frm.elements[i].name &&
         validationSet[frm.elements[i].name]) {
```

Next, we see some code that prepares the in-page error message elements; it's the same as the code we used in `checkValid`.

Now, let's start to display the error message(s) to the user.

File: **genericValidation.js** (excerpt)

```
         if (failedE && errDisplay) {
            errDisplay.innerHTML =
               validationSet[failedE.name]['error'];
         }
```

In this first case, validation failed and a `span` for the field does exist, so we write the error message in-page, as before.

File: **genericValidation.js** (excerpt)

```
         if (!failedE && errDisplay) {
            errDisplay.innerHTML = '';
         }
```

In this second case, there's no error but there is a `span`, so we clean up any lingering error text that was previously displayed in-page.

Whenever we have an error, we also want to collect up the message for display in a single summary. That's what this next piece of code does:

File: **genericValidation.js** (excerpt)

```
if (failedE) {
  var labels = document.getElementsByTagName('label');
  errText[errText.length] =
      validationSet[failedE.name]['error'];
  for (var j = 0; j < labels.length; j++) {
    if (labels[j].htmlFor == failedE.id) {
      errText[errText.length - 1] +=
          ' (field \'' + labels[j].firstChild.nodeValue +
          '\')';
    }
  }
}
```

If you look at this code closely, you'll see that we're not only grabbing the message associated with the field: we're also adding the content of the field's label to the error message. That will tie what the user sees on the screen with what they see in the error message.

Sadly, there is no `document.getLabelElementsByForValue`, so we are forced to iterate through each `label` element on the page and compare its `htmlFor`[5] property with the `id` of the given form element. If we find a match, we extract the label's content (the `nodeValue` of the `firstChild`, which is the text node), and use the content to add an extra hint, such as "(field 'Phone number')" or similar, to the end of the error message for that field. If no corresponding `label` can be found, we simply do not add the hint, so the script degrades gracefully.

Once the `for` loop is finished, the script should show any errors that were collected:

File: **genericValidation.js** (excerpt)

```
if (errorsList.length > 0) {
  alert('Please fix the following errors and resubmit:\n' +
      errText.join('\n'));
```

The `join` method of the `errText` array is used to combine the collected error messages into a single string, separated by line breaks (`\n`) for readability.

Of course, if any errors were caught, we don't want the form to submit. To this end, we must cancel the event, which we have to do differently for the Internet Explorer and standards-compliant event models.

---

[5]Note that this property is *labelElement*.`htmlFor`, not *labelElement*.`for`. This is because `for` is a JavaScript keyword.

File: **genericValidation.js** (excerpt)

```
    frm.submitAllowed = false;
    if (e && e.stopPropagation && e.preventDefault) {
        e.stopPropagation();
        e.preventDefault();
    }
    if (window.event) {
        window.event.cancelBubble = true;
        window.event.returnValue = false;
        return false;
    }
} else {
    frm.submitAllowed = true;
}
```

In addition to cancelling the event, this code sets a `submitAllowed` property on the form to indicate whether the submission should go ahead. This is used by the `checkSubmit` method, the old-style `onsubmit` event handler that runs after our listener and cancels the event in the Safari browser:

File: **genericValidation.js** (excerpt)

```
checkSubmit: function() {
    return this.submitAllowed;
},
```

Note the use of `this` to reference the `form` element in this event handler. Don't be fooled into doing the same in a modern DOM event listener—`this` usually just points to the `window` object in an event listener. As we have already seen, you need to get the target element from the event object.

Notice that the `checkValid` and `checkSubmitValid` methods we've built contain no references at all to the page content. Instead, they contain references to the `validationSet` object, which will hold all the page-specific information required by the script.

File: **exampleValidation.html**

```
<!DOCTYPE HTML PUBLIC "-//W3C//DTD HTML 4.01//EN"
    "http://www.w3.org/TR/html4/strict.dtd">
<html>
  <head>
    <title>Client-side form validation</title>
    <script type="text/javascript" src="exampleValidation.js"
      ></script>
    <script type="text/javascript" src="genericValidation.js"
```

```
    ></script>
  <link type="text/css" rel="stylesheet"
      href="exampleValidation.css">
 </head>
 <body>
  <h1>Client-side form validation</h1>
  <form action="">
    <p><label for="email">Email address</label>
      <input type="text" name="email" id="email">
      <span id="error_email" class="errormessage"></span></p>

    <p><label for="phone">Phone number</label>
      <input type="text" name="phone" id="phone"></p>

    <p><label for="country">Country code</label>
      <input type="text" name="country" id="country" size="2"
          maxlength="2"></p>

    <p><input type="submit" value="submit"></p>
  </form>
 </body>
</html>
```

This page makes reference to two external JavaScript files: exampleValidation.js and genericValidation.js. The first sets up the validationSet object for the form(s) on this page:

File: **exampleValidation.js**

```
var validationSet = {
  'email': {
    'regexp': /^.+?@.+?\..+$/,
    'error': 'This email address is invalid. ' +
        'It should be of the form someone@example.com.'
  },
  'phone': {
    'regexp': /^[-0-9 ]+$/,
    'error': 'A phone number must be digits only.'
  },
  'country': {
    'regexp': /^[a-zA-Z][a-zA-Z]$/i,
    'error': 'Country codes are two letters only. ' +
        'Examples are US, UK or FR.'
  }
};
```

The JavaScript code that generally handles form validation has been put in a separate JavaScript file, `genericValidation.js`, so that it can be shared by multiple pages. It's wrapped up in an `fV` object to prevent namespace clashes with other JavaScript code (as described in the previous chapter). So that you have it all in one place, here's the complete listing of this script:

File: **genericValidation.js**

```
var fV = {
  addEvent: function(elm, evType, fn, useCapture) {
    // cross-browser event handling for IE5+, NS6 and Mozilla
    // By Scott Andrew
    if (elm.addEventListener) {
      elm.addEventListener(evType, fn, useCapture);
      return true;
    } else if (elm.attachEvent) {
      var r = elm.attachEvent('on' + evType, fn);
      return r;
    } else {
      elm['on' + evType] = fn;
    }
  },

  init: function() {
    for (var i in validationSet) {
      if (document.getElementsByName(i)) {
        var formField = document.getElementsByName(i)[0];
        fV.addEvent(formField, 'blur', fV.checkValid, false);

        if (!formField.form.validateSubmit) {
          fV.addEvent(formField.form, 'submit',
            fV.checkValidSubmit, false);
          formField.form.onsubmit = fV.checkSubmit; // Safari
          formField.form.validateSubmit = true;
        }
      }
    }
  },

  checkValidSubmit: function(e) {
    var frm = window.event ? window.event.srcElement : e ?
      e.target : null;
    if (!frm) return;
    var errText = [];

    for (var i = 0; i < frm.elements.length; i++) {
```

```
   if (frm.elements[i].name &&
       validationSet[frm.elements[i].name]) {

     var failedE = fV.handleValidity(frm.elements[i]);

     var errDisplay = document.getElementById('error_' +
         frm.elements[i].name);
     if (failedE && errDisplay) {
       errDisplay.innerHTML =
           validationSet[failedE.name]['error'];
     }
     if (!failedE && errDisplay) {
       errDisplay.innerHTML = '';
     }

     if (failedE) {
       var labels = document.getElementsByTagName('label');
       errText[errText.length] =
           validationSet[failedE.name]['error'];
       for (var j = 0; j < labels.length; j++) {
         if (labels[j].htmlFor == failedE.id) {
           errText[errText.length - 1] +=
               ' (field \'' + labels[j].firstChild.nodeValue +
               '\')';
         }
       }
     }
   }  /* end 'if' */
 } /* end 'for' */

 if (errText.length > 0) {
   alert('Please fix the following errors and resubmit:\n' +
       errText.join('\n'));
   frm.submitAllowed = false;
   if (e && e.stopPropagation && e.preventDefault) {
     e.stopPropagation();
     e.preventDefault();
   }
   if (window.event) {
     window.event.cancelBubble = true;
     window.event.returnValue = false;
     return false;
   }
 } else {
   frm.submitAllowed = false;
 }
```

```
  },

  checkSubmit: function() {
    return this.submitAllowed;
  },

  checkValid: function(e) {
    var target = window.event ? window.event.srcElement : e ?
        e.target : null;
    if (!target) return;

    var failedE = fV.handleValidity(target);

    var errDisplay = document.getElementById('error_' +
        target.name);
    if (failedE && errDisplay) {
      errDisplay.innerHTML =
          validationSet[failedE.name]['error'];
      failedE.focus();
    }
    if (failedE && !errDisplay) {
      alert(validationSet[failedE.name]['error']);
    }
    if (!failedE && errDisplay) {
      errDisplay.innerHTML = '';
    }
  },

  handleValidity: function(field) {
    if (!field.value) {
      return null;
    }
    var re = validationSet[field.name]['regexp'];
    if (!field.value.match(re)) {
      return field;
    } else {
      return null;
    }
  }
}

fV.addEvent(window, 'load', fV.init, false);
```

This page also uses a style sheet to provide styling for the form. Here's that style
sheet:

File: **exampleValidation.css**

```
input {
  border-width: 1px;
  border-style: solid;
  border-color: #ccc #666 #666 #ccc;
  padding: 3px;
  color: #666;
}

span.errormessage {
  color: red;
}
```

Figure 6.1 shows how the page displays if the first two fields receive bad data.

Figure 6.1. Field-level validation error messages.

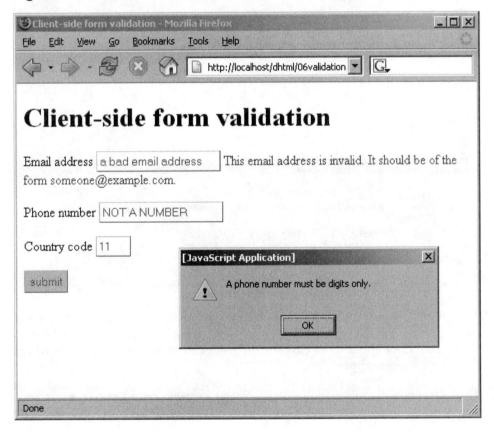

In Figure 6.1, the "Email address" field has a span element to contain its errors, and an error is displayed because the field was filled in incorrectly. The "Phone number" field does not offer space in which an error can display, so the error is presented in a dialog. Figure 6.2 shows the same form after the user hits the submit button.

Figure 6.2. Submitting an invalid form.

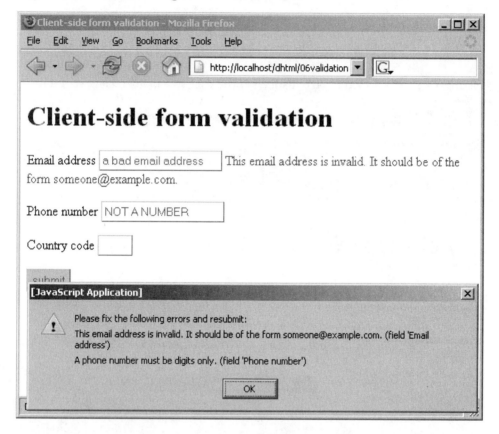

As Figure 6.2 shows, when the form is submitted, the error messages are collated together into one dialog; that dialog lists each error and identifies the field to which each error applies. It's easy for the reader to work out the fields to which the error messages apply.

This information could equally be displayed in-page. For example, some sites display error messages at the top of a form entry page to indicate the fields that need extra attention. In order to do that, you'd need to make both the general-purpose `fV` object and the `validationSet` object a little smarter. The `validationSet` object would need to have an extra property to hold the IDs of the elements alongside which the in-page messages should be added. The general-purpose object must have its `checkValidSubmit` method slightly enhanced so it can retrieve that extra property and use it to write the in-page messages. It's a fairly simple enhancement: experiment with it yourself.

Client-Server Coordination

Let's briefly look at the other half of the validation story: server-side validation.

Dangers of Validating on the Client Only

Client-side validation is very useful, but at the risk of belaboring the point, it's extremely important that you don't rely on it. You must always ensure that the input to your server-side code (the bit that actually does something with the data) is valid and as expected. A user may be using a browser that doesn't support JavaScript; they may have switched JavaScript off (about 10% of Web users do); they may be using a browser that doesn't support the DOM methods required for this script; worst of all, they may maliciously have submitted information to your server-side code from a page they created themselves with the intention of breaching security. Your client-side code provides a better interface for your users, but the server-side code is the bit that must be right. Of course, it would be good to integrate the server-side with the client-side, so you didn't need to write both separately.

Full Example: Server Fallback Validation

The server-side page that actually generates the form should integrate neatly with the client-side code. We can store a list of the regular expressions appropriate to each field in the server code. The server code can write these expressions into the JavaScript section of the generated page, and use the expressions to check the fields when the page is submitted. As such, the required regular expressions can be specified once and used on both the server side and the client side.

If an error occurs upon submission (i.e. a field does not match its regular expression), the server-side page generator writes the form out again, placing the error text in the appropriate `span` element.

The key benefit here is that changing the field validation is as simple as changing the regular expression list in the server code: this automatically makes the client-side code work, without any extra effort. If the two are maintained separately, it's reasonably easy for them to get out of sync. In that case, either the client-side code will allow some values that the server code will not (which is a usability problem), or the client-side code will correctly block some values that the server does not. The latter case has the potential to cause security problems if someone circumvents the client code by turning off JavaScript or writing their own form.

Here's an example implementation of these principles in PHP. First, here's the HTML starting point:

File: **phpValidation.php**

```
<!DOCTYPE HTML PUBLIC "-//W3C//DTD HTML 4.01//EN"
    "http://www.w3.org/TR/html4/strict.dtd">
<html>
  <head>
    <title>Client and Server-side form validation</title>
    <link type="text/css" rel="stylesheet"
        href="exampleValidation.css">
  </head>
  <body>
    <h1>Client and server-side form validation</h1>
    <?php
      include 'serverValidation.php';
    ?>
  </body>
</html>
```

We could simply put all the code that generates the page in this one file, but splitting the form generation code into the included serverValidation.php file makes the code simpler to read, and concentrates all the form technology in one place. Here's an outline of this script:

File: **serverValidation.php** (excerpt)

```
<?php

  $form_variables = array( … );

  function build_javascript( … ) { … }

  function build_form( … ) { … }

  if ($_POST) {
```

```
    // validate the data and collect error messages
  if ( … any error … ) {
      // generate the form content with in-page error messages
  } else {
      // generate "form submission underway" content
  }
  } else {
      // A simple page fetch. Generate the form content normally
  }
?>
```

The `$form_variables` variable will contain our regular expressions and error messages. The functions prefixed with `build_` will translate that PHP-based data into HTML and JavaScript content as required. The last set of `if`s perform the form submission logic, generating one of three separate pages depending on what's happening. Here's the full listing, a piece at a time:

File: **serverValidation.php** (excerpt)

```php
<?php

  $form_variables = array(
    'email' => array(
      'regexp' => '/^.+?@.+?\..+$/',
      'error' => 'This email address is invalid. ' .
          'It should be of the form someone@example.com.'
    ),
    'phone' => array(
      'regexp' => '/^[- ()0-9]+$/',
      'error' => 'A phone number must be digits only.'
    ),
    'country' => array(
      'regexp' => '/^[a-zA-Z][a-zA-Z]$/',
      'error' => 'Country codes are two letters only. ' .
                'Examples are US, UK or FR'
    )
  );
```

In the case of JavaScript, we used objects to implement a set of sets. Here in PHP, we're using nested arrays to achieve the same effect.

File: **serverValidation.php** (excerpt)

```php
function build_javascript($form_variables) {
  $js = "var validationSet = {\n";
  $entries = array();
```

```
        foreach ($form_variables as $name => $properties) {
          $entry = "    '$name': {\n";
          $entry .= "      'regexp': {$properties['regexp']},\n";
          $entry .= "      'error': '" .
              addslashes($properties['error']) . "'\n";
          $entry .= "    }";
          $entries[] = $entry;
        }
        $js .= join(",\n", $entries) . "\n";
        $js .= "}\n";
        return $js;
    }
```

This function scans the PHP data and creates a PHP string containing JavaScript code that has the same meaning.

File: **serverValidation.php** (excerpt)

```
    function build_form($form_variables, $errors=array(),
        $data=array()) {
      // Ensure $errors and $data have empty strings for incorrect
      // fields
      foreach (array_keys($form_variables) as $name) {
        $data[$name] = isset($data[$name]) ?
            htmlspecialchars($data[$name]) : '';
        if (!isset($errors[$name])) {
          $errors[$name] = '';
        } elseif ($errors[$name]) {
          $data[$name] = ''; // Don't redisplay invalid data
        }
      }
```

The first part of this function initializes a PHP array for form data and errors. All unused fields are set to empty, and any form values that resulted in an error are cleared.

File: **serverValidation.php** (excerpt)

```
    $javascript = build_javascript($form_variables);

    echo <<<EOD
      <script type="text/javascript">
        $javascript
      </script>
      <script type="text/javascript" src="genericValidation.js"
          ></script>
      <form action="" method="post">
```

```
        <p>
          <label for="email">Email address</label>
          <input type="text" name="email" id="email"
              value="{$data['email']}">
          <span id="error_email" class="errormessage"
              >{$errors['email']}</span>
        </p>
        <p>
          <label for="phone">Phone number</label>
          <input type="text" name="phone" id="phone"
              value="{$data['phone']}">
          <span id="error_phone" class="errormessage"
              >{$errors['phone']}</span>
        </p>
        <p>
          <label for="country">Country code</label>
          <input type="text" name="country" id="country"
              size="2" maxlength="2" value="{$data['country']}">
          <span id="error_country" class="errormessage"
              >{$errors['country']}</span>
        </p>
        <p><input type="submit" value="submit"></p>
      </form>
EOD;
  }
```

The rest of the function specifies the HTML's form content, inserting any retained
form data and any required error messages. Note the <script> tags, which include
a reference to the client-side validation library (genericValidation.js) we built
earlier in this chapter.

Finally, here's the section that generates the page:

File: **serverValidation.php (excerpt)**

```
// Now generate the form or POST response page
if ($_POST) {
  $errors = array();
  foreach ($form_variables as $name => $properties) {
    $value = isset($_POST[$name]) ? $_POST[$name] : '';
    if (!preg_match($properties['regexp'], $value)) {
      $errors[$name] = $properties['error'];
    }
  }
  if ($errors) {
    // Redisplay the form
    echo build_form($form_variables, $errors, $_POST);
```

```
      } else {
      // Process contents
      echo 'Processing...';
      echo '<pre>'; print_r($_POST); echo '</pre>';
    }
  } else {
    echo build_form($form_variables);
  }

?>
```

Inside the first `if`, the code loops through the form's submitted data and tests each item using the PHP copies of the regular expressions for the form. If any step in the validation process fails, the matching errors are passed to the `build_form` function. Otherwise, the form is processed without complaint.

To see this code at work, first, load the page normally. Enter some bad data, and the client-side JavaScript will catch the errors, preventing the form from being submitted. Next, turn JavaScript off in your browser and reload the form. Re-enter some bad data and press submit. This time, the validation is performed on the server-side, in PHP. Either way, the regular expressions used originate from the same place in PHP.

Improving Form Usability

Web applications are increasingly responsible for the user interfaces with which people work, day in, day out, on their computers. One of the downsides of this approach is the set of widgets—buttons, drop-down lists, text boxes, and radio buttons—that make up HTML forms. It's a limited repertoire when compared with the richness of today's desktop applications.[6] It's possible, using DHTML, to make up for some of these deficiencies. In the coming pages, we'll review some form widget enhancements that already exist, and experiment with a new one that you can add to your toolbox.

Standing on the Shoulders of Giants

The problem of HTML form widgets not being quite as fancy as those in normal client-side applications is well known, and numerous widget enhancements have already been developed with DHTML.

---

[6]People are working to improve this. One example is the WHAT Working Group, at http://whatwg.org/, which is building a set of specifications for extensions to HTML that will improve Web applications.

Rich-Text Editors

Internet Explorer has had a built-in rich-text editor for some time. This allows users to edit text in a textarea-like element, but also gives them the ability to format that text. Mozilla-based browsers have also implemented the same rich-text editor internally.

Such editors can be built using DHTML, but, while there are many DHTML-based editors on the market, not all have been revised to work in Mozilla-based browsers as well as IE. Popular open-source options include HTMLArea[4] (the status of which is a little shaky as this book goes to print), and FCKeditor[5]. Figure 6.3 shows HTMLArea at work:

Figure 6.3. A cross-browser rich-text editor at work.

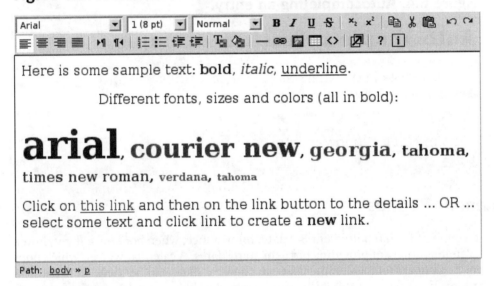

Autocomplete Text Boxes

A popular enhancement to text boxes in client-side applications is an entry history: the text box remembers previous entries, and offers matching entries from that list as alternatives when the user starts to make a new entry.

[4] http://www.dynarch.com/projects/htmlarea/
[5] http://www.fckeditor.net/

Web browsers often provide this enhancement as part of their user interfaces. You can see it at work on the address or location text box: when you begin to enter a URL, the box auto-completes the partial entry with a previous entry if they match, making it easier to get back to a page that has been visited before.

Some browsers also offer this functionality on text boxes in HTML forms on a page. Nicholas Zakas emulated this autocomplete functionality in DHTML in his article *Make Life Easy with Autocomplete Text Boxes*[6]. You can create a text box and record possible autocomplete values for it; typing into the text box will autocomplete those values. In Figure 6.4 below, the user has entered "br" into the text box, and it has autocompleted to "brown," which is the sole match in a list of choices that includes "red," "orange," "yellow," "green," "blue," "indigo," "violet," and "brown."

Figure 6.4. Autocompleting an entry.

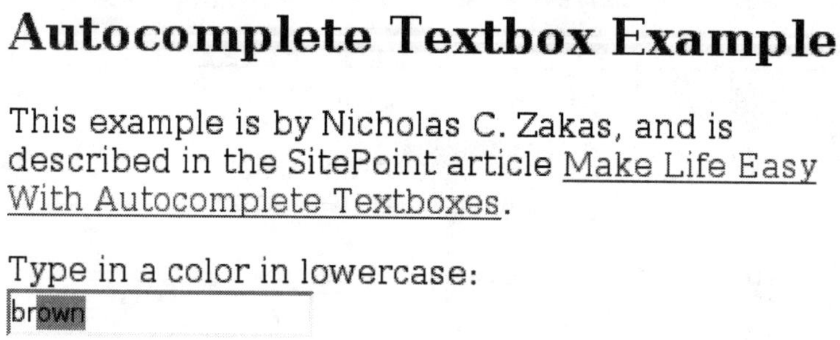

Autocomplete Textbox Example

This example is by Nicholas C. Zakas, and is described in the SitePoint article Make Life Easy With Autocomplete Textboxes.

Type in a color in lowercase:
brown

Calendar Popups

A common form requirement is a date, for instance, when booking a flight, hotel, or train journey, or providing birth- or start- dates. A calendar widget, which pops up a calendar from which the user can choose a date, can be useful in these situations. Such widgets should be used when the date is not too far from today's date, since navigating to a previous time can be awkward. They're also culture-specific: Gregorian, solar calendars with English month-names are only used in the English-speaking world.

A good example of a cross-browser DHTML calendar widget is available from mishoo's site[7]. Figure 6.5 shows this calendar at work.

---

[6] http://www.sitepoint.com/article/life-autocomplete-textboxes
[7] http://www.dynarch.com/projects/calendar/

Figure 6.5. The DHTML calendar at work.

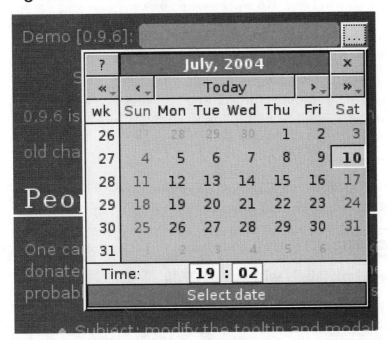

Text Boxes with Suggestions

A common approach for text boxes in forms on HTML pages has been to pre-populate the text box with instructions for completion (e.g. "Enter your surname here"), then to remove those instructions when the user clicks into the box to enter some text. If the user clicks away from the text box without completing it, the instructions are restored.

This technique was often executed with suspect JavaScript techniques: using `onclick` and `onblur` listeners on the tags themselves, and hardcoding the instructions into the JavaScript in the listeners. This approach makes the technique degrade well, but hides the instructions from browsers that don't support JavaScript.

Aaron Boodman built an enhancement[8] that automatically uses the content from the label element related to a given text box to populate that text box. The instructions are, therefore, available to non-JavaScript-capable browsers (as they're

[8] http://www.youngpup.net/2001/labels

located in the label element), but are placed in the text box itself in DOM browsers, as can be seen in Figure 6.6 and Figure 6.7 below.

Figure 6.6. Text box labels with DHTML.

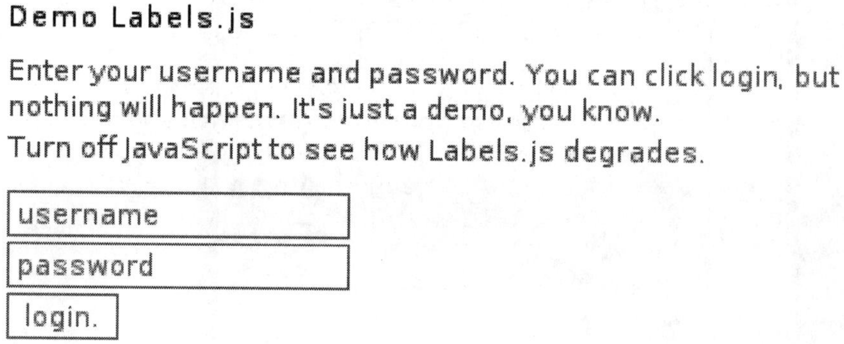

Demo Labels.js

Enter your username and password. You can click login, but nothing will happen. It's just a demo, you know.
Turn off JavaScript to see how Labels.js degrades.

```
username
password
login.
```

Figure 6.7. Text box labels without DHTML.

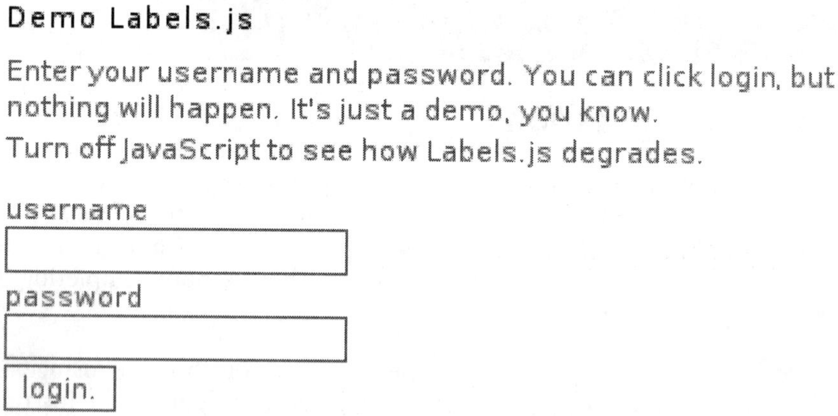

Demo Labels.js

Enter your username and password. You can click login, but nothing will happen. It's just a demo, you know.
Turn off JavaScript to see how Labels.js degrades.

```
username

password

login.
```

While the use of this technique needs to be approached with care (there are usability implications associated with providing users with instructions to fill in a text box, and having those instructions disappear when users try to do so!), this technique takes a common, "old-style" DHTML staple and uses unobtrusive DHTML techniques to rebuild it for the modern age.

How to Find Scripts

Countless JavaScript snippets and scripts are available on the Web, ready to be used to enhance your Website. Those mentioned in this chapter, in common with those developed throughout this book, use modern DOM scripting techniques, rather than outdated or browser-specific approaches.

When reviewing scripts yourself, it's important to know what to look for so that your sites can stay compliant and cross-browser compatible, giving you the widest audience and avoiding user dissatisfaction. The easiest way to confirm that a script uses modern, rather than legacy, techniques is to test it in more than one modern DOM browser. If it works in Mozilla Firefox and in Internet Explorer, that's a start; if it also works in Opera, Safari on OS X, and Konqueror on Linux, it's definitely using new techniques.

Be aware that the latter group of browsers may not implement the standards as completely as Firefox and Internet Explorer (although they may implement the standards more correctly!). This means that a script may fail to work in Konqueror (for example) because the browser isn't as comprehensive as it could be, rather than because the script is poor. Key features of DOM scripting, as we have seen time and again, are the `document.getElementBy` methods; a script using these functions will almost certainly be a DOM script. Equally, a key feature of legacy scripting techniques is the use of the `document.all` and `document.layers` properties. Any script using these is likely to be outdated, and may not work in DOM browsers (at best, it may be attempting to retain backwards compatibility with old browsers).

Type-Ahead Drop-Down Lists

We conclude this chapter's discussion on forms with a new widget.

Short drop-down lists in Web pages are reasonably easy to deal with. But what about long ones? Usability experts tell us that we should avoid select elements that contain more than a few elements: long lists are bad. Although this is true, almost every Web user has probably used one of those huge drop-downs containing country names. Some have worked around the problem of locating particular countries in these long lists by putting the more frequently-selected countries at the top,[7] but this is hardly an ideal solution.

---

[7]Sometimes, developers place just one country at the top—the United States—leaving UK residents such as myself, and other non-Americans, to scroll through the ridiculously long list. Hmph. (Australians don't mind—Ed.)

It is possible to press the key that corresponds with the initial letter of an entry in the list in order to jump to that entry; repeatedly hitting that key will move between list entries that begin with that letter. This suggests an improvement: perhaps instead of keypresses triggering initial-letter searches only, they should accumulate into a string, which is matched as a whole. While typing "k," "i," "n" in a standard drop-down will result in a jump to the first list entry beginning with "k," then the first beginning with "i," then the first beginning with "n," this could be changed so that those keypresses jump the selection to the first entry containing the string "kin." That would probably be the United Kingdom (or the Kingdom of Tonga!), in the countries example.

Functionality very similar to this is actually already present in both Safari and Firefox. Both of those browsers let you type a series of letters to match the *start* of an entry in a drop-down list. This example takes this feature a step further by searching for the string anywhere in the list item. And it works in Internet Explorer to boot! Unfortunately, Safari does not support handling keyboard events on drop-down lists with JavaScript. As a result, the enhancement we will undertake in this section will not apply to that browser.

A number of further enhancements also suggest themselves: the current accumulated string should be displayed somewhere so that the user can see what they've entered, similar to Firefox's "type-ahead find" feature. It should also be possible, as with type-ahead find, to press **Backspace** to remove the most recently-added letter from the accumulated string. Finally, after a period without typing, the accumulated string should be reset to blank to allow typing from scratch.

Here's an example HTML file containing the countries list:

File: **typeahead.html**

```
<!DOCTYPE HTML PUBLIC "-//W3C//DTD HTML 4.01//EN"
    "http://www.w3.org/TR/html4/strict.dtd">
<html>
  <head>
    <title>Type-ahead drop-down lists</title>
    <script type="text/javascript" src="typeahead.js"></script>
  </head>
  <body>
    <h1>Type-ahead drop-down lists</h1>
    <form action="">
      <p>
        <select name="country">
          <option value="AFG">Afghanistan</option>
          <option value="ALB">Albania</option>
          <option value="DZA">Algeria</option>
```

```
      …
      <option value="ZAR">Zaire</option>
      <option value="ZMB">Zambia</option>
      <option value="ZWE">Zimbabwe</option>
    </select>
  </p>
  </form>
  </body>
</html>
```

The associated JavaScript should attach an event listener to each `select` element in the document. Browsers offer three events for handling pressed keys: `keyup`, `keydown`, and `keypress`. As we saw in Chapter 3, despite being the best-supported of these properties, `keypress` is nonstandard, and a little limited. In particular, in some browsers it does not fire for "control" keys such as **Backspace**, which is required by this script. We'll therefore use `keydown` for this script.

In summary, we'll create a library object as follows:

File: **typeahead.js**

```
var tADD = {
  addEvent: function(elm, evType, fn, useCapture) { … },
  init: function() { … },
  addKey: function(e) { … }
}
tADD.addEvent(window, 'load', tADD.init, false);
```

This is mostly standard setup. As only a single listener is required, we'll put it all in `typeahead.js`. There's nothing else in that file. Here's the `init` method:

File: **typeahead.js (excerpt)**

```
init: function() {
  if (!document.getElementsByTagName) return;
  var selects = document.getElementsByTagName('select');
  for (var i = 0; i < selects.length; i++) {
    tADD.addEvent(selects[i], 'keydown', tADD.addKey, false);
    tADD.addEvent(selects[i], 'keypress',
        function(e) { if (e) e.preventDefault(); }, false);
  }
},
```

This decorates all `select` elements with a `keydown` event listener and a `keypress` event listener. The `keydown` listener, `addKey`, will implement the type-ahead behavior. The `keypress` listener is in place for one reason only: the Firefox browser will navigate to the previous page when the user types **Backspace**, even if the keydown event listener calls `preventDefault` to cancel the event. To prevent this, the `keypress` event must be cancelled by its own listener.

Here's the keydown event listener:

File: **typeahead.js** (excerpt)

```
addKey: function(e) {
  var t = window.event ? window.event.srcElement : e ?
      e.target : null;
  if (!t) return;

  if (e && e.which) {
    var code = e.which;
  } else if (e && e.keyCode) {
    var code = e.keyCode;
  } else if (window.event && window.event.keyCode) {
    var code = window.event.keyCode;
  } else {
    return;
  }

  var character = String.fromCharCode(code).toLowerCase();
  if (t.timeout_key)
    clearTimeout(t.timeout_key);

  if (!t.keyword)
    t.keyword = '';

  if (code == 8) {
    if (t.keyword != '')
      t.keyword = t.keyword.substr(0, t.keyword.length - 1);
  } else if (code >= 32) {
    t.keyword += character;
  }

  if (t.keyword == '') {
    window.status = t.keyword = '';
  } else {
    window.status = 'Searching: ' + t.keyword;

    t.timeout_key = setTimeout(
        function() { window.status = t.keyword = ''; },
        5000);

    var gotoIndex = t.selectedIndex;
    for (var i = 0; i < t.options.length; i++) {
```

```
      if (t.options[i].text.toLowerCase().indexOf(t.keyword)
          != -1) {
        gotoIndex = i;
        break;
      }
    }
    setTimeout(function() { t.selectedIndex = gotoIndex; }, 1);
  }

  if (window.event) {
    window.event.cancelBubble = true;
    window.event.returnValue = false;
  } else if (e) {
    e.stopPropagation();
    e.preventDefault();
  }
}
```

As described in Peter Paul Koch's Event Properties summary[9], the code of the pressed key is available from the `keyCode` or `which` properties of the event object (we get that object in the normal cross-browser way). Here's the code that ensures that we have both an event object and a key at the end:

File: **typeahead.js (excerpt)**

```
var t = window.event ? window.event.srcElement : e ?
    e.target : null;
if (!t) return;

if (e && e.which) {
  var code = e.which
} else if (e && e.keyCode) {
  var code = e.keyCode;
} else if (window.event && window.event.keyCode) {
  var code = window.event.keyCode;
} else {
  return;
}
```

Next, we convert the supplied code into a lowercase character: the character is converted to lowercase because the search through the drop-down will be case-insensitive. There are also serious browser issues with case-sensitive keystroke detection.

---

[9] http://www.quirksmode.org/

File: **typeahead.js (excerpt)**
```
var character = String.fromCharCode(code).toLowerCase();
```

Below, `setTimeout` is used to implement the five-second string reset timer mentioned; if a timer is currently running, we cancel it, because a key has just been pressed. We don't want the typed-in string cleared halfway through the user typing it, even if they are a bit slow.

File: **typeahead.js (excerpt)**
```
if (t.timeout_key)
  clearTimeout(t.timeout_key);
```

The accumulated string of characters will be stored in a property of the `select` element named `keyword`. This property is created by the code, using (again) JavaScript's handy ability to attach arbitrary properties to objects. If the property does not exist, it is created as an empty string:

File: **typeahead.js (excerpt)**
```
if (!t.keyword)
  t.keyword = '';
```

The **Backspace** key has a `keyCode` of 8. If **Backspace** has been pressed, and some letters have accumulated, we remove the last accumulated letter:

File: **typeahead.js (excerpt)**
```
if (code == 8) {
  if (t.keyword != '')
    t.keyword = t.keyword.substr(0, t.keyword.length - 1);
```

If a key other than **Backspace** was pressed, then we add the corresponding character to the accumulated string (as long as the key isn't a control character; we don't want to add a line feed if **Enter** is pressed).[8]

File: **typeahead.js (excerpt)**
```
} else if (code >= 32) {
  t.keyword += character;
}
```

---

[8]http://www.js-x.com/syntax/key_codes.php provides a table of keycodes, including those generated by control characters.

Next, we set the message in the browser's status bar to display the accumulated string, providing visual feedback to the user.[9] If the accumulated string is empty (i.e. if we've just backspaced away the last character), we empty the status bar to match.

File: **typeahead.js (excerpt)**

```
if (t.keyword == '') {
  window.status = '';
} else {
  window.status = 'Searching: ' + t.keyword;
```

Set a timeout to blank the accumulated string in five seconds' time. Note the use of an anonymous function for simplicity.

File: **typeahead.js (excerpt)**

```
t.timeout_key = setTimeout(
    function() { window.status = t.keyword = ''; },
    5000);
```

Finally, we'll iterate through the list entries in the drop-down until one that contains the accumulated string is found. If one is found, we set it as the selected entry. If not, we set the selected entry to remain as the currently selected entry. In either case, we set the selected entry after a tiny delay, because Mozilla browsers will do their own type ahead navigation immediately after this event listener runs (there is currently no way to prevent it), so our selection assignment must come in after that.

File: **typeahead.js (excerpt)**

```
var gotoIndex = t.selectedIndex;
for (var i = 0; i < t.options.length; i++) {
  if (t.options[i].text.toLowerCase().indexOf(t.keyword)
      != -1) {
    gotoIndex = i;
    break;
  }
}
setTimeout(function() { t.selectedIndex = gotoIndex; }, 1);
```

---

[9]This may not work in all browsers: the browser status bar has been so misused for hiding URLs or for scrolling messages that manipulation of its contents from JavaScript is now sometimes disabled by default.

Like many DHTML enhancements, this is a simple improvement over the existing in-browser functionality, and degrades neatly to doing nothing in browsers that do not support it.

The script does have the disadvantage that it's not necessarily very discoverable; the only hint that a given drop-down list is using this new, more-usable method of finding items is that the status bar changes to display the accumulated string, and, as noted, this may not take effect in some browsers. On public Websites, therefore, this script won't cause a problem, but it may not enhance usability as much as you might have expected. On an intranet, or some other environment in which users can undergo training that includes a description of how the enhanced drop-down works, this feature can seriously improve the usability of long drop-down lists. It may also be possible to display a tooltip, rather than a status bar message, when the user scrolls through the list with the keys, which would make the new behavior more apparent. That's an exercise for you to try for yourself!

Summary

In this chapter, we've seen the ways that DHTML can enhance form-filling, one of the most common activities in any Web application. We've seen how to implement the regular expression-based validation of form fields through DOM techniques. We've also learned how to make life easier on developers by integrating that validation with the equivalent validation that must be completed on the server. There's no need to write the same code twice in two languages.

We then looked at enhancing individual form widgets to work in more complex ways, or to emulate more useful widgets from client-side applications. Those enhancements help overcome some limitations of Web browsers' rather basic form implementations. We also highlighted work that others have already done in this area. Finally, a new technique was presented for enhancing the use of large drop-down lists.

7

Advanced Concepts and Menus

Why didn't you bring... something more advanced? Show me a piece of future technology.
—Dr Silberman, *The Terminator*

In this chapter, we'll explore a DHTML idea that seems quite complex: a multi-level animated menu. These menus abound on the Web—in fact, some firms do a roaring trade selling code to generate DHTML menus for use in Website navigation. But, as it turns out, such menus aren't complex at all.

The principles of unobtrusive DHTML and the power of the DOM mean that the actual code required to create a multi-level animated navigation system can be quite short; nevertheless, advanced concepts are at work in such systems. Understanding these concepts is a key aspect of large-scale DOM programming.

A multi-level animated menu is a big project, so let's see what we're aiming for. Figure 7.1 shows the menu we're about to develop.

Normally, the menu shows only the two leftmost menu items visible in the figure. In the figure, the user has moused over the second of those two items (DHTML Tutorials), causing a submenu to show. The user then moused over the first item in the submenu (By Simon Willison) to reveal the rightmost submenu. The top of this final menu is level with that of the middle one because the first item of the middle menu was chosen.

Without further ado, let's start development! There's quite a lot of code involved, but we'll step through it one small piece at a time.

Figure 7.1. The goal: a multi-level menu.

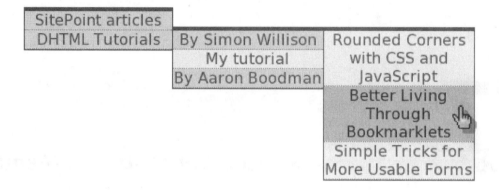

Creating Menu Content

The first step is to create the raw HTML content; then, we'll bash it into shape with some CSS styling.

Create Semantic Menu Content

As we've seen through earlier chapters, laying out HTML so that it's semantically correct makes dealing with the code much simpler. We want the menus to appear as shown in Figure 7.1, which means that, like most other navigation systems, each level of this menu must contain either links or submenus. The ideal way to lay out this kind of multi-level menu is to use the unordered list tag, <ul>. So, first, let's lay out the menu.

File: **menu-stage-1.html**

```
<!DOCTYPE HTML PUBLIC "-//W3C//DTD HTML 4.01//EN"
    "http://www.w3.org/TR/html4/strict.dtd">
<html>
  <head>
    <title>Client-side form validation</title>
    <base href="http://www.sitepoint.com/">
  </head>
  <body>
```

```
<ul class="slidingmenu">
  <li>
    <a href="http://www.sitepoint.com/">SitePoint articles</a>
    <ul>
      <li><a href="article/search-engine-spam-techniques"
          >Latest Search Engine Spam Techniques</a></li>
      <li><a href="article/free-web-design-apps"
          >Free Web Design Apps You Can't Live Without!</a>
      </li>
      <li><a href="article/securing-apache-2-server-ssl"
          >Securing Your Apache 2 Server with SSL</a></li>
    </ul>
  </li>
  <li>
    <a href="subcat/javascript">DHTML Tutorials</a>
    <ul>
      <li>
        <a href="articlelist/345">By Simon Willison</a>
        <ul>
          <li><a href="article/rounded-corners-css-javascript"
              >Rounded Corners with CSS and JavaScript</a>
          </li>
          <li><a href="article/bookmarklets"
              >Better Living Through Bookmarklets</a></li>
          <li><a href="article/simple-tricks-usable-forms"
              >Simple Tricks for More Usable Forms</a></li>
        </ul>
      </li>
      <li><a href="article/smooth-scrolling-javascript"
          >My tutorial</a></li>
      <li><a href="article/behaved-dhtml-case-study"
          >By Aaron Boodman</a>
        <ul>
          <li><a href="article/behaved-dhtml-case-study"
              >Well-Behaved DHTML: A Case Study</a></li>
        </ul>
      </li>
    </ul>
  </li>
</ul>

</body>
</html>
```

Notice that the topmost `ul` has a special class of `slidingmenu`. This hook is all we should need to unobtrusively implement the menu's behavior: the code can simply look for a `ul` with this class. We'll come back to this later.

Now, if you display this page, there are no surprises, as Figure 7.2 shows:

Figure 7.2. Unstyled content for the animated menu.

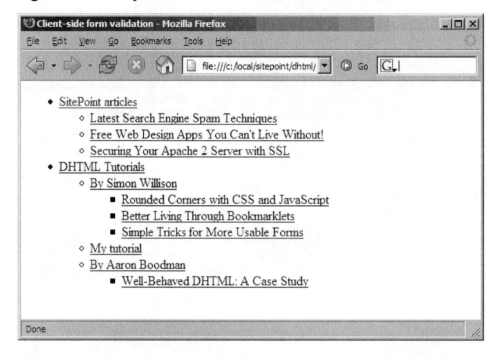

As you can see, the menu hierarchy is laid out in nested lists. The key point to remember about unordered lists is that a `ul` element can contain only `li` elements. Nothing else is allowed. This is especially critical for our complex menus. If you don't follow that rule, the animated effects won't work properly.

It directly follows that to nest one list inside another, the second-level list's `ul` must appear inside an `li`. Here's an example code snippet:

```
<ul class="toplevel">
  <li>This is the top level
    <ul class="submenu">
      <li>This is the second level</li>
    </ul>
```

```
    </li>
    <li>This is also the top level</li>
</ul>
```

Note that the submenu ul is entirely contained within the (bold) li element!

Styling the Menu's Layout

Having created the content, let's apply CSS styling so that the pieces of the menu appear as they should (with all parts of the menu expanded). To begin, we add a line to the head of the document:

File: **menu-stage-2.html** (excerpt)

```
<link type="text/css" rel="stylesheet"
    href="sliding-menu-2.css">
```

We'll put pure layout information into the CSS file—just to start with.

File: **sliding-menu-2.css**

```
ul.slidingmenu,
ul.slidingmenu ul,
ul.slidingmenu li,
ul.slidingmenu a {
  padding: 0;
  margin: 0;
  display: block;
}

ul.slidingmenu,
ul.slidingmenu ul {
  width: 10em;
}

ul.slidingmenu li {
  list-style-type: none;
  position: relative;
}

ul.slidingmenu a {
  width: 100%;
}

ul.slidingmenu ul {
  position: absolute;
  left: 100%;
```

```
    top: 0;
}
```

Five style rules are at work here, using various features of CSS2. Now, some cooks don't like to reveal their recipes, but we're not holding back here: we'll go through every ingredient! Let's analyze each rule in turn.

The first rule applies to all of the elements in the menu content. The rule is responsible for stripping off all padding and/or margins that browsers add to lists and list items in order to make them look like lists.

The second rule sets a fixed width for both the sliding menu list and all of the lists it contains. If it weren't for a bug in Internet Explorer that adds an unwanted margin to the bottom of list items, we could set the width in the first rule and have it apply to all elements.

The third rule works on individual list (menu) items. It takes away the list item marker, and prepares the menu item for animation effects by setting it to use CSS relative positioning.

The fourth rule assigns a `width` of `100%` to links, so that they fill the list items that contain them, making the entire rectangle of each menu item clickable. Again, if it weren't for Internet Explorer's list item spacing bug, this could be handled by the first rule.

Figure 7.3. Menus styled with CSS layout rules.

SitePoint articles
DHTML Tutorials

Latest Search
Engine Spam
Techniques
5 Free Windows
Web Design Apps
You Can't Live
Without!
Securing Your
Apache 2 Server
with SSL

Rounded Corners
with CSS and
JavaScript
Better Living
Through
Bookmarklets
Simple Tricks for
More Usable
Forms

The last rule addresses any list that's a submenu. Rather than have that submenu disrupt the stacking of the current menu's items (the "normal flow"), this rule positions the element absolutely. Normally, absolute positioning would see the element located exactly on top of the current menu, but, as we move it by 100% of the width of the current menu, it sits to the side. Figure 7.3 shows the results of these style rules:

You can see that all the menu items appear at once, in their final locations. Some menus are overlaid on top of others, but that isn't a problem because, in the finished application, they won't be displayed simultaneously.

With these changes in place, we've got the content where we want it. It's still ugly, though.

Styling the Menu's Appearance

Adding some style for appearance, rather than layout, makes the menus look attractive *and* makes it easier for us to see where each one is located. Here are the CSS additions:

File: **sliding-menu-3.css** (excerpt)

```css
body {
  font-family: sans-serif;
}

ul.slidingmenu, ul.slidingmenu ul {
  border: 1px solid #666;
  border-width: 4px 1px 1px 1px;
}

ul.slidingmenu li {
  background: #efe;
  text-align: center;
  border-bottom: 1px dotted #999;
}

ul.slidingmenu a {
  color: #666;
  background: #efe;
  text-decoration: none;
}

ul.slidingmenu a:hover {
  background: #cdc;
  color: #333;
}
```

There's nothing magical about these styles: they just apply block coloring and provide a little feedback when users mouseover a link. The only slightly tricky bit is that we've made sure to set a background color on the links as well as the list items. If we set the background color on the list items alone, Internet Explorer would not detect that the mouse was positioned over a link unless it was over the text of that link. Setting the background color ensures that the entire link rectangle is active for mouseover purposes (this will be important later).

Figure 7.4 shows the result of this styling; as a bonus, it's now easier to recognize the overlapping submenus.

Figure 7.4. The menus styled for appearance.

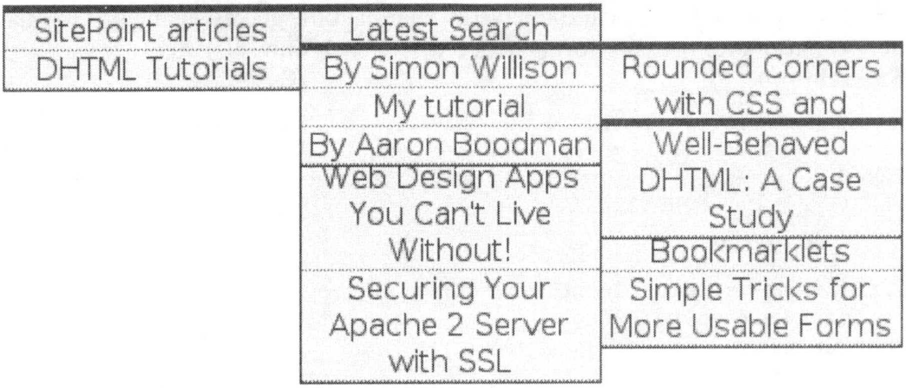

Hiding the Secondary Content

Finally, we need to tuck away all the menus except for the first one. Here's the modified rule as it appears in the style sheet:

File: **sliding-menu-4.css (excerpt)**

```
ul.slidingmenu ul {
  position: absolute;
  top: -4px; /* the height of the top border */
  left: 100%;
  display: none;
}
```

We've set the `display` property to `none`, and made a last-minute positioning adjustment so that the top border width doesn't throw the submenu items out of alignment with their parent menu item. Figure 7.5 shows the result.

Figure 7.5. The final styled sliding menu content.

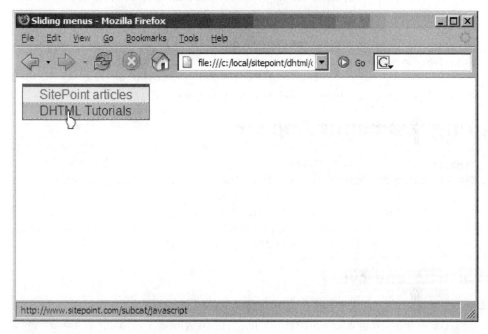

Okay, but there's a problem: we can't see any of the submenu content! We'll fix that with JavaScript, and provide a fallback solution for cases in which JavaScript isn't available.

Making the Menu Work

The HTML and graphic design sections of the work are over; it's time to make the menus actually work like menus. When a menu item that leads to a submenu is moused over, the submenu should display. Moving the cursor off a menu should hide it, but not immediately. A delay is needed to avoid the common problem of users accidentally moving the cursor off a menu and having it disappear immediately.

Advanced CSS Menu Alternatives

Before we examine the DOM scripting required to finish the menu, it's important to note that dynamic menus can be achieved without any scripting at all, using pure HTML and CSS. Eric Meyer first popularized this technique, naming it Pure CSS Menus[1]. However, the technique isn't appropriate here, for two reasons: it doesn't support menu animation (it unmasks all items in a hidden menu in one hit), and, more importantly, it requires a decent level of CSS support from the browser. Specifically, the browser must support the :hover pseudo-class on any element. Sadly, Internet Explorer only supports :hover on links—not all elements—so this technique is not as popular as it could be.

Making Submenus Appear

In essence, all submenus should be hidden to start with. When a submenu's header li (the li element that contains the submenu) is moused over, the submenu ul should appear. When the cursor leaves that submenu, or the submenu header, the submenu should disappear. This is a long-winded way of describing how menus work, but breaking the process down into steps can sometimes reveal tricky bits that you might not have thought about otherwise.

Simplistic Menu Events

Exposing these menus is trickier than it may seem at first. As our first option, let's try some straightforward thinking. The obvious approach is to attach a listener to each of the li's **mouseover** and **mouseout** events, which show and hide the submenus. The structure for this approach involves a standard technique: iterate through all the lis in each ul of class **slidingmenu**, setting **mouseover** and **mouseout** listeners. Here's that experimental code:

File: **sliding-menu-5.js** (excerpt)

```
function init() {
  var uls = document.getElementsByTagName('ul');
  for (var u = 0; u < uls.length; u++) {
    if (uls[u].className.search(/\bslidingmenu\b/) == -1)
      continue;
    var lis = uls[u].getElementsByTagName('li');
    for (var i = 0; i < lis.length; i++) {
      var node = lis[i];
      if (node.nodeName.toLowerCase() == 'li' &&
```

[1] http://www.meyerweb.com/eric/css/edge/menus/demo.html

```
            node.getElementsByTagName('ul').length > 0) {
        addEvent(node, 'mouseover', mover, false);
        addEvent(node, 'mouseout', mout, false);
        node.getElementsByTagName('a')[0].className +=
            ' subheader';
      }
    }
  }
}

addEvent(window, 'load', init, false);
```

The outer loop finds all the uls on the page (there may be more than one); the first if checks whether or not each list has the special slidingmenu class. The inner loop steps through the menu items looking for those that have submenus, and lodging listeners on them. The functions mover and mout are the mouseover and mouseout listeners, respectively; we'll declare these shortly. The inner loop also adds a CSS class of subheader to the links inside these elements. We add a rule in our style sheet for this class to make such links look a little different:

File: **sliding-menu-5.css (excerpt)**

```
ul.slidingmenu a.subheader {
  background: #ded;
}
```

Now, the two listener functions seem trivial. Here's the mouseover case:

File: **sliding-menu-5.js (excerpt)**

```
function mover(e) {
  var el = window.event ? window.event.srcElement : e ? e.target :
      null;
  if (!el) return;
  for (var i = 0; i < el.childNodes.length; i++) {
    var node = el.childNodes[i];
    if (node.nodeName.toLowerCase() == 'ul') {
      node.style.display = 'block';
    }
  }
}
```

Here's the corresponding mout mouseout listener, which hides the submenu:

File: **sliding-menu-5.js (excerpt)**

```
function mout(e) {
  var el = window.event ? window.event.srcElement : e ? e.target :
```

```
      null;
  if (!el) return;
  for (var i = 0; i < el.childNodes.length; i++) {
    var node = el.childNodes[i];
    if (node.nodeName.toLowerCase() == 'ul') {
      node.style.display = 'none';
    }
  }
}
```

Unfortunately, though, it's not quite as simple as this. Try it and see for yourself just how spectacularly it fails. We'll discuss why it doesn't work in the next section.

Mouse Event Complexities

Imagine we have a simple unordered list styled with chunky padding:

```
<ul>
  <li>LI
    <a>This is a link</a>
  </li>
</ul>
```

This arrangement is shown in Figure 7.6.

Now, suppose the user moves the cursor onto the li (the darker area). This will fire the li element's mouseover listener, as we'd expect. What happens, though, when the cursor moves onto the link, as shown in Figure 7.7?

When the cursor moves onto the link, several events occur, but, importantly, the li's mouseout listener fires. Even though the link is contained within the li, the browser sees mousing onto the link as movement off the list item. This poses something of a problem in our simple model above: since each of our menu items is a link within a list item, movement of the cursor onto a submenu header causes the submenu quickly to appear (as the cursor enters the li area) and disappear (as the cursor enters the link area).

Figure 7.6. A list with a link.

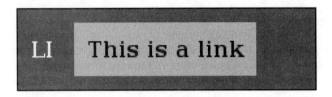

Figure 7.7. Mousing over the link.

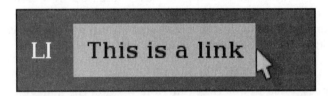

In fact, the situation is even more complicated than I've just explained. The transition described above will fire three(!) separate events:

1. The li's mouseout listener (with the li as the target).

2. The link's mouseover listener (with the link as the target).

3. The li's mouseover listener (with the link as the target).

Odd as it may seem, that's the way it works. Your code is notified of the cursor leaving the list item, entering the link, then entering the list item again; the most deeply-nested element over which the cursor is located is the target of the event in each case.

Part of the problem is that the listeners assume they're getting a reference to the submenu header li as the target of the event. As I've just explained, this isn't always the case. Depending on the position of the mouse, the target can be any of the elements contained in the li, including all the elements that make up the submenu and its contents!

What we need is to ascertain the element to which the event listener was assigned. According to the W3C DOM event model, this can be found with the currentTarget property of the event object:

```
function mover(e) {
  var el = window.event ? window.event.srcElement : e ?
    e.currentTarget : null;
  ...
```

This works fine for browsers that support the standard event model, but remember that Internet Explorer doesn't. And although IE uses `window.event.srcElement` as equivalent to the standard `target` property, IE has no equivalent to the `currentTarget` property.

In order to get the element to which the event listener was assigned in IE, we'll have to be slightly more creative. Instead of using the `mover` and `mout` functions directly as the mouse event listeners for all of the submenu headers, we'll create a custom pair of listener functions for each one. Those custom listener functions will, in turn, call `mover` and `mout`, but will pass them the reference to the particular `li` that we need.

Let's look at the code changes. First, in our `init` function, we alter the `addEvent` calls that assign our event listeners:

File: **sliding-menu-6.js (excerpt)**

```
addEvent(node, 'mouseover', getMoverFor(node), false);
addEvent(node, 'mouseout', getMoutFor(node), false);
```

Instead of assigning `mover` and `mout` as the listeners, we call new functions `getMoverFor` and `getMoutFor`. These functions will create custom listener functions for the submenu header in question (`node`):

File: **sliding-menu-6.js (excerpt)**

```
function getMoverFor(node) {
  return function(e) { mover(e, node); };
}

function getMoutFor(node) {
  return function(e) { mout(e, node); };
}
```

As you can see, `getMoverFor` and `getMoutFor` create and return new event listener functions that call `mover` and `mout`, respectively, passing not only the event object, but a reference to the submenu header element, `node`.

Because this listener function is created inside the `getMoverFor/getMoutFor` function, it can access any of the local variables that exist in that environment, including the `node` argument. The act of taking a function that has access to a private environment and making it accessible (as an event listener) from outside that environment is known in computer science circles as "creating a **closure**." We've actually done this once before, in Chapter 5, when we created a function that had access to a local variable and passed it to `setTimeout`.

If you're curious about closures, an excellent (if heavy-going) discussion of them, written by Richard Cornford, is available online.[2] For the purposes of this example, however, it's sufficient to understand that creating a custom event listener for each of the submenu headers allows us to reference that header when the listener is called.

Speaking of referencing the header, we now need to modify `mover` and `mout` to make use of the reference that's passed as a second argument by the custom event listeners:

File: **sliding-menu-6.js** (excerpt)

```
function mover(e, targetElement) {
  var el = window.event ? targetElement : e ? e.currentTarget :
      null;
  if (!el) return;
  ...
}

function mout(e, targetElement) {
  var el = window.event ? targetElement : e ? e.currentTarget :
      null;
  if (!el) return;
  ...
}
```

These functions use the `currentTarget` property on W3C DOM-compliant browsers; in Internet Explorer, where this property is not available, the second argument, `targetElement`, contains the needed value.[1]

Try this updated script and you'll find that it works rather well (though not quite perfectly). The changes we've made allow the submenus to appear and stay visible, but the succession of events still hides the submenu, then shows it again very quickly, which causes a lot of flicker.

---

[2] http://jibbering.com/faq/faq_notes/closures.html

[1]Indeed, you could use `targetElement` on all browsers and do away completely with the code that detects and uses the **currentTarget** property, but I prefer to bow to the DOM standard where possible, and look forward to the day when all browsers support it.

Before we address this flickering, there's one more Internet Explorer problem that still needs to be fixed.

Fixing the IE Memory Leak

Just when you thought we'd overcome all the idiosyncrasies Internet Explorer could throw at us, there's one last problem we need to solve, and it's a doozy.

A particularly nasty bug in Internet Explorer (versions 4 through 6) is that the browser will leak memory when the user navigates away from a page after a script has set up a circular reference that includes a DOM node. What does this mean, exactly? Well, we actually have a prime example in the current version of our menu script.

Each of the submenu header elements has an event listener, and that listener contains a reference to the header element. This is a circular reference. And, because the submenu header elements are DOM nodes, Internet Explorer will fail to clear the memory they utilize when the user navigates to another page.

Now, a few DOM nodes won't use up much memory, but put this menu on all the pages of your site and the leaks will start to add up. The next thing you know, the computers of site visitors who use Internet Explorer will slow to a crawl.

The solution to this problem is to unhook all of the event listeners when the page is unloaded in Internet Explorer. Web developer Mark Wubben published on his site an excellent summary of the problem, along with a simple script called Event Cache[3] that implements the solution.

The script is a single file, `event-cache.js`, which must be loaded by the HTML document:

File: **menu-stage-7.html (excerpt)**

```
<head>
  <title>Sliding menus</title>
  <link type="text/css" rel="stylesheet"
      href="sliding-menu-7.css">
  <script type="text/javascript" src="event-cache.js"></script>
  <script type="text/javascript" src="sliding-menu-7.js">
  </script>
```

---

[3] http://novemberborn.net/javascript/event-cache

Now, in our JavaScript, whenever we add an event listener using Internet Explorer's `attachEvent` method, we register the listener with the `EventCache` object:

File: **sliding-menu-7.js (excerpt)**

```
function addEvent(elm, evType, fn, useCapture) {
  // cross-browser event handling for IE5+, NS6 and Mozilla
  // By Scott Andrew
  if (elm.addEventListener) {
    elm.addEventListener(evType, fn, useCapture);
    return true;
  } else if (elm.attachEvent) {
    var r = elm.attachEvent('on' + evType, fn);
    EventCache.add(elm, evType, fn);
    return r;
  } else {
    elm['on' + evType] = fn;
  }
}
```

When the page is unloaded, we call the `EventCache`'s `flush` method to unhook all the event listeners:

File: **sliding-menu-7.js (excerpt)**

```
addEvent(window, 'unload', EventCache.flush, false);
```

And, just like that, Internet Explorer releases memory as it should.

Smarter Menu Events

Although the menus are now effectively working, the sheer number of events that are flying around cause the submenus to flicker in and out of visibility. In certain browsers, the order of events can even get mixed up, causing a menu to stay open when it shouldn't, or to disappear when it should remain visible.

One way to solve these problems is to ignore some of the events that cause the listeners to fire. That's the approach we'll take here.

To do this, we introduce a delay in the code's reactions to `mouseout` events. Instead of instantly taking the appropriate action (hiding the submenu), the code can note that the event occurred, but delay doing anything for a short time. If the same `li` fires a `mouseover` event within that time period, we know that the mouse is still on the `li` element. In that case, the `mouseover` event can cancel the delayed `mouseout` processing, leaving the submenu visible.

Delaying particular reactions for a short time is accomplished with `setTimeout`, which we looked at in detail in Chapter 5. In the present case, we want the code to wait for 300 milliseconds (or 300ms) to see if a `mouseover` event occurs; if it doesn't, we want to run the delayed listener that hides the submenu. The simplest way to accomplish this is to store the return value from `setTimeout` (recall that this value can be used to cancel the timeout).

It works like this: on `mouseout`, the `mout` listener will set a timeout for 300ms; this calls another function, `mout2`, which will hide the submenu. On `mouseover`, `mover` will cancel any existing timeout. If the `mouseover` event fires inside the 300ms time limit, `mout2` will not run, so the submenu will not be hidden.

These kinds of tricks are a great way to get longer lunches, because, though they sound complex, they take very little code! Here are the tiny modifications required to get it all working:

File: **sliding-menu-8.js** (excerpt)

```
function mover(e, targetElement) {
  var el = window.event ? targetElement : e ? e.currentTarget :
      null;
  if (!el) return;
  clearTimeout(el.outTimeout);
  for (var i = 0; i < el.childNodes.length; i++) {
    var node = el.childnodes[i];
    if (node.nodeName.toLowerCase() == 'ul') {
      node.style.display = 'block';
    }
  }
}

function mout(e, targetElement) {
  var el = window.event ? targetElement : e ? e.currentTarget :
      null;
  if (!el) return;
  el.outTimeout = setTimeout(function() { mout2(el); }, 300);
}

function mout2(el) {
  for (var i = 0; i < el.childNodes.length; i++) {
    var node = el.childNodes[i];
    if (node.nodeName.toLowerCase() == 'ul') {
      node.style.display = 'none';
    }
  }
}
```

The return value from `setTimeout` is saved as `outTimeout`, a newly-created property of the `li` node itself; the `mouseover` listener uses this value to cancel the timeout if it is still pending. In fact, `clearTimeout` is designed in a handy way: it will clear a timer if a valid timeout reference is passed to it; otherwise, it will do nothing. So we don't have to examine `outTimeout` in any way before we pass it to `clearTimeout`.

The rest of the `mout` logic has been moved (or delegated) to the `mout2` function.

We now have a fully functioning menu.

Adding Animation

We now have the menu working, albeit in a fairly pedestrian way:[2] submenus appear as you mouse toward them and disappear as you mouse away, much as they should do. To spruce it up a little, the menus could be animated. What might be appropriate is a "billboard" effect in which the top border of the menu scrolls into view, then the menu itself appears below the border. We're calling this a sliding menu, but the movement is also similar to the way a flag unfurls. Figure 7.8 shows the progressive display of such a menu:

One of the reasons why you might choose this effect is that it's easy to produce, thanks to CSS's `clip` property. This property restricts which portion of an element is shown on-screen. By repeatedly changing the size of the clipping rectangle applied to an element, that element can be made to appear to "wipe" into view, as shown above.

A submenu's animated display is started with a 0x4-pixel clip area. That menu is 100% clipped, since it's zero pixels wide. Animation widens the rectangle bit by bit. When that's done, it changes tactics, growing the rectangle to the full height of the submenu, again, bit by bit. At this point, the whole submenu is visible. You can see the process at work in Figure 7.8.

---

[2]Some people may be thinking "in a *usable* way" at this point and wondering why animation would be useful. Those people may stop reading this chapter at this point. We won't think any less of you.

Figure 7.8. The billboard effect in action.

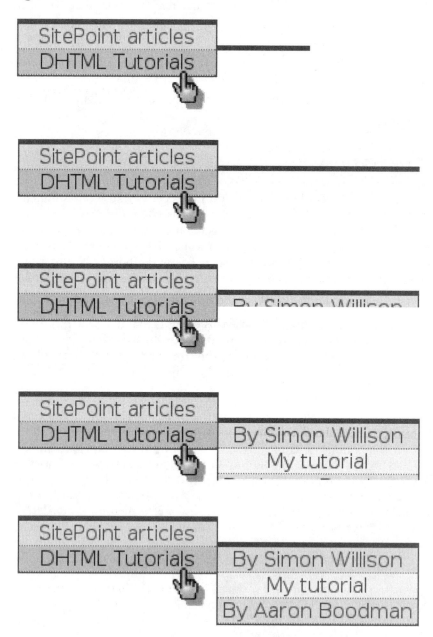

Preparing the Library Object

As in previous chapters, we intend to keep our JavaScript organized. We'll therefore package our entire script into a library object as we add the animation. Here's the object signature that we'll fill out as we go:

File: **sliding-menu.js** (excerpt)

```
sM = {
  init: function() { ... },

  getMoverFor: function(node) { ... },
  getMoutFor: function(node) { ... },
  mover: function(e, targetElement) { ... },
  mout: function(e, targetElement) { ... },
  mout2: function(el) { ... },

  showMenu: function(el) { ... },
  hideMenu: function(el) { ... },

  addEvent: function(elm, evType, fn, useCapture) { ... }
};

sM.addEvent(window, 'load', sM.init, false);
sM.addEvent(window, 'unload', EventCache.flush, false);
```

The code we've already written does most of the work for the first six methods shown here. So, instead of dwelling on these event-handling methods, let's plunge into the animation effect. It's produced by the showMenu and hideMenu methods.

Implementing the Animation

Animation, as we've seen, is a series of small steps, and is thus an ideal use case for the setInterval function. To make a submenu appear, the mover method should start an interval timer, which will "wipe" the submenu into existence instead of simply setting its display to block. The mout2 method should do the reverse: start an interval that will wipe the submenu out of existence. So, in all, three timers will operate in our script: the wipe-in timer, the wipe-out timer, and the timer that calls mout2 after a delay, which we've already written.

We'll need to track the animation's progress so that each time one of the timers fires, it knows what the next step of the animation should be. We can get some of that information from the JavaScript object for the element that's being animated. We must store other information on the node ourselves. Here's the extra information we're going to need:

```
node.savedOW = node.offsetWidth;
node.savedOH = node.offsetHeight;
node.clippingRectangle = [0, 0, 4, 0];
node.intervalID = setInterval(...);
```

The first two properties save the value of the full "opened width" and "opened height" of the menu in pixels. `clippingRectangle` is an array of four items (*top*, *right*, *bottom*, *left*) representing the current visible size of the element in pixels. `intervalID` holds whichever of the menu show or menu hide interval timers is currently in effect. We'll put these assignments in place shortly; for now, let's look at how the `showMenu` and `hideMenu` methods use them to produce the animation.

Here's `showMenu`:

File: **sliding-menu.js (excerpt)**

```
showMenu: function(el) {
  el.clippingRectangle[1] += 20;
  if (el.clippingRectangle[1] >= el.savedOW) {
    el.clippingRectangle[1] = el.savedOW;
    el.clippingRectangle[2] += 20;
    if (el.clippingRectangle[2] >= el.savedOH) {
      el.clippingRectangle[2] = el.savedOH;
      clearInterval(el.intervalID);
      // reset the clip: browser-specific
      if (document.all && !window.opera) {
        el.style.clip = 'rect(auto)';
      } else {
        el.style.clip = '';
      }
      return;
    }
  }
  el.style.clip = 'rect(' + el.clippingRectangle.join('px ') +
    'px)';
  el.style.display = 'block';
},
```

This method is called once for each step of the animation. All it does is update `clippingRectangle`, then write that rectangle's values to the CSS `clip` property in `el.style.clip`. If the animation has progressed to the point where the entire submenu is visible, the clipping is removed entirely. We'll discuss the details of this process in just a moment.

Here's `hideMenu`:

File: **sliding-menu.js (excerpt)**

```
hideMenu: function(el) {
  el.clippingRectangle[2] -= 20;
  if (el.clippingRectangle[2] <= 4) {
    el.clippingRectangle[2] = 4;
    el.clippingRectangle[1] -= 20;
    if (el.clippingRectangle[1] <= 0) {
      clearInterval(el.intervalID);
      // reset the clip: browser-specific
      if (document.all && !window.opera) {
        el.style.clip = 'rect(auto)';
      } else {
        el.style.clip = '';
      }
      el.style.display = 'none';
      return;
    }
  }
  el.style.clip = 'rect(' + el.clippingRectangle.join('px ') +
    'px)';
},
```

The logic is exactly the same as `showMenu`, except that the order of clip adjustment is reversed (height, then width, rather than width, then height).

In both cases, the `clippingRectangle` is applied to the element with the following line:

File: **sliding-menu.js (excerpt)**

```
el.style.clip = 'rect(' + el.clippingRectangle.join('px ') +
  'px)';
```

Here's a calculation that explains how this works. Suppose `clippingRectangle` is the array of four numbers: `[20, 30, 40, 50]`. JavaScript arrays have a `join` method that joins the items in the list into a string. It takes a parameter—the separator—which is used to join the elements. So `[20, 30, 40, 50].join('px ')` is `'20px 30px 40px 50'`.

An element's `clip` is set as a string in the form: `'rect(20px 30px 40px 50px)'`. So we join together the numbers in `clippingRectangle` with a separator of `'px`

', then add `'rect('` to the start and `'px)'` to the end to give the final string of `'rect(20px 30px 40px 50px)'`. Easy. The reason we go to all this trouble is that it's easy to do calculations on an array of four numbers, especially when compared to working directly on a `rect()` string.

When the menu is fully displayed (or fully hidden), `showMenu` (or `hideMenu`) turns off the clipping[3] and cancels the interval, because the animation is finished.

Starting the Animation

As soon as any code starts using long-running, step-wise processes like this, a very common problem with animation is likely to rear its head: what if the user mouses back out of the submenu when it's only half-displayed?

Some close analysis is needed to address this question. We conclude that only one animation can occur on a menu at any given time. If the menu is in the process of wiping into view when the user mouses away, then it should stop wiping into view and start wiping out of view. If the wipe-into-view animation isn't cancelled, the menu will simultaneously be wiping in *and* wiping out. This could make the menu jitter about on the screen, or freeze completely.

We can handle this problem by tracking the animation in progress on any given submenu. Like `setTimeout`, `setInterval` returns a value that can be used to cancel the interval timer. We'll put that value into an `intervalID` property on the submenu header element so that the `mover` and `mout2` methods can cancel any existing animation when they're invoked. So, if the wipe-into-view animation is already running when `mout2` is called, `mout2` will cancel the wipe-into-view before it starts the wipe-out-of-view animation. No more jitter! Let's update `mout2` and `mover` now.

The `mover` method needs to complete these extra tasks:

1. Cancel any existing animation when called, so that if the submenu is currently wiping out of view, it will stop doing so.

2. Set the `clippingRectangle` to the starting size for the menu.

---

[3]The code for this is unpleasantly browser-specific, but IE requires `clip = 'rect(auto)'`, while Mozilla/Opera/Safari require `clip=''` to mean "apply no clipping at all." Mozilla and Opera also support `clip='auto'`, the most standards-compliant method, but we've used `clip=''` instead to make Safari cooperate.

3. Save the full `offsetHeight` and `offsetWidth` of the fully-expanded menu in properties `savedOH` and `savedOW` for future reference.

4. Start the new wipe-into-view animation, saving its interval timer.

Here's the updated method:

File: **sliding-menu.js (excerpt)**

```
mover: function(e, targetElement) {
  var el = window.event ? targetElement : e ? e.currentTarget :
      null;
  if (!el) return;
  clearTimeout(el.outTimeout);
  if (!el.isIn) {
    for (var i = 0; i < el.childNodes.length; i++) {
      var node = el.childNodes[i];
      if (node.nodeName.toLowerCase() == 'ul') {
        clearInterval(node.intervalID);
        node.clippingRectangle = [0, 0, 4, 0];
        node.style.display = 'block';
        node.savedOW = node.offsetWidth;
        node.savedOH = node.offsetHeight;
        node.style.display = 'none';
        node.intervalID = setInterval(function() {
            sM.showMenu(node); }, 10);
        break;
      }
    }
  }
  el.isIn = true;
},
```

As we've seen, this method will be called over and over in response to mouseover events as the mouse moves around within the submenu; however, we don't want to start a new animation in response to every event. Setting the `isIn` flag at the end of this method, then checking it before we start any new animation, stops that from happening.

Notice also that we can calculate the width and height of the menu by setting its `display` property to `block` without the menu ever showing. Because the screen isn't updated until the script ends, we can get away with making the menu visible temporarily, so we can measure its dimensions, then hiding it again. The new mout2 is a little simpler. It does not need to save offsetHeight/offsetWidth properties, nor does it need to set a clippingRectangle.[4]

File: sliding-menu.js (excerpt)

```
mout2: function(el) {
    for (var i = 0; i < el.childNodes.length; i++) {
        var node = el.childNodes[i];
        if (node.nodeName.toLowerCase() == 'ul') {
            clearInterval(node.intervalID);
            node.intervalID = setInterval(function() {
                sM.hideMenu(node); }, 10);
            break;
        }
    }
    el.isIn = false;
},
```

This code simply says: find the submenu, stop what it's doing, and start to hide it. It also sets the isIn property to false, so that a new wipe-in animation can begin if need be.

The Benefit of Object-Based Programming

That completes the significant code changes required to produce the animated effects. Here's the completed code, for your reference:

File: sliding-menu.js

```
sM = {
    init: function() {
        var uls = document.getElementsByTagName('ul');
        for (var u = 0; u < uls.length; u++) {
            if (uls[u].className.search(/\bslidingmenu\b/) == -1)
                continue;
            var lis = uls[u].getElementsByTagName('li');
            for (var i = 0; i < lis.length; i++) {
                var node = lis[i];
                if (node.nodeName.toLowerCase() == 'li' &&
                        node.getElementsByTagName('ul').length > 0) {
                    sM.addEvent(node, 'mouseover', sM.getMoverFor(node),
                        false);
                    sM.addEvent(node, 'mouseout', sM.getMoutFor(node),
```

---

[4]It doesn't need to, because mout2 can only be called on a menu that has already been displayed and, therefore, the menu will already have a clippingRectangle from the wipe-into-view process.

```
            false);
        node.getElementsByTagName('a')[0].className +=
            ' subheader';
        node.isIn = false;
      }
    }
  }
},

getMoverFor: function(node) {
  return function(e) { sM.mover(e, node); };
},

getMoutFor: function(node) {
  return function(e) { sM.mout(e, node); };
},

mover: function(e, targetElement) {
  var el = window.event ? targetElement : e ? e.currentTarget :
      null;
  if (!el) return;
  clearTimeout(el.outTimeout);
  if (!el.isIn) {
    for (var i = 0; i < el.childNodes.length; i++) {
      var node = el.childNodes[i];
      if (node.nodeName.toLowerCase() == 'ul') {
        // Stop current animation
        clearInterval(node.intervalID);
        // Assign initial visible area
        node.clippingRectangle = [0, 0, 4, 0];
        // Save full width and height
        node.style.display = 'block';
        node.savedOW = node.offsetWidth;
        node.savedOH = node.offsetHeight;
        node.style.display = 'none';
        // Start animation
        node.intervalID = setInterval(function() {
            sM.showMenu(node); }, 10);
        break;
      }
    }
  }
  el.isIn = true;
},

mout: function(e, targetElement) {
```

```
      var el = window.event ? targetElement : e ? e.currentTarget :
          null;
    if (!el) return;
    el.outTimeout = setTimeout(function() { sM.mout2(el); }, 300);
  },

  mout2: function(el) {
    for (var i = 0; i < el.childNodes.length; i++) {
      var node = el.childNodes[i];
      if (node.nodeName.toLowerCase() == 'ul') {
        // Stop current animation
        clearInterval(node.intervalID);
        // Start animation
        node.intervalID = setInterval(function() {
            sM.hideMenu(node); }, 10);
        break;
      }
    }
    el.isIn = false;
  },

  showMenu: function(el) {
    el.clippingRectangle[1] += 20;
    if (el.clippingRectangle[1] >= el.savedOW) {
      el.clippingRectangle[1] = el.savedOW;
      el.clippingRectangle[2] += 20;
      if (el.clippingRectangle[2] >= el.savedOH) {
      el.clippingRectangle[2] = el.savedOH;
      clearInterval(el.intervalID);
      // reset the clip: browser-specific
      if (document.all && !window.opera) {
        el.style.clip = 'rect(auto)';
      } else {
        el.style.clip = 'auto';
      }
      return;
      }
    }
    el.style.clip = 'rect(' + el.clippingRectangle.join('px ') +
        'px)';
    el.style.display = 'block';
  },

  hideMenu: function(el) {
    el.clippingRectangle[2] -= 20;
    if (el.clippingRectangle[2] <= 4) {
```

```
      el.clippingRectangle[2] = 4;
      el.clippingRectangle[1] -= 20;
      if (el.clippingRectangle[1] <= 0) {
        clearInterval(el.intervalID);
        // reset the clip: browser-specific
        if (document.all && !window.opera) {
          el.style.clip = 'rect(auto)';
        } else {
          el.style.clip = 'auto';
        }
        el.style.display = 'none';
        return;
      }
    }
    el.style.clip = 'rect(' + el.clippingRectangle.join('px ') +
      'px)';
  },

  addEvent: function(elm, evType, fn, useCapture) {
    // cross-browser event handling for IE5+, NS6 and Mozilla
    // By Scott Andrew
    if (elm.addEventListener) {
      elm.addEventListener(evType, fn, useCapture);
      return true;
    } else if (elm.attachEvent) {
      var r = elm.attachEvent('on' + evType, fn);
      EventCache.add(elm, evType, fn);
      return r;
    } else {
      elm['on' + evType] = fn;
    }
  }
};

sM.addEvent(window, 'load', sM.init, false);
sM.addEvent(window, 'unload', EventCache.flush, false);
```

As we saw previously, wrapping the code in an object is a good way to ensure that it's isolated from other JavaScript code that may be running on a page. JavaScript, unlike some more rigorous object-oriented languages, allows properties to be set arbitrarily on any object. This means that it is easy—and encouraged—to store a piece of data relating to an element as a property of that element. This technique can be extremely useful, as with the storage of the savedOW and savedOH properties on each node, and the similar storage of the interval for a given node on the node itself.

In fact, it is this ability of JavaScript that makes it so easy to manage multiple animations on a single page. Since each object maintains the data required to manage its own animation, having more than one object animated at any time is not a problem.

Summary

Large DHTML projects like cascading menus require a step-by-step developmental approach. That statement applies to all DHTML effects, but menus require a little extra care if we are to get the timing details right. The important ideas of timed listeners and delegation help to make this task easy, if not actually trivial.

Writing successful DHTML applications or Website enhancements involves a combination of neat tricks and good programming practices. Web scripts have traditionally been small, simple, and poorly integrated, but as the complexity of your DHTML grows, more disciplined programming is required to ensure that your code fits together properly.

A good understanding of the concepts of objects, delegation, and the power of CSS, combined with a sound background knowledge of JavaScript's particular strengths, will create a firm foundations for your DOM scripting—foundations that will give you the freedom to build the latest and greatest thing. You need both theory and practice if you want to avoid worrying about it all crashing down around you!

8

Remote Scripting

I am one of the four Kings of the Dark Kingdom! Out of my pride I will not yell refresh!
—Kunzite, *Sailor Moon*

HTML is static and unchanging. So far, we've looked at ways to make HTML dynamic through use of the DOM. In this chapter, we'll explore some more advanced ways to add dynamism to a Web page, incorporating better coordination between the Web browser and the server. This chapter investigates a number of techniques that retrieve content from the server without serving a whole replacement page.

Most Websites rely upon some manner of server-side work to change HTML. For example, think of data being delivered from a database, or a list of emails in a Webmail application. The "standard" way to handle this kind of "dynamic" HTML—data that changes based on something on the server—has been simply to generate a whole new page on the server-side. While this technique undoubtedly works, it has a disadvantage: a whole page refresh is a laborious process, especially if your application only wants to change a small portion of the current display.

Suppose you could have the server send only the specific page data that has changed. In that case, your pages could alter their own content through the DOM, rather than requiring the server to build a whole new page from scratch. This approach would eliminate two key usability issues associated with sites that are heavily server-reliant: the large amount of time involved in retrieving a new, complete page from the server, and the amount of time required to update the display in the browser.

Problems with Frames

In the past, the established way to refresh part of a page was to use a frameset. The frameset divided the viewing area into frames, each of which contained a separate HTML document. Only one frame had to be refreshed at a time.

While this approach is still common, and undoubtedly works, frameset pages have usability problems.

Bookmarking a frameset page is awkward, because browsers only bookmark the initial state of each frame (rather than the current state). Bookmarking doesn't work because the current state of a frameset page can't be expressed as a URL. This makes it a lot more difficult to share links with friends by email, or to collaborate in other ways.

Framesets are also problematic in lower-specification devices, such as text browsers, screen readers, PDAs and mobile phones, and they make use of the Back and Forward buttons difficult. The buttons step back or forward through each frame change; returning to a page that displayed before the frameset can take a lot of clicks if the frames have changed repeatedly.

Frameset documents also require the pages they hold to be aware that they're displayed within a frameset. Otherwise, external links will appear within the frameset, rather than replacing it.

While a frameset can be an acceptable approach in some circumstances, the disadvantages outweigh any advantages when the goal is simply to grab minor data changes from the server. There are better ways, so framesets are no longer recommended for use in applications that request only minor changes from the server.

Remote Scripting Methods

There are several major techniques for sending messages to, and obtaining minor data changes from a server, without resorting to a full page refresh:

❏ an `iframe`

❏ a hidden image

☐ a 204 response

☐ XMLHTTP.

Each of these techniques requires a server-side component as well as client-side code, although the server-side component is usually very simple. Each has advantages, disadvantages, and varying levels of browser support. Let's look at these techniques in detail.

Using `<iframe>`

An `iframe` element is a floating frame: it takes up an area of the page, just like any normal HTML element, but it displays a different URL, as does a frame in a frameset. `iframe`s can be used to display dynamic content in two ways: we can use the frameset approach, displaying an entirely different document inside the `iframe`, or we can pass pure data back to the main page through the `iframe`.

Simple `iframe` Display

Displaying a separate page in an `iframe` is easy: just set the `iframe`'s `src` attribute to the URL of the page.

```
<iframe src="http://www.google.com/"></iframe>
```

This adds to your page a small, scrollable area in which the designated document is shown.[1] Like other elements, an `iframe` can be sized with CSS; you can specify its `width` and `height` property values, and even apply a border.

File: **simple-iframe.html**

```
<!DOCTYPE HTML PUBLIC "-//W3C//DTD HTML 4.01//EN"
    "http://www.w3.org/TR/html4/strict.dtd">
<html>
  <head>
    <title>A simple iframe example</title>
    <style type="text/css">
      #myframe {
        width: 300px;
        height: 100px;
        border: 2px solid red;
      }
```

---

[1] Note that you can also add HTML between the `<iframe>` and `</iframe>`; this content will display in browsers that don't support `iframe`s at all.

```
    </style>
  </head>
  <body>
    <h1>A simple iframe</h1>
    <p>Below is an iframe, styled in size with CSS and
      displaying a different document.</p>
    <iframe id="myframe" src="simple-iframe-content.html">
    </iframe>
  </body>
</html>
```

The HTML document displayed by the iframe is trivial and unstyled:

File: **simple-iframe-content.html**

```
<!DOCTYPE HTML PUBLIC "-//W3C//DTD HTML 4.01//EN"
   "http://www.w3.org/TR/html4/strict.dtd">
<html>
  <body>
    <p>This is a document <em>in</em> the iframe.</p>
  </body>
</html>
```

Figure 8.1 shows the page display.

Figure 8.1. The document with an iframe that displays another document.

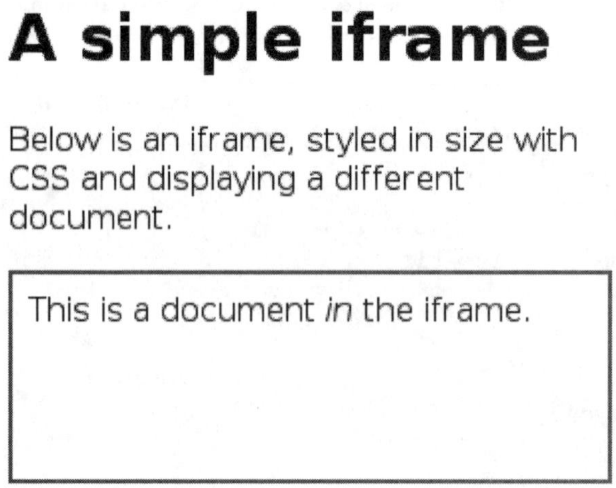

A simple iframe

Below is an iframe, styled in size with CSS and displaying a different document.

This is a document *in* the iframe.

There's no sign that the `iframe` document is separate from that which surrounds it.

Replacing `iframes`

You can change the document that displays inside the `iframe` using a script located in the surrounding document. If the `iframe` is styled so as not to draw attention to itself, this technique creates the illusion that part of the parent document has changed.

The `iframe` element's `src` attribute is, like other attributes on HTML elements, available as a property of the corresponding DOM object. Here's a simple script that can be called from a button press or link click; it merely changes the document displayed in the `iframe`:

```
<script type="text/javascript">
function changeIFrame() {
  document.getElementById('myframe').src =
      'http://www.google.com/';
}
</script>
```

This example is so simple it doesn't even need JavaScript. `iframes` act like normal frames and can therefore be the target of any hyperlink. You can display a link's destination in an `iframe` by setting the `target` attribute on the link to the name of the `iframe`.

Retrieving Data with `iframes`

With further scripting, it's possible for the `iframe`'s newly-loaded page to pass data back to its parent page. Scripts in the `iframe` content page can call functions in the parent page by referring to those parent-page functions as `window.parent.functionName`. This means that we can put any number of smart scripts in the parent page, ready for triggering by the `iframe` content as needed.

Let's look at a simple example. First, the main page:

File: **simple-iframe-2.html**
```
<!DOCTYPE HTML PUBLIC "-//W3C//DTD HTML 4.01//EN"
    "http://www.w3.org/TR/html4/strict.dtd">
<html>
  <head>
    <title>A simple iframe example</title>
```

```
    <link type="text/css" rel="stylesheet"
        href="simple-iframe-2.css">
    <script type="text/javascript">
      function receiveData(data) {
        document.getElementById('response').firstChild.nodeValue =
          data;
      }
    </script>
  </head>
  <body>
    <p>An iframe to which we send requests</p>
    <iframe id="scriptframe" name="scriptframe" src=""></iframe>
    <p><a href="simple-iframe-content-2.html"
        target="scriptframe">Send a request</a></p>
    <div>
      <h2>Response data received</h2>
      <p id="response">No data yet.</p>
    </div>
  </body>
</html>
```

There's a lot going on in this document, so let's pick through it slowly. First, there's a link to a style sheet. It's trivial stuff:

File: **simple-iframe-2.css**

```
div {
  border: 1px solid black;
  padding: 0 0 1em 0;
  width: 20em;
}

h2 {
  background-color: black;
  color: white;
  text-align: center;
  margin: 0;
}

div p {
  padding: 0 1em;
}

#scriptframe {
  width: 300px;
  height: 100px;
```

```
  border: 2px solid red;
}
```

Second, there's a JavaScript function, `receiveData`. Notice that it's not called from anywhere in this page—it's not even installed as an event listener. It's just sitting there, waiting for someone else to use it. After that, there's content. Figure 8.2 shows the page as it appears when it first loads.

Figure 8.2. The page ready for data exchanges via `iframe`.

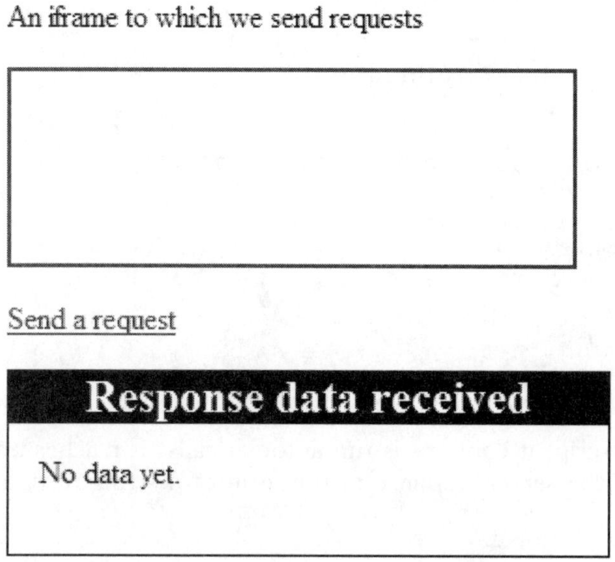

An iframe to which we send requests

Send a request

Response data received

No data yet.

Let's look at the page's content tags closely. First is the `iframe`. Notice that both its `id` (for styling) and `name` (for links) are set to `scriptframe`. This `iframe` will be the target that receives the HTML document generated by the server in response to a request for information made by this page.

Second, there's a link. It has a `target` of `scriptframe`, which matches the `iframe`. This link will produce the request for information from the server.

Third, we see a p element with `id="response"`. This paragraph will display the data that has been retrieved from the server. If you look closely, you'll see that the `receiveData` function declared at the top of the page will do most of the work:

File: **simple-iframe-2.html (excerpt)**

```
function receiveData(data) {
  document.getElementById('response').firstChild.nodeValue =
      data;
}
```

All that's missing is something that will call the function, and pass to it the data to be displayed. The response received from the server—and displayed in the iframe—will do just that:

File: **simple-iframe-content-2.html**

```
<!DOCTYPE HTML PUBLIC "-//W3C//DTD HTML 4.01//EN"
    "http://www.w3.org/TR/html4/strict.dtd">
<html>
  <body>
    <p>This iframe contains the response from the server.</p>
    <script type="text/javascript">
      if (window.parent.receiveData) {
        window.parent.receiveData(
            'some data sent from the iframe content page!');
      }
    </script>
  </body>
</html>
```

When this page loads, the script it contains is run automatically; it reaches up into the parent, delivering the server response in the form of a string of data ('some data...').

Figure 8.3 shows the page after the user has clicked the link.

To summarize, clicking the Send a request link on the main page loads the content page into the iframe (note the target attribute on the link); that content page contains JavaScript that calls the receiveData function in the main page. The end result is that content from the server is put into the current page without requiring that the whole page be reloaded. If the requested page was a PHP-, ASP-, or other server-generated page, it could pass back from the server any dynamic data required.

Figure 8.3. Updated `iframe` page after the link is clicked.

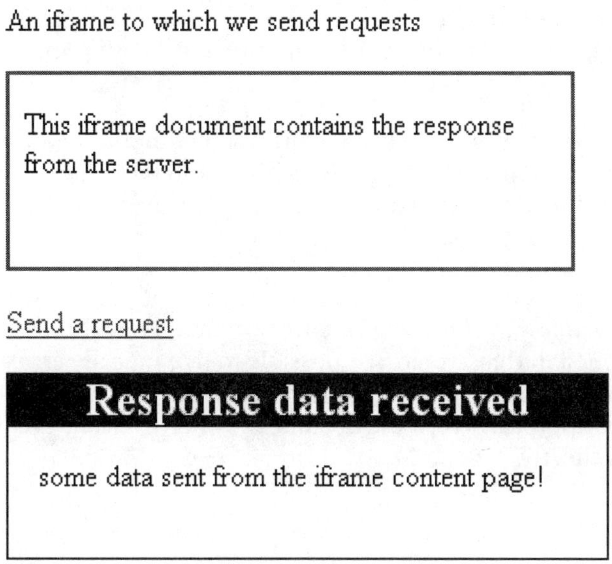

An iframe to which we send requests

This iframe document contains the response
from the server.

Send a request

Response data received

some data sent from the iframe content page!

Overcoming `iframe` Restrictions

There's an obvious flaw with this method, though: that big, ugly `iframe` sitting in the middle of the page. Although you wouldn't need to apply the thick border shown above, it's still there in the page.

You might think that an easy solution would be to style the `iframe` to zero size,[2] and indeed, that does work. Setting the `width` and `height` properties of the `iframe` to 0 will effectively hide the `iframe` from view. Links on the page can then load other pages into the `iframe` and receive data from them.

Since a page is loaded into the `iframe` via a linked URL, it's even possible to pass data in the request by adding it to the URL's query string. So, for example, a link in the page could look up an item in a database by requesting `iframe-content.php?id=32`; the HTML generated by that PHP script would call back the `receiveData` function in the main page with details of item number 32 from the (server-side) database.

---

[2]You might also think of hiding it from view entirely with `display: none`, until you discovered that Netscape 6 entirely ignores `iframe`s that are undisplayed and, therefore, that approach, sadly, doesn't work.

The next notable flaw with this `iframe` approach is that it breaks the Back and Forward buttons in the user's browser. The loading of a page into an `iframe` is added to the browser history, so, from the user's perspective, the Back button (which simply undoes the page load within the invisible `iframe`) doesn't appear to do anything.

A solution is to use JavaScript's `window.location.replace` method to load the new document into the `iframe`, replacing the current history item rather than adding to the history list. This means that the browser history is unaffected and the Back (and Forward) buttons continue to work properly.

This variation is described in great detail on Apple's Developer Connection site, in an article called *Remote Scripting with IFRAME*[1]. One further, extremely useful and elegant variation is outlined in that article. It's possible to dynamically create the `iframe` element with the DOM, rather than rely on it already being present in the HTML document; this approach keeps the document's HTML clean. We'll see this technique in action shortly.

Example: Autoforms

Let's conclude the discussion of `iframe`s with a more advanced example.

A recent trend in desktop environments has been to move away from dialog boxes with Apply buttons, and move towards a new type of dialog box: one which applies changes as soon as they are made by the user. This feature provides a kind of "real time" awareness of the user interactions, which take effect immediately. When users finish making changes, they simply close the dialog box.

Nested Form Design

Real-time forms are difficult to duplicate on the Web, because there needs to be an active Apply Changes button to submit the form—complete with the user's changes—to the server. Remote scripting provides a means to implement this dynamic functionality on the Web.

The core of the problem is this: the page that contains the form for dynamic submission (which I'll christen an **autoform**) needs to be able to submit that form data to the server without submitting the whole page.

---

[1] http://developer.apple.com/internet/webcontent/iframe.html

One way to achieve this is for the page to open a copy of itself in an `iframe`. When the user changes a form element, the autoform reflects that change in the corresponding field in the copy. Once the copy is updated, the page causes the copy's autoform to submit, thus saving the data on the server without submitting the main page.

Since this technique is an alteration to the way in which Web forms normally work, progress hints should be supplied to the user. At the very least, you should indicate that the user's change has been processed. Ideally, when the user changes a field, that field should indicate that the data is being processed; when the response is received, the field should update again to indicate that the processing is complete. Figure 8.4 shows these steps.

Figure 8.4. Editing, saving, and a saved autoform field.

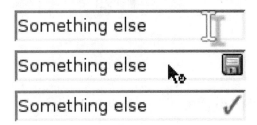

In Figure 8.4, the first field is untouched. Below it, we see a field from which the user has clicked away, moving the focus to another field. Note how the field changes: a floppy disk symbol is displayed, indicating that the field's value is being saved (i.e. the duplicate form in the `iframe` is being submitted). Below that field we see another field, which was changed earlier. That data has been saved to the server, so the indicator has changed again to display a check mark. Choose your own icons if you don't like these ones.

Avoiding Infinite Forms

Since the page is loaded twice—once in the browser window, and once in the hidden `iframe`—it needs special logic. The version that's loaded into the browser window (the "parent") needs to create the `iframe` and load the second copy (the "child") into that `iframe`. The child, however, mustn't do the same thing, or else the browser will descend into an infinitely nested set of pages.[3] Our script's `init` method must contain some logic to prevent such nesting:

---

[3]It might be fun to try, just to see what happens, though!

```
if (parent.document.getElementById('autoform_ifr')) {
  aF.init_child();
} else {
  aF.init_parent();
}
```

This code determines whether the current document should be initialized as the main form, or as a duplicate form loaded in an `iframe`. It does this by looking for a containing `iframe` with ID `autoform_ifr` in the parent document.

If this `iframe` is detected, then the page running this code must be the "child" containing the duplicate form; hence, we call the `init_child` method to initialize the page accordingly. Otherwise, we call the method `init_parent`.

Let's now take a step back and look at the basic structure of the page. We'll then be equipped to write our parent and child initialization methods.

Setting up Content and Scripts

In the finished example, we'll generate our form page using a server script, for reasons we'll see shortly. For the moment, however, let's work with a static version of the page:

```
<!DOCTYPE HTML PUBLIC "-//W3C//DTD HTML 4.01//EN"
    "http://www.w3.org/TR/html4/strict.dtd">
<html>
  <head>
    <title>A very simple form</title>
    <link type="text/css" href="autoform.css" rel="stylesheet">
    <script type="text/javascript" src="autoform.js"></script>
  </head>
  <body>
    <h1>A simple form</h1>
    <form method="post" id="f1" class="auto">
      <p>
        <label for="name">Name</label>
        <input type="text" name="name" id="name">
      </p>
      <p>
        <label for="age">Age</label>
        <input type="text" name="age" id="age">
      </p>
```

```
      <p>
        <label for="shoesize">Shoe size</label>
        <input type="text" name="shoesize" id="shoesize">
      </p>
      <input type="submit">
    </form>
  </body>
</html>
```

Notice that the form has a Submit button, just like a standard Web form, and that there's no iframe tag in the page. Once our script gets to the page, these things will change.

Here's the style sheet for the page. It's quite simple, except that it contains rules for some classes and elements that are not yet present in the page:

File: **autoform.css**

```
input {
  padding-right: 20px;
  display: block;
}

.autoform_pending {
  background: url(autoform_save.png) center right no-repeat;
}
.autoform_saved {
  background: url(autoform_saved.png) center right no-repeat;
}

#autoform_ifr {
  border: none;
  width: 0;
  height: 0;
}
```

The second and third rules will apply to fields being auto-submitted, and fields for which auto-submission is complete, respectively. The last rule guarantees that the iframe will be invisible to the user.

With the basic HTML and CSS in place, we're ready to consider the JavaScript. As in all the projects in this book, we're aiming for neatly stored, reusable code, and a library object is the way we'll achieve this. Here's the object signature for our autoform library object.

File: **autoform.js (excerpt)**

```
var aF = {
  addEvent: function(elm, evType, fn, useCapture) { ... },
  init: function() { ... },

  init_parent: function() { ... },
  init_child: function() { ... },

  cancel_submit: function(e) { ... },
  parent_load_child: function() { ... },
  parent_callback: function(elementNames) { ... },
  parent_document_callback: function(docObj) { ... },
  parent_element_change: function(e) { ... }
}

aF.addEvent(window, 'load', aF.init, false);
```

The addEvent and init methods serve the same purposes as always. Initialization is a big task for this example, so, as we've seen, init gets help from one of two other methods: init_parent or init_child.

We'll meet the remaining methods as we progress, but be aware that two of them are **callbacks**. Callbacks are methods that are called from outside this script by code that the script launches. In this example, the callback methods in the parent document will be called by the child document contained in the hidden iframe.

To kick things off, here's the full text of the init method; it's a little more complete than the brief snippet we saw before:

File: **autoform.js (excerpt)**

```
init: function() {
  if (!document.getElementById ||
      !document.createElement ||
      !document.getElementsByTagName ||
      !document.getElementsByName) return;
  if (parent.document.getElementById('autoform_ifr')) {
    aF.init_child();
  } else {
    aF.init_parent();
  }
},
```

This code tests for all the DOM facilities that our autoform might need. If there's a lack of support, the iframe and scripting will not be used: a plain HTML form results.

Coordinating Parent and Child Pages

The parent page, which displays the form for the user, is initialized by the method init_parent:

File: **autoform.js (excerpt)**

```
init_parent: function() {
  var load_child = false;
  var frms = document.getElementsByTagName('form');
  for (var i = 0; i < frms.length; i++) {
    if (frms[i].className &&
        frms[i].className.search(/\bauto\b/) != -1) {
      load_child = true;

      aF.addEvent(frms[i], 'submit', aF.cancel_submit, false);
      frms[i].onsubmit = function() { return false; }; // Safari
      for (var j = frms[i].elements.length - 1; j > 0; j--) {
        var el = frms[i].elements[j];
        if (el.nodeName.toLowerCase() == 'input' &&
            el.type.toLowerCase() == 'submit') {
          el.parentNode.removeChild(el);
        }
      }

      // attach an onchange listener to each element
      for (var j = 0; j < frms[i].elements.length; j++) {
        var el = frms[i].elements[j];
        aF.addEvent(el, 'change', aF.parent_element_change,
            false);
      }
    }
  }
  if (load_child) aF.parent_load_child();
},
```

The method keeps a flag, load_child, so that the loading of the iframe can be done, at most, once at the end of the script—even if the page contains several forms. The body of the method searches for forms with class="auto". If one or more is found, a submit event listener is attached to the form(s); this will block submission of the form, as we saw in Chapter 6:

File: **autoform.js (excerpt)**

```
cancel_submit: function(e) {
  if (window.event) {
    window.event.cancelBubble = true;
```

```
      window.event.returnValue = false;
      return false;
    } else if (e) {
      e.stopPropagation();
      e.preventDefault();
    }
  },
```

Additionally, `init_parent` attaches an old-style event handler that will block the submission in Safari, which does not support doing so with an event listener:

File: **autoform.js (excerpt)**

```
frms[i].onsubmit = function() { return false; }; // Safari
```

Finally, any Submit buttons in the form are found and removed from the document.

As a replacement for normal form submission, each field gains a `change` event listener: the `parent_element_change` method, which we'll look at shortly.

Finally, the dirty work of loading the child page is handed to `parent_load_child`. Here's that method:

File: **autoform.js (excerpt)**

```
parent_load_child: function() {
  var b = document.getElementsByTagName('body')[0];
  var i = document.createElement('iframe');
  i.id = 'autoform_ifr';
  i.name = 'autoform_ifr';
  b.appendChild(i);
  if (i.contentDocument && i.contentDocument.location) {
    // For DOM2 compliant
    var subdoc = i.contentDocument;
  } else if (i.contentWindow) {
    // For IE5.5 and IE6
    var subdoc = i.contentWindow.document;
  } else if (window.frames) {
    // Safari
    var subdoc = window.frames['autoform_ifr'].document;
  } else {
    return;
  }
  subdoc.location.replace(location.href);
},
```

Most of the work is done in the five lines, in which we create a new `iframe` element and insert it at the end of the document. Next, we complete some object detection in order to get a reference to the `iframe`'s `document` object, using either the `contentDocument` property of the DOM2 standard, the Internet Explorer-specific `contentWindow` property, or for Safari, which in some versions has an incomplete implementation of `contentDocument`, the corresponding entry in `window.frames`. We then use this reference to get the `iframe`'s `location` object, and replace the default blank page with a copy of the current page (`location.href`).[4]

The parent page has now been loaded and prepared for operation as an autoform. Let's now turn our attention to the duplicate copy of the page that's contained in the `iframe`.

When loaded into the `iframe`, the duplicate page will execute the `init` method above and, detecting that it is the child, will execute `init_child`:

File: **autoform.js** (excerpt)

```
init_child: function() {
  parent.aF.parent_document_callback(document);

  if (aF.changedElements && aF.changedElements.length > 0) {
    parent.aF.parent_callback(aF.changedElements);
  }
},
```

This method has two purposes. The first is to call the parent, supplying a reference to the child's document object (via `parent_document_calback`); this document reference will be used by the parent later. Here's the `parent_document_callback` method, which is called in the parent document to store the document reference:

File: **autoform.js** (excerpt)

```
parent_document_callback: function(docObj) {
  aF.childDocument = docObj;
},
```

The second task of `init_child` is to notify the parent of any form fields whose changes have successfully been submitted to the server. We're skipping ahead a little, here, so bear with me.

---

[4] Unfortunately, this causes a new step to be recorded in the navigation history of Mozilla browsers. As we'll see, this isn't that big a deal because navigation history is going to be a problem for this example across all browsers.

When the child document is loaded into the `iframe` for the first time, no form values have been changed or submitted, so there's nothing to do in this case. Later, however, when changes made to the parent form cause the child document's form to submit, the page will be reloaded, with the names of the submitted fields listed in an array called `aF.changedElements`. We want to notify the parent document when that happens, so that it can update the fields in the main form to show that they were successfully submitted. To do this, `init_child` must pass `aF.changedElements` to the `parent_callback` method in the parent document.

In simpler terms, the parent document tells the child document to submit some values. Once it has done so, the child document notifies the parent document of its success by calling the parent's `parent_callback` method, and passing it a list of the form fields that were submitted.

Naturally, we need a `parent_callback` method:

File: **autoform.js** (excerpt)

```
parent_callback: function(elementNames) {
  for (var i = 0; i < elementNames.length; i++) {
    var el = document.getElementsByName(elementNames[i])[0];
    el.className = el.className.replace(/\b ?autoform_[a-z]+\b/,
        '');
    el.className += ' autoform_saved';
  }
},
```

This method loops through the supplied array of form element names, and sets `class="autoform_saved"` on each of the corresponding elements.

But, as I said, we're jumping ahead here. Before we start handling stuff that happens after form submission, we should first implement the logic that actually submits the form!

Submitting Forms Indirectly

When the user changes a field in the main form, the change event listener, `parent_element_change`, is called. It's the last of the JavaScript methods we need to implement:

File: **autoform.js** (excerpt)

```
parent_element_change: function(e) {
  var el = window.event ? window.event.srcElement : e ?
      e.target : null;
```

```
    if (!el) return;
    el.className = el.className.replace(/\b ?autoform_[a-z]+\b/,
        '');
    el.className += ' autoform_pending';
    var child_form = aF.childDocument.getElementById(el.form.id);
    aF.childDocument.getElementsByName(el.name)[0].value =
        el.value;
    child_form.submit();
}
```

After removing any `autoform_` CSS class that may already be applied to the form field, the method assigns the class `autoform_pending` to it. This causes the "saving" icon to appear in the field, as specified by the style sheet.[5] The method then changes the value of this field *in the child document* to match the newly-changed value in the parent. It finds the corresponding element in the child by calling `getElementsByName` on the handy `aF.childDocument` reference that was created during document setup. The method then submits the form in the child, which sends the data to the server but does not alter the parent (displaying in the browser window).

Unfortunately, this is where our attempts to keep the navigation history clean fall apart. No matter what we do, the form submission in the child document will add a step to the browser's navigation history. So if a user makes three changes to field values, he or she will get three new steps in the browser history while apparently sitting on a single page. For this reason, if you want to make practical use of this technique in your application, I recommend displaying the autoform page in a popup window with no back/forward buttons.

On the server, the form submission is processed just like any form submission, returning a slightly modified copy of the form page to the browser. This modified page contains a little extra JavaScript that fills `aF.changedElements` with the names of the fields that the server noted as having changed from the previous values. An example of the JavaScript that the server might write follows:

```
aF.changedElements = ['name', 'age'];
```

Next, `init_child` will execute, passing these values to the parent (specifically, to the `parent_callback` method). That method uses the names to set the appropriate fields to have the `autoform_saved` class, which displays the "saved" check mark icon.

---

[5]Safari, which does not permit styling of form fields, will not display the icon. For maximum usability, you might want to adjust this example to display the icon outside the field.

This whole procedure is complicated somewhat by the fact that the page is loaded twice (and, therefore, needs to be able to handle two code paths: parent and child), but the underlying idea of loading a page into an `iframe` can be put to many uses.

Serving up the Page

The key complexity here, which may take time to get your head around, is that the server page that generates the form (repeatedly), and the server page that's called by the client-side script to save the data, are in fact *the same* page.

Here's the PHP script that does everything we need to produce a working auto-form with the necessary server-side logic:

File: **autoform.php**

```php
<?php
  // File containing a serialized key => value array
  $data_file = '/tmp/serialized.dat';

  // If the data file doesn't exist, create it with default values
  if (!file_exists($data_file)) {
    // Initialize file with default array keys
    $fp = fopen($data_file, 'w');
    fwrite($fp,
        serialize(array('name' => '', 'age' => '',
        'shoesize' => '')));
    fclose($fp);
  }

  // Load data from the data file to populate the form
  $from_file = unserialize(file_get_contents($data_file));

  // If the form has been submitted, and there were changes,
  // save the new data back to the file
  $changed_keys = array();
  if ($_POST) {
    foreach (array_keys($from_file) as $key) {
      if (array_key_exists($key, $_POST)
          && $_POST[$key] != $from_file[$key]) {
        $changed_keys[] = $key;
        $from_file[$key] = $_POST[$key];
      }
    }
    if (count($changed_keys) > 0) {
      // Write data back to file
```

```php
      $fp = fopen($data_file, 'w');
      fwrite($fp, serialize($from_file));
      fclose($fp);
    }
  }
?>
<!DOCTYPE HTML PUBLIC "-//W3C//DTD HTML 4.01//EN"
    "http://www.w3.org/TR/html4/strict.dtd">
<html>
  <head>
    <title>A very simple form</title>
    <link href="autoform.css" rel="stylesheet" type="text/css">
    <script type="text/javascript" src="autoform.js"></script>
    <script type="text/javascript">
      aF.changedElements = [<?php
        if (count($changed_keys) > 0) {
          echo "'" . implode("', '", array_map('addslashes',
              $changed_keys)) . "'";
        }
      ?>];
    </script>
  </head>
  <body>
    <h1>A simple form</h1>
    <form method="post" id="f1">
      <p>
        <label for="name">Name</label>
        <input type="text" name="name" id="name"
            value="<?php
            echo htmlspecialchars($from_file['name']); ?>">
      </p>
      <p>
        <label for="age">Age</label>
        <input type="text" name="age" id="age"
            value="<?php echo htmlspecialchars($from_file['age']);
            ?>">
      </p>
      <p>
        <label for="shoesize">Shoe size</label>
        <input type="text" name="shoesize" id="shoesize"
            value="<?php
            echo htmlspecialchars($from_file['shoesize']); ?>">
      </p>
      <input type="submit">
    </form>
```

```
    </body>
</html>
```

This relatively simple PHP page loads a batch of data from a file, `/tmp/serialized.dat`, and writes out an HTML page with a form containing the values loaded from that file. When the form is submitted, it saves the submitted values (if any have changed) back into the file, and keeps track of the altered fields in a PHP array variable named `$changed_keys`. Essentially, the file acts as a database.[6]

Most of the work that makes this into an autoform is done by our library script, so we have included it, along with its complementary style sheet:

File: **autoform.php (excerpt)**

```
<link href="autoform.css" rel="stylesheet" type="text/css">
<script type="text/javascript" src="autoform.js"></script>
```

And now for the tricky bit! The PHP script has to generate the `aF.changedElements` array, which must contain the names of all the form fields whose values were changed with the last submission. As such, PHP must write out some JavaScript of its own.

`aF.changedElements` is a list of all the values that changed when the form was last submitted, i.e. every value in the submitted form which differed from the previously saved value. The PHP code needs to make this list of changed elements available to JavaScript, so it should write out a JavaScript snippet containing a JavaScript list of the names of the changed elements. So, if the user had just submitted the form with new values for `name` and `shoesize`, the PHP should write out the following snippet:

```
<script type="text/javascript">
    aF.changedElements = ['name', 'shoesize'];
</script>
```

The script builds up a list of the changed fields in `$changed_keys`, so it uses this to print out the necessary JavaScript:

File: **autoform.php (excerpt)**

```
<script type="text/javascript">
    aF.changedElements = [<?php
```

---

[6]PHP's `serialize` and `unserialize` functions do all the work here, converting the data to a format that's suitable for storage in a file, and then restoring the data when it's read from the file. For more information on how this works, you may refer to the PHP Manual, or you might prefer to implement it in your own choice of language.

```
    if (count($changed_keys) > 0) {
        echo "'" . implode("', '", array_map('addslashes',
            $changed_keys)) . "'";
    }
  ?>];
</script>
```

The rest of the work is carried out by the JavaScript library as described above. The writing out of the `aF.changedElements` value is the only thing that's required to make the form an autoform; exactly how the data is saved on the server-side doesn't affect the autoform nature of the page, and can be done any way you like—even via a database.

Hidden Cookie Updates

The hidden `iframe` technique is quite general in that it allows any amount of content or script to be loaded at the click of a link. If you only need a small amount of data, there are other techniques on offer—one variation uses cookies to send data.

Using such techniques, you don't have to create a separate `iframe` document to communicate with the server—the main document will do fine. Let's look at two of these techniques now.

Image Swaps

A similar but more restrictive approach to the hidden `iframe` technique is to use hidden images. JavaScript can load images into an `Image` object without those images being displayed on the page.[7] Since the image is being served from an HTTP server, it can set a cookie when it is loaded; JavaScript can read the cookies that were set by the server. So the technique creates an `Image` object and sets as its `src` property the server-side page that returns data. This server-side page sets a cookie that contains the data that's to be passed back to the client, and the client page reads the data straight out of that cookie. The `Image` object itself is never used; it's simply requested in order that the cookie can be set by the server.

This approach has been neatly wrapped up by Brent Ashley into his easy-to-use RSLite library[2]. In a moment, we'll look at an example that illustrates its use.

---

[7]Anyone who has used an old-school JavaScript image rollover will be familiar with the concept of "preloading" the images to be used for the rollover; this is exactly the same.
[2] http://www.ashleyit.com/rs/rslite/

204 Piggybacks

Even simpler than the image swap technique is to use the HTTP 204 "No Content" response. Using this technique, instead of changing the src of an image to a new document, we simply navigate to a special link. That link runs a server script that returns a 204 response code (and no content at all), along with useful cookie data. Browsers know to leave the current page in place when a 204 response is received. This approach is otherwise very similar to the image swap technique.

Example: Name Resolution

Many email clients have an address book with a "nickname" feature; enter the nickname into the To or Cc boxes, and the email client replaces it with the email address attached to that nickname. Webmail systems don't often provide this functionality, but it's a clear example of the sort of problem that the RSLite library is designed to answer.

To create this functionality, we pass a small amount of data (a nickname) to the server via the RSLite library; the server then does all the work, resolving the nickname to an email address. RSLite then passes the results of that work (the email address) back to the client for display.

Here's a sample Web mail page. It looks just like an ordinary Web application:

File: **nameresolution.html**

```
<!DOCTYPE HTML PUBLIC "-//W3C//DTD HTML 4.01//EN"
    "http://www.w3.org/TR/html4/strict.dtd">
<html>
  <head>
    <title>Name Resolution</title>
    <link type="text/css" rel="stylesheet"
        href="nameresolution.css">
    <script src="rslite.js" type="text/javascript"></script>
    <script src="nameresolution.js" type="text/javascript">
    </script>
  </head>
<body>
    <h1>Name resolution</h1>
    <form>
      <p>
        <label for="to">To:</label>
        <input type="text" name="to" id="to">
      </p>
```

```
    <p>
      <label for="cc">Cc:</label>
      <input type="text" name="cc" id="cc">
    </p>
    <p>
      <label for="Subject">Subject:</label>
      <input type="text" name="subject" id="subject">
    </p>
    <p>
      <textarea id="message" name="message"></textarea>
    </p>
    <p>
      <input type="submit" value="Send">
    </p>
  </form>
  </body>
</html>
```

The styles in nameresolution.css are decorative only: they have no impact on the DHTML effect. Figure 8.5 shows this page in action:

Figure 8.5. A Webmail interface.

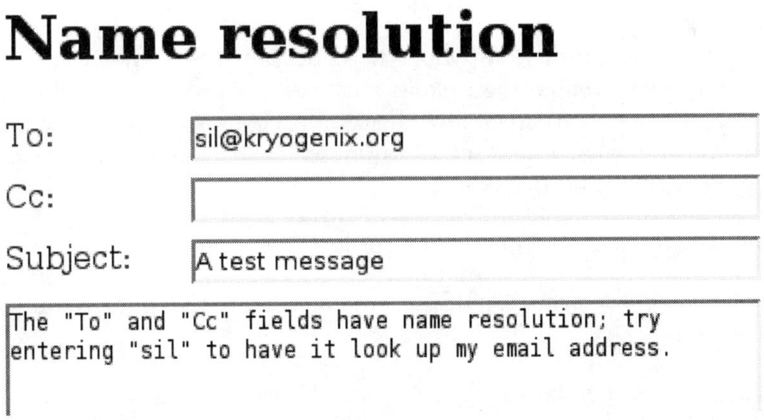

Name resolution

To:	sil@kryogenix.org
Cc:	
Subject:	A test message

The "To" and "Cc" fields have name resolution; try
entering "sil" to have it look up my email address.

Any code that we add should watch the To and Cc fields for changes. Whenever they change, our code will pass the contents back to the server using RSLite. RSLite will hand us back a resolved email address to go with the passed nickname (assuming an email address if found); otherwise, it will not hand back anything. Here's the very simplified server script:

File: **resolver.php**

```php
<?php

$names = array(
    'sil' => 'sil@kryogenix.org',
    'simon' => 'simon@incutio.com',
    'simonm' => 'simon@sitepoint.com',
    'nigel' => 'nrm@kingtide.com.au',
    'kev' => 'kevin@sitepoint.com'
);


$p = @$_GET['p'];


if (isset($names[$p]))
  setcookie('RSLite', $names[$p]);
?>
```

Obviously, in a real application, the $names array would not be hardcoded; instead, the code might look up the passed nickname ($_GET['p']) in a database.

Here's our scripting plan. The HTML includes the rslite.js library to make RSLite calls possible. Our script should then attach a change listener to the To and Cc fields so that it is notified of changes. Our script must also tell RSLite about callbacks.

RSLite is an asynchronous library, so when the code calls the server, that call does not return with the server's response data. Instead, the call returns immediately with no data. RSLite then repeatedly checks for a cookie set by the server (using setInterval) and, when one is set, a nominated callback function is called with the new cookie value from the server.

Here's an example of the required processing for just one field change:

1. Initialization code in the page tells RSLite which callback to call if any values arrive from the server.

2. The change event listener calls RSLite when a change occurs.

3. RSLite uses a JavaScript Image object to make a request to the server, sets up an interval timer to watch for responses, and finishes.

4. The server returns a cookie with its response to the request.

5. The interval timer notices the cookie and calls the callback function specified in Step 1.

As usual, let's start with the signature of the library object for which we're aiming:

File: **nameresolution.js** (excerpt)

```
var nR = {
  init: function() { ... },
  addEvent: function(elm, evType, fn, useCapture) { ... },

  resolve: function(e) { ... },
  resolve_callback: function(response) { ... },
  resolve_failure: function() { ... }
}

nR.addEvent(window, 'load', nR.init, false);
```

init and addEvent have the same roles as always. resolve is the listener that will kick off the name resolution. The other two methods are callbacks that are passed to RSLite.

Here's the init method that sets everything up:

File: **nameresolution.js** (excerpt)

```
init: function() {
  if (!document.getElementById) return;
  if (!RSLiteObject) return;
  window.RSLite = new RSLiteObject();
  // Set the "to" and "cc" fields to have name resolution
  var to_field = document.getElementById('to');
  if (to_field) nR.addEvent(to_field, 'change', nR.resolve,
      false);
  var cc_field = document.getElementById('cc');
  if (cc_field) nR.addEvent(cc_field, 'change', nR.resolve,
      false);
  // Set up the callbacks
  window.RSLite.callback = nR.resolve_callback;
  window.RSLite.failure = nR.resolve_failure;
}
```

The resolve method is registered as a listener on every field that supports name lookup, and RSLite is told about the two callback methods. Have a read of the RSLite code if you want to see how it stores those methods for later processing.

The `resolve` method is the event listener for the `change` event on the To and Cc fields. Here it is:

File: **nameresolution.js** (excerpt)

```
resolve: function(e) {
    var target = window.event ? window.event.srcElement: e ?
        e.target : null;
    if (!target || !target.value) return;
    nR.currentTarget = target;
    if (target.value.indexOf('@') != -1) return; // email address
    // Try and resolve the entered value to a proper value by
    // calling the server for name resolution
    window.RSLite.call('resolver.php', target.value);
}
```

This method retrieves the target element as usual, then saves that target element in an object property for later use. This is required so that the callback method can find out which field changed. The method then checks that the value does not contain an @ symbol; if it does, the code returns on the assumption that if the value in the field is already an email address, it does not need resolving. Finally, it uses RSLite to pass the value[8] back to the server. `nR.RSLite.call` takes two parameters: the name of the server page that's to be called (`resolver.php`), and the value to pass to that page (which, in this case, is the content of the field for resolution). This method then immediately exits; it does not wait for the value returned from the server. Instead, when the server returns a value, that value is passed to the callback method, `resolve_callback`. Here it is:

File: **nameresolution.js** (excerpt)

```
resolve_callback: function(response) {
    nR.currentTarget.value = response;
},
```

This method receives the server response, and sets the value of the field to that response. This is why `resolve`, above, saved the field into a variable. The field automatically changes from an entered nickname ("sil") to a resolved email address ("sil@kryogenix.org") when the user clicks or tabs out of it.

RSLite also allows for a failure callback function, which is called if the server returns nothing. In the server code above, the server will return nothing if the

---

[8]The function assumes, for simplicity, that the user has only entered one nickname into the field. Extending the function to allow for multiple (comma-separated) addresses or nicknames is an exercise that I've left to you.

passed nickname is not in the $names array; the code can use this to flag to the user that the entered nickname is unknown:

File: **nameresolution.js (excerpt)**

```
resolve_failure: function() {
  var errorSpan = document.createElement('span');
  errorSpan.className = 'error';
  errorSpan.appendChild(document.createTextNode(
      'Address ' + nR.currentTarget.value + ' invalid'));
  nR.currentTarget.errorSpan = errorSpan;
  nR.currentTarget.parentNode.appendChild(errorSpan);
},
```

An invalid address is flagged with the addition of a new span to the document containing the text, "Address *foo* invalid". A tiny extra customization to resolve is also required:

File: **nameresolution.js (excerpt)**

```
resolve: function(e) {
  var target = window.event ? window.event.srcElement: e ?
      e.target : null;
  if (!target || !target.value) return;
  nR.currentTarget = target;
  if (nR.currentTarget.errorSpan) {
    nR.currentTarget.errorSpan.parentNode.removeChild(
        nR.currentTarget.errorSpan);
    nR.currentTarget.errorSpan = null;
  }
  if (target.value.indexOf('@') != -1) return; // email address
  // Try and resolve the entered value to a proper value by
  // calling the server for name resolution
  window.RSLite.call('resolver.php', target.value);
},
```

The additional lines above remove any existing error message span before checking for a new address.

XMLHTTP

The methods presented so far have the disadvantage that they're oriented towards transferring small amounts of data from server to client: short strings, numbers, and the like. Transferring a larger quantity of data would be problematic using these methods; the hidden image technique, for example, is limited to data quantities of four kilobytes: the maximum size of a cookie.[9] For notifications, for small amounts of data, for a flag saying merely "yes" or "no", these methods are sufficient. When the client wants to retrieve a larger amount of data from the server, a different technique is called for. The best alternative is XMLHTTP.

Origins of XMLHTTP

XMLHTTP was originally implemented by Microsoft in Internet Explorer. It allows JavaScript to request an arbitrary URL,[10] receive the returned content, and do anything with it that you wish. The data returned from that URL can obviously be anything: it can be as long as you like, and anything you like. Although the method is called XMLHTTP, you are not limited to sending or returning XML. It is, therefore, a technique that's useful where other methods fall short.

Other methods fall short from time to time because they're essentially hacks—they use side-effects of other techniques to perform data transfer. XMLHTTP was specifically designed to do this transfer, so, if you want to pass a lot of data from the server back to the client, XMLHTTP is the way to go.

Even though the technique is called XMLHTTP, the class invented by Microsoft is called `XMLHttpRequest`. Since HTTP is also an acronym it should really be called `XMLHTTPRequest`. It's not though, so we're stuck with using `XMLHttpRequest` in our code. We'll continue to use XMLHTTP as the name of the technique, though.

The XMLHTTP technique relies entirely on HTTP requests and responses, as does the rest of the Web. There's no new form of communication between the Web browser and the Web server, there's just a new way to make requests from scripts—that's all.

Browser Variations

XMLHTTP has some compatibility issues; it's implemented a little differently in Gecko-based browsers (Mozilla, Firefox, Camino, and so on) than it is in IE.[11] Apple's Safari implements the Mozilla method, while other browsers may not support it at all. Opera is introducing support in its latest releases; Opera 7.6 will also implement the Mozilla approach.

---

[9]It would, of course, be possible to re-engineer the server code and the library to use multiple cookies to transfer data to get around this limit, but it would be a lot of work for not much benefit.
[10]The JavaScript security rules apply here; briefly, you can only request URLs from the server from which this HTML page was served. You can't just grab any URL from anywhere on the Web.
[11]IE 5.5 and above: IE5.0 does not support the technique.

By far the easiest way to work around these issues is to use one of the existing libraries that "wrap" the XMLHTTP objects provided by each browser. Including the library and using its objects, instead of the browser objects, to make requests neatly hides the varying browser implementations.

XMLHTTP, AJAX, and the Future

Since XMLHTTP has become widely supported across the browser market, more and more applications use it. Jesse James Garrett at Adaptive Path has coined the term "AJAX"[3] for applications using XMLHTTP, as a shorthand for "Asynchronous JavaScript And XML". Use of AJAX by famous Websites like Google (on the Google Suggest page) has helped to accelerate its popularity.

XMLHTTP has great potential because it breaks down the page-based model that most Web-based applications use. Before the Web came along, most applications used static data entry screens that weren't page-oriented. XMLHTTP allows that earlier kind of design to be re-expressed on the Web. If it worked once, probably it will work again.

XMLHTTP also has its issues. It reduces the accessibility of Web pages somewhat. That, however, was also said about DHTML when it first came on the scene. In this book, we've explained ways to ensure the accessibility of a site while exploiting the possibilities of DHTML. The same sorts of techniques are likely to evolve for XMLHTTP as well.

Sarissa: a Cross-Browser Library

One of the better XMLHTTP libraries is Sarissa[4], which wraps up both the `XMLHttpRequest` class for making HTTP requests, and the DOM `Document` class for interpreting the response, as an XML DOM tree.

Making a request for a URL with Sarissa is simple. First, include the Sarissa library in your code:

```
<script type="text/javascript" src="sarissa.js"></script>
```

Next, create a cross-browser XMLHTTP object:

```
var xmlhttp = Sarissa.getXmlHttpRequest();
```

---

[3] http://www.adaptivepath.com/publications/essays/archives/000385.php
[4] http://sarissa.sourceforge.net/

Third, specify the page to request:

```
xmlhttp.open('GET', 'url-of-page', true);
```

This call does not actually send the HTTP request; it merely specifies what it will be when it's sent. The request can, in theory, use any HTTP request type. The type is specified in the first parameter to the **open** call.[12] The request should be made asynchronously, so that the browser doesn't lock up while it's being made. An asynchronous request is performed by making the third parameter in the open call above **true**. The callback function, which is called when the request returns with data, is defined as follows:

```
xmlhttp.onreadystatechange = function() {
  if (xmlhttp.readyState == 4) {
    // place your callback code here
  }
}
```

That's an anonymous (nameless) callback function. It uses the number **4** because the returning response goes through a number of different states; state 4 means "the response is complete." Finally, to send the request, we use the following:

```
xmlhttp.send(null);
```

send returns immediately. When the request returns (later on, in its own time), your callback code is called, and the data from the requested URL is available in **xmlhttp.responseText**. Easy!

Example: Checking Usernames

Lots of Websites have signup forms that require a name, address, email address, username, and so forth. In signing up for a popular site, it's not uncommon to find that the username you wanted, or even your second and third choices, have already been taken. Of course, to find that out, you have to complete the whole form and then wait while it's submitted to the server. Then, finally, you're presented with the dreaded, "That username is already in use" message. In this example, we'll try to improve that user experience.

A nice enhancement to these forms might use remote scripting to check if the username you entered is already in use while you're filling in the rest of the form. That solution saves time and effort. We could achieve it using the above methods;

---

[12] In practice, browser support for request verbs other than GET and POST is lacking. Other verbs, such as PUT and DELETE, can be used with REST-style APIs, but they're not very common as yet.

RSLite, for example, would be an ideal approach. Simply pass the entered username back to the server asynchronously, and have the server pass back `true` or `false`, meaning already-in-use or available-for-use, respectively.

An extra enhancement could see the server, which knows the names already in use, suggest some alternatives that are not currently taken. Passing back this larger quantity of data, as already discussed, is an ideal use case for XMLHTTP.

Imagining the Solution

To make this work, there would first have to be a server-side page. When passed a name and a possible username, that page would return a simple list of suggested alternatives. Implementation of this server-side page is left as an exercise for the reader;[13] for now, assume that it is called with username and name parameters in the query string, and that it returns a list of possible alternative unused usernames as XML, like so:

```
<usernames>
  <username>StuartLangridge</username>
  <username>SLangridge</username>
  <username>sil194</username>
</usernames>
```

For the sake of completeness, here's a naïve implementation of such a script in PHP:

File: **check-username.php**

```php
<?php

// A quick and dirty XMLHTTP response script

header('Content-type: text/xml');
$username = $_GET['username'];
$name = $_GET['name'];
$names = explode(' ', $name);
$initial = substr(trim($name), 0, 1);
$surname = $names[count($names) - 1];
$firstname = $names[0];

?>
<usernames>
```

---

[13]Obviously it also needs to return an indication that the suggested username is available if, in fact, it is. This is also left as an exercise for the reader.

```
  <username><?php echo htmlspecialchars($firstname) .
      htmlspecialchars($surname); ?></username>
  <username><?php echo htmlspecialchars($initial) .
      htmlspecialchars($surname); ?></username>
  <username><?php echo htmlspecialchars($username);
      ?>194</username>
</usernames>
```

The signup form itself requires very simple HTML:

File: **check-username.html**

```
<!DOCTYPE HTML PUBLIC "-//W3C//DTD HTML 4.01//EN"
    "http://www.w3.org/TR/html4/strict.dtd">
<html>
  <head>
    <title>Check a username for uniqueness</title>
    <link type="text/css" rel="stylesheet"
        href="check-username.css">
    <script type="text/javascript" src="sarissa.js"></script>
    <script type="text/javascript" src="check-username.js">
    </script>
  </head>
  <body>
    <form action="">
      <div>
        <label for="name">Your name</label>
        <input type="text" class="text" id="name" name="name">
      </div>
      <div id="usernamecontainer">
        <label for="username">Your chosen username</label>
        <input type="text" class="text" id="username"
            name="username">
      </div>
      <div>
        <label for="address">Address</label>
        <textarea id="address" name="address"></textarea>
      </div>
      <div><input type="submit" class="submit"></div>
    </form>
  </body>
</html>
```

The username field (indicated in bold above) is the key here; when the field's value changes, the server should be called to confirm or deny the availability of the supplied username.

Here's the style sheet that controls the layout of the form:

```css
form {
  margin-left: 200px;
}

form div {
  margin: 0 0 0.25em 0;
}

label {
  float: left;
  margin-left: -200px;
}

label.para {
  float: none;
  display: block;
}

label.radio {
  float: none;
  margin-left: 0;
}

ul.radio {
  margin: 0;
  padding: 0;
  list-style-type: none;
}

input.text {
  width: 15em;
}

textarea {
  width: 20em;
  height: 10em;
}

input.submit {
  margin-left: -200px;
}
```

This style sheet contains a few rules for elements that the document does not yet contain, but they will come into play by the time we finish building this example. Since this isn't a book about style sheets, I'll leave you to examine the rules in detail if you wish.

Figure 8.6 shows the form before the server has been called.

Figure 8.6. Entering a username.

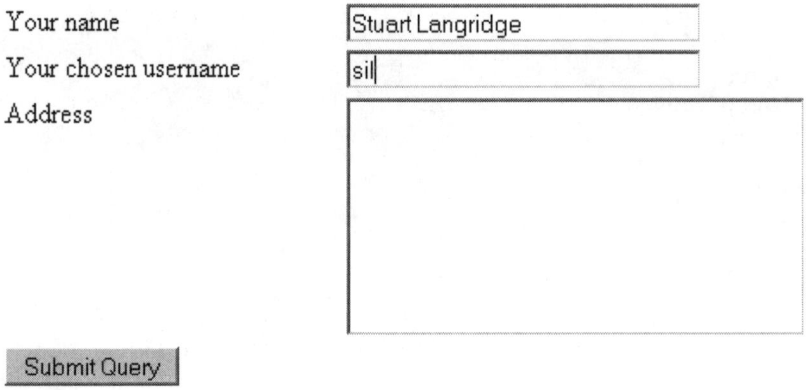

Building the JavaScript Scripts

We'll use the standard approach to attach an event listener to the change event on the username field, and to store some variables for later use. Here's our library object signature:

File: **check-username.js** (excerpt)

```
var cU = {
  init: function() { ... },
  addEvent: function(elm, evType, fn, useCapture) { ... },
  checkUsername: function() { ... },
  receiveUsernames: function(dom) { ... }
}

cU.addEvent(window, 'load', cU.init, false);
```

checkUsername will ask the server to perform the check. receiveUsernames is the callback method that handles the server response. Here's the init method that sets this up:

```
init: function() {
  if (!document.getElementById) return;
  if (!Sarissa) return;
  cU.name = document.getElementById('name');
  cU.username = document.getElementById('username');
  cU.usernamecontainer = document.getElementById(
    'usernamecontainer');
  if (!cU.name || !cU.username) return;
  if (!cU.usernamecontainer.innerHTML) return;
  cU.addEvent(cU.username, 'change', cU.checkUsername, false);
}
```

All this does is store references to the form fields, and to the div element where results will be displayed; it also installs a change event listener on the username field.

Note that init checks for the presence of the Sarissa object before proceeding—it's very easy to forget to load the library!

The checkUsername method, the event listener, constructs the appropriate URL for the server-side page (check-username.php?username=*A*&name=*B*) and initiates the XMLHTTP request.

```
checkUsername: function() {
  var xmlhttp = Sarissa.getXmlHttpRequest();
  var qs = '?username=' + cU.username.value +
    '&name=' + cU.name.value;
  xmlhttp.open('GET', 'check-username.php' + qs, true);
  xmlhttp.onreadystatechange = function() {
    if (xmlhttp.readyState == 4) {
      cU.receiveUsernames(xmlhttp.responseXML);
    }
  };
  xmlhttp.send(null);
},
```

The callback function shown in bold simply calls receiveUsernames with the returned XML document structure, responseXML.

The receiveUsernames method can, when called, obtain the suggested usernames from the returned XML, and then present them to the user in some way. Let's break receiveUsernames down.

The list of usernames can be obtained from the XML DOM in the same way as it would be obtained from the HTML DOM when parsing a Web page:

File: **check-username.js (excerpt)**

```
receiveUsernames: function(dom) {
  var alternatives = dom.getElementsByTagName('username');
```

The `alternatives` variable now holds a set of elements. A suitable way to present the list of alternative usernames to the user might involve adding a set of labeled radio buttons to the page. The page must also leave the text box in place (so the user is not forced to choose one of the presented alternatives), along with a message to explain that the selected username is unavailable.

This is quite a lot of HTML to add to the page. In theory, the script should use DOM methods like `document.createElement`, and `document.appendChild` to create each element, build the elements together into a DOM tree, and then insert that DOM tree into the page. This would be exceedingly tedious.

Instead, let's make use of the proprietary (but widely supported) property, `innerHTML`. While using this property is frowned upon by standards-bearers, it is a much simpler way of creating a block of HTML on-the-fly than is building it with DOM methods.[14] Since we're already using XMLHTTP—a nonstandard browser feature—we might as well use `innerHTML` as well.

The HTML block that is to be inserted looks like this:

File: **check-username.js (excerpt)**

```
var usernameHTML = '<label for="username" class="para">' +
  'The username \'USERNAME\' is already in use. ' +
  'Please choose one of the alternatives below, or ' +
  'enter another username.</label>' +
  '<ul class="radio">ALTERNATIVESLIST<li>' +
  '<label class="radio"><input type="radio" ' +
  'name="unchoice" checked="checked" value="username"> ' +
  'Another choice:</label> ' +
  '<input type="text" class="text" id="username" ' +
  'name="username"></li></ul>';
usernameHTML = usernameHTML.replace('USERNAME',
  cU.username.value);
```

---

[14]The new E4X standard provides an easy, standards-based solution. It's only available in Mozilla 1.8 and Firefox 1.1 and above, though.

As you can see, the HTML code placed in `usernameHTML` initially contains two placeholders: `USERNAME` and `ALTERNATIVESLIST`. The username is added with the string's `replace` method.

The `ALTERNATIVESLIST` placeholder is a little more complicated. We must construct the list of alternative usernames by iterating through the elements in `alternatives` and building it up:

File: **check-username.js** (excerpt)

```
var alternativeslist = '';
for (var i = 0; i < alternatives.length; i++) {
  var thisAL = '<li><label class="radio"><input ' +
      'type="radio" name="unchoice" checked="checked" ' +
      'value="USERNAME"> USERNAME</label></li>';
  thisAL = thisAL.replace(/USERNAME/g,
      alternatives[i].firstChild.nodeValue);
  alternativeslist += thisAL;
}
usernameHTML = usernameHTML.replace('ALTERNATIVESLIST',
    alternativeslist);
```

Each time through the loop, we create the HTML code for a radio button for one username in the `alternatives` array. We collect all that content together in `alternativeslist` and stick that set of list items into the HTML content string we prepared earlier.

Finally, we add the HTML to the page. Note that this replaces the current content of the `usernamecontainer` div, removing the previously-contained elements from the document entirely.

File: **check-username.js** (excerpt)

```
cU.usernamecontainer.innerHTML = usernameHTML;
```

Since the previous username text box was removed from the document and replaced with a new one by the `innerHTML` assignment, there will no longer be a `change` event listener attached to it. We'll have to put one back in. Instead of reassigning it directly, we delay that assignment for a short time with `setTimeout`; the browser occasionally takes a little time to make DOM nodes available after adding them to the document with `innerHTML`, so we give it time to catch up.

File: **check-username.js** (excerpt)

```
// reattach the event, giving browsers time to do the
// innerHTML work
setTimeout(function() {
```

```
      cU.username = document.getElementById('username');
      cU.addEvent(cU.username, 'change', cU.checkUsername, false);
  }, 200);
}
```

Altogether, the `receiveUsernames` method looks like this:

File: **check-username.js** (excerpt)

```
receiveUsernames: function(dom) {
  var alternatives = dom.getElementsByTagName('username');
  var usernameHTML = '<label for="username" class="para">' +
    'The username \'USERNAME\' is already in use. ' +
    'Please choose one of the alternatives below, or ' +
    'enter another username.</label>' +
    '<ul class="radio">ALTERNATIVESLIST<li>' +
    '<label class="radio"><input type="radio" ' +
    'name="unchoice" checked="checked" value="username"> ' +
    'Another choice:</label> ' +
    '<input type="text" class="text" id="username" ' +
    'name="username"></li></ul>';
  usernameHTML = usernameHTML.replace('USERNAME',
      cU.username.value);
  var alternativeslist = '';
  for (var i = 0; i < alternatives.length; i++) {
    var thisAL = '<li><label class="radio"><input ' +
        'type="radio" name="unchoice" checked="checked" ' +
        'value="USERNAME"> USERNAME</label></li>';
    thisAL = thisAL.replace(/USERNAME/g,
        alternatives[i].firstChild.nodeValue);
    alternativeslist += thisAL;
  }
  usernameHTML = usernameHTML.replace('ALTERNATIVESLIST',
      alternativeslist);
  cU.usernamecontainer.innerHTML = usernameHTML;

  // reattach the event, giving browsers time to do the
  // innerHTML work
  setTimeout(function() {
    cU.username = document.getElementById('username');
    cU.addEvent(cU.username, 'change', cU.checkUsername, false);
  }, 200);
}
```

Figure 8.7 shows the result of this manipulation for the example alternatives presented earlier.

Figure 8.7. The username alternatives looked up with XMLHTTP.

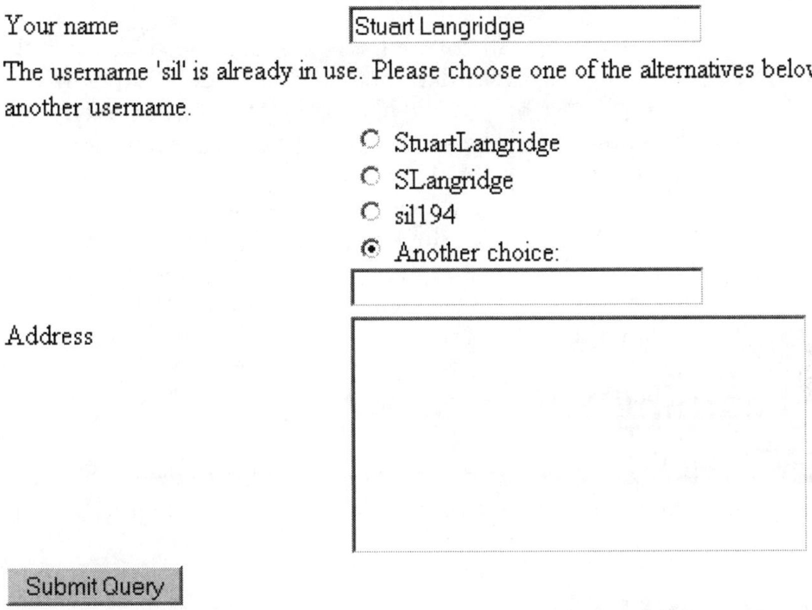

Your name

Stuart Langridge

The username 'sil' is already in use. Please choose one of the alternatives below, or enter another username.

○ StuartLangridge

○ SLangridge

○ sil194

◉ Another choice:

Address

Submit Query

Other Client-Server Options

Finally, we should point out that there exists another class of solutions for drawing data from the server. These all rely on more traditional client-server architecture, and have more to do with programming than with Web development. We'll just point them out here, and do no more than that.

The first option in this class of solutions is Web services. XML-based messaging systems like XML-RPC and SOAP provide options for communicating with servers without replacing the current page.

The second option is in-page components. If Web content is digitally signed, then alternatives like Microsoft ActiveX controls and Mozilla XPCOM components can be used. Even without digital signatures, a Java applet that takes up no screen space at all can be used to "phone home" to its server in the background.

These are all specialized solutions and are not intended for typical Web pages. Nevertheless, they are part of the picture of DHTML.

Drawing Code from Servers

The methods described so far are all focused on passing pure data from the server, then doing something with that data on the client-side. It's possible to make your application run faster by passing back from the server something a bit more structured than pure data. The server might pass back some formatted HTML; the client can then just drop this HTML directly into the page without having to do any work—an approach which makes for speed. Similarly, the server could pass back JavaScript code; the client can then execute that code directly by passing it to the JavaScript `eval` function. While these methods are a bit less "pure" than passing simple data back-and-forth, they can really accelerate the client work in your application.

Example: Learning about Beer

A simple demonstration is in order. Imagine an online guide to beer, which displays a number of beers and provides information about each. Figure 8.8 illustrates:

Figure 8.8. The beer guide.

If developed in a traditional style, the HTML for the body of the page might look like this:

File: **first-beer.html** (excerpt)

```
<div id="characters">
  <h2>Beer characters</h2>
  <ul>
    <li>
      <a id="hoppy"
```

```
        href="character.php?character=hoppy">hoppy</a>
    </li>
    <li>
      <a id="malty"
          href="character.php?character=malty">malty</a>
    </li>
    ...
  </ul>
</div>

<div id="beers">
  <h2>The beers</h2>
  <ul>
    <li>
      <a id="adnamsbitter"
          href="beer.php?beer=adnamsbitter">Adnams Bitter</a>
    </li>
    <li>
      <a id="draughtbass"
          href="beer.php?beer=draughtbass">Draught Bass</a>
    </li>
    ...
  </ul>
</div>
```

Each description of a character forms a link to a new page, which describes beers that exhibit that character (`character.php`). Each beer is also a link to a page (`beer.php`) that describes that beer.[15] There's lots of CSS styling at work, but the only tricky bit is this:

File: **first-beer.css (excerpt)**

```
#characters {
  width: 25%;
  float: left;
  margin-right: 5px;
  overflow: hidden;
}

#beers {
  width: 40%;
  float: left;
  margin-right: 5px;
  overflow: hidden;
}
```

[15]These pages aren't described; I'm sure you can imagine roughly what they'd be like.

```
a {
  width: 100%;   /* IE Hack */
  ...
}

h2 {
  width: 100%;   /* IE Hack */
  ...
}
```

These styles align the two `divs` left-to-right by floating them against the left side of the page. To prevent whitespace from appearing underneath each `li` in Internet Explorer, we use the trick we saw in Chapter 7: set the `li` contents to occupy the full width of the `li`. That wrecks the layout slightly for standards-compliant browsers, so we set `overflow: hidden` to tidy up there.

Planning the DHTML Beer Pages

Let's update this tiny application so that it doesn't need to send us off to different pages for information. We'll add a new section to the page itself to display data about a particular beer, and we'll change it so that clicking a beer character highlights it, and all the beers that have it.

These are the steps we'll take:

1. Generate the page dynamically, based on server data.

2. Add a new page element in which beer descriptions will be displayed.

3. Create a script to fetch data on an individual beer from the server.

4. Create a script to display the data from step 3 in the new section on the page.

5. Create a script to fetch data about which beers share a particular character.

6. Create a script to highlight those beers that are indicated by data from step 5.

As usual, we'll require a set of JavaScript methods, so let's jump forward for a second and see what those are going to look like:

File: **final-beer.js** (excerpt)

```
bG = {
  init: function() { ... },
  addEvent: function(elm, evType, fn, useCapture) { ... },
  geturl: function(u, fn) { ... },

  clickCharacter: function(e) { ... },
  clickBeer: function(e) { ... },

  display: function(beer) { ... },
  display2: function(beerdata) { ... },

  highlight: function(character) { ... },
  highlight2: function(charjs) { ... }

}

bG.addEvent(window, 'load', bG.init, false);
```

geturl will draw data back from the server. The click... methods are event listeners. display and display2 drive the beer selection feature, and highlight and highlight2 drive the character highlighting feature. But one step at a time is more than enough!

Generating the Starting Page from Data

Step 1, generating the page from server data, requires the same tactics as past examples. We'll keep all the data about beer in a separate PHP data structure. We imagine that $beers is an array populated as follows, perhaps from a database:

File: **beers.php** (excerpt)

```
$beers = array(
  'beerid1' => array(
    'beername',
    'beerdescription',
    'beercharacter'),
  'beerid2' => array(...
)
```

Here's an example of a single beer:

```
'guinness' => array(
  'Guinness',
```

```
  'An evil but habit-forming stout, best drunk near the Irish',
  'malty')
```

We also have a set of beer characters, which match those mentioned within the various beers' records:

File: **beers.php** (excerpt)

```
$beercharacters = array('hoppy', 'malty', 'fruity');
```

These arrays provide the data with which we'll generate the HTML for the page. The script will start like this:

File: **second-beer.php** (excerpt)

```
<?php
  include 'beers.php';
?>
```

We can now generate the lists for the beers' characters, and for the beers themselves, dynamically. Here's the code for the beers themselves:

File: **second-beer.php** (excerpt)

```
<div id="beers">
  <h2>The beers</h2>
  <ul>
    <?php foreach (array_keys($beers) as $beer) { ?>
      <li>
        <a id="<?php echo htmlspecialchars($beer); ?>"
           href="beer.php?beer=<?php
           echo htmlspecialchars($beer); ?>"><?php
           echo htmlspecialchars($beers[$beer][0]); ?></a>
      </li>
      <?php } ?>
  </ul>
</div>
```

This is no more than a simple loop that drags the beers out of the data structure.

Step 2—somewhere to put extra beer data—is trivial. We'll add a new HTML block at the end of the page, though we won't do much with it yet:

File: **second-beer.php** (excerpt)

```
<div id="beerdata">
  <h2>Beer data</h2>
  <p id="beerdef"></p>
</div>
```

This extra content requires an extra style rule:

File: **second-beer.css** (excerpt)

```
#beerdata {
  width: 25%;
  float: left;
  margin-right: 5px;
  overflow: hidden;
  border-left: solid 5px #f0f;
}
```

With those changes, we now have a dynamically generated page: one based on server data that we can share with other server scripts. That shared server data will make our lives much easier.

Fetching HTML Fragments

For step 3, the code needs to be able to fetch data about a specific beer. This is simply done. We need a server page that can print the data for a specific beer:

File: **beerserver1.php**

```
<?php
  include 'beers.php';

  if ($_GET['action'] == 'beer') {
    $beer = $_GET['beer'];
    // Write out the beer definition
    echo $beers[$beer][1];
  }
?>
```

Our JavaScript can now request beerserver1.php?action=beer&beer=*beerid* with Sarissa, and get back the beer description. Although the beer descriptions are plain text in this example, they could actually comprise formatted HTML if you so desired. Either way, to display a beer description, the JavaScript code is as follows, assuming the returned data is stored in the variable beerdata:

```
document.getElementById('beerdef').innerHTML = beerdata;
```

And indeed that's exactly what happens for step 4 of our requirements, in which we have to display the server data. Here's the relevant JavaScript:

File: **third-beer.js (excerpt)**

```
clickBeer: function(e) {
  var target = window.event ? window.event.srcElement : e ?
      e.target : null;
  if (!target) return;
  if (target.nodeName.toLowerCase() != 'a')
    target = target.parentNode;

  bG.display(target.id);

  if (window.event) {
    window.event.cancelBubble = true;
    window.event.returnValue = false;
    return;
  }
  if (e) {
    e.stopPropagation();
    e.preventDefault();
  }
},

display: function(beer) {
  bG.geturl('beerserver1.php?action=beer&beer=' +
      escape(beer), bG.display2);
},

geturl: function(u, fn) {
  var xmlhttp = Sarissa.getXmlHttpRequest();
  xmlhttp.open('GET', u, true);
  xmlhttp.onreadystatechange = function() {
    if (xmlhttp.readyState == 4) {
      fn(xmlhttp.responseText);
    }
  };
  xmlhttp.send(null);
},

display2: function(beerdata) {
  document.getElementById('beerdef').innerHTML = beerdata;
}
```

Processing starts with the `clickBeer` method, which we'll install as an event listener later. It simply calls `display` with the ID of the clicked link, which we set to be a beer ID when generating the page.

display, in turn, calls geturl, a utility method that takes a URL and a function object, makes a request to the URL, and passes the result to the function. In this case, the display2 method is the function that will be called.

display2 simply takes the beer description returned by the server and inserts it into the beerdef element by setting its innerHTML property.

In summary, our event listener passes a beer ID to display; the description of that beer, as returned from beerserver1.php, is inserted into the beerdef element by display2. display and display2 work as a pair.

The complexity of this example may obscure an otherwise useful piece of design: the geturl method, while complicated, contains no code specific to the current page. That's fantastic, because it means that geturl is written in a general-purpose way. We can use it over and over again in other applications, just as we do addEvent.

Finally, we need an init method that sets up the event listener:

File: **third-beer.js (excerpt)**

```
init: function() {
  if (!Sarissa || !document.getElementsByTagName) return;

  var beerlinks = document.getElementById('beers').
      getElementsByTagName('a');
  for (var i = 0; i < beerlinks.length; i++) {
    bG.addEvent(beerlinks[i], 'click', bG.clickBeer, false);
    // Safari
    beerlinks[i].onclick = function() { return false; };
  }
},
```

By now, this code should be self-explanatory.

Figure 8.9 shows what we have so far in terms of functionality.

Figure 8.9. Displaying beer data with the DOM.

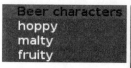

The beer guide

Beer characters	The beers	Beer data
hoppy	Adnams Bitter	A golden, straw
malty	Draught Bass	coloured beer in
fruity	Boddington's Bitter	which the grainy
	Cain's Traditional Bitter	malt, hop and bitter
	Charles Wells Bombardier	character can be
	Hydes Bitter	spoiled by a cloying
		sweetness.

Fetching and Running JavaScript

The remaining part of the beer project involves highlighting beers that have a particular character. This addresses steps 5 and 6 in our list, and they're a little more complicated than what we've done so far. Instead of retrieving some new data and adding it to the page, clicking a beer character needs to alter some of the data that's already *in* the page.

One way to do this is with an extension of the above technique; instead of fetching HTML from the server and dropping it directly into the page, the script could fetch JavaScript code from the server and run it. JavaScript provides the function `eval` for exactly this purpose; it takes a string and executes that string as JavaScript code. If a URL can return just JavaScript code, then that URL can be fetched with Sarissa, and the code executed with `eval`.

For this example, the server page should take a beer character as a parameter, and return JavaScript code like the following:

```
document.getElementById('beerid').className = 'highlight';
```

There should be one line for each beer with the character in question. This code will set the class `highlight` on each matching beer; we'll use this class in the style sheet to highlight them. Here's the new style:

File: **fourth-beer.css (excerpt)**

```
a.highlight {
  background-color: #0dd;
  border-left: 5px solid #0ff;
}
```

And here's the PHP code that will generate the necessary JavaScript to set the highlight class on the appropriate elements. Again, this script works from the $beers array that contains the test data:

File: **beerserver2.php**

```php
<?php
  include 'beers.php';

  if ($_GET['action'] == 'character') {

    $character = $_GET['character'];

    // highlight one character
    foreach ($beercharacters as $bc) { ?>
      document.getElementById('<?php
        echo addslashes($bc); ?>').className = '';
    <?php } ?>
    document.getElementById('<?php echo addslashes($character);
      ?>').className = 'highlight';
    <?php

    // highlight beers of that character
    foreach (array_keys($beers) as $beer) { ?>
      document.getElementById('<?php echo addslashes($beer);
        ?>').className = '';
      <?php if ($beers[$beer][2] == $character) { ?>
        document.getElementById('<?php echo addslashes($beer);
          ?>').className = 'highlight';
      <?php }
    }
  }
?>
```

First, the code loops through all of the available characters, generating JavaScript that unsets any CSS classes that may have been applied to the character elements. It then sets the highlight class on the selected character element.

Next, it loops through the array of beers, removing highlighting from all of them. But when a beer is found that has the selected character, it is highlighted.

That takes care of step 5—generating code from the server. Step 6 involves application of the retrieved lines of script.

Fetching and executing this JavaScript is very similar to fetching and displaying the HTML in the beer description case above. Just as we had clickBeer, display and `display2` methods to do that, we have `clickCharacter`, `highlight` and `highlight2` methods for this task. Here's the code:

File: **fourth-beer.js** (excerpt)

```
clickCharacter: function(e) {
  var target = window.event ? window.event.srcElement : e ?
      e.target : null;
  if (!target) return;
  if (target.nodeName.toLowerCase() != 'a')
    target = target.parentNode;

  bG.highlight(target.id);

  if (window.event) {
    window.event.cancelBubble = true;
    window.event.returnValue = false;
    return;
  }
  if (e) {
    e.stopPropagation();
    e.preventDefault();
  }
},

highlight: function(character) {
  bG.geturl('beerserver2.php?action=character&character=' +
      escape(character), bG.highlight2);
},

highlight2: function(charjs) {
  eval(charjs);
}
```

Just like `clickBeer`, `clickCharacter` passes an ID (this time for a beer character) to a method, `highlight`. `highlight` calls `geturl`, `geturl` calls Sarissa, and Sarissa passes the results to `highlight2`. The content of the fetched URL is then passed directly to `eval` to be executed as JavaScript code.

Notice how we've managed to reuse `geturl`, even though the URL, the callback handler, the data returned, and in fact everything else, is different from the `clickBeer` case. That's very handy.

All that's left is to adjust `init` to set up our new event listener:

File: **fourth-beer.js (excerpt)**

```
init: function() {
  if (!Sarissa || !document.getElementsByTagName) return;
  var beerlinks = document.getElementById('beers').
    getElementsByTagName('a');
  for (var i = 0; i < beerlinks.length; i++) {
    bG.addEvent(beerlinks[i], 'click', bG.clickBeer, false);
    // Safari
    beerlinks[i].onclick = function() { return false; };
  }
  var charlinks = document.getElementById('characters').
    getElementsByTagName('a');
  for (var i = 0; i < charlinks.length; i++) {
    bG.addEvent(charlinks[i], 'click', bG.clickCharacter, false);
    // Safari
    charlinks[i].onclick = function() { return false; };
  }
},
```

Figure 8.10 shows the updated script at work.

Figure 8.10. Matching beers highlighted.

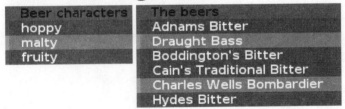

This small application is now more user-friendly and quicker to run, because the user doesn't need to wait for a page refresh after clicking a link. Most importantly, though, it will still work in exactly the same way when visited by a user whose browser doesn't support DOM techniques.

To see the final code in action, try the `fourth-beer.php` script provided in the code archive.

Summary

Remote scripting is potentially one of the most powerful tools in the DOM developer's toolbox. It's important to remember that, except in limited environments, it can only be an enhancement to Web applications and sites. It may not be supported by all visiting browsers. Nevertheless, the ability to query the server for data *without* a time-consuming page refresh makes serious usability improvements available to Web applications.

Communicating With The Server

Your wish, Captain, my Captain, is my keystroke, colon, double backslash, execute, command.
—Sparks, *Enter The Matrix*

The previous chapter explained how to dynamically retrieve data from the server through your pages, then use that data to alter sections of the page without a full page refresh. An extra level of interactivity can be brought into your Websites beyond this technique. In addition to using the server as a source of data, we can call back to say, "something interesting has happened here on the client." This makes it possible to take a dynamic Website right into the realms of a client-side application.

The distinction between the two modes of operation is subtle, but becomes clearer if we consider who's giving the orders. The traditional, non-interactive model has the server giving out data, and the client receiving it passively. In Chapter 8, the client sometimes asked for new orders. Here, we'll discuss the process by which the client gives orders back to the server—do this, do that—and the server responds with an indicator of success or failure.

Example: Managing Files

In addition to FTP access to a Website's directories, Web hosting companies often provide a "file manager" that allows users to add, manipulate, and delete files through their browsers. While this can be convenient, it's an awkward and fiddly way to work with files; a "real" file manager, such as Windows Explorer, doesn't require its users to check a checkbox next to a file, then click a Move button, in order to move a file around. Instead it allows users to move files by dragging them between folders. This functionality could be adapted for Web-based file managers: display a list of files and folders on-screen, allow the user to drag a file to a folder and, when they do so, send a message to the server saying, "move the dragged file to the dragged-to folder."

Specifying the File Manager

Critical to project planning is a clear specification of what the desired piece of software should do. While this file manager script is not a particularly big project, specifying its details up-front can help clarify exactly what the script should do, and what it shouldn't.

Such a script should display a list of folders on the left-hand side of the page. This list should be expandable and collapsible; clicking on a folder should show (or hide) the folders it contains. Clicking on a folder should also display, to the right of the page, a list of the files in that folder. Filenames should be draggable. Dragging a file onto a folder should highlight that folder; dropping a file on a folder should remove that filename from the page (because it should have been moved to a different folder), and send a command to the server to move the file to that folder. Dropping a file somewhere other than on a folder should make the filename return to its place in the right-hand-side file list.[1]

This specification can help us to break the script into components, each of which does just one thing. Let's break the above description into separate points:

The script should display a list of folders on the left-hand side of the page.
We need a way to obtain a list of folders from the server.

---

[1] At first glance, it might seem that it would be easier to put the folder list and the file list into separate frames; that way, each can be scrolled separately. However, you can't drag-and-drop a JavaScript object between one frame and another, so that solution won't work.

This list should be expandable and collapsible.
A component to expand and collapse lists is required.

Clicking on a folder should also display a list of the files in that folder.
We need a way to get a list of the files in any folder from the server.

Filenames should be draggable.
A component that facilitates the dragging of HTML elements is required.

Dropping a file on a folder...
The drag component needs to recognize when one element is dragged over another, and when one is dropped on another.

...should send a command to the server to move the file to that folder.
We must be able to send a move-file command to the server.

Planning the Technology

Figure 9.1 shows a view of the file manager: on the left is a folder tree, showing an expanded list of nested folders. On the right appears the list of files in the currently selected folder, ready to be dragged and dropped. Normally, drag-and-drop operates on icons. In this case, we'll be dragging and dropping pieces of text. We could add icons using CSS if we really wanted to.

Figure 9.1. A two-pane window layout showing folder hierarchy.

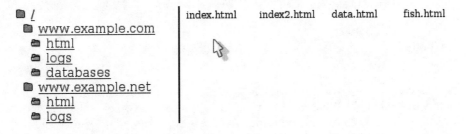

Here's the HTML code for our example, which includes a simpler set of just three folders:

File: **fileman.html** (excerpt)

```html
<!DOCTYPE HTML PUBLIC "-//W3C//DTD HTML 4.01//EN"
    "http://www.w3.org/TR/html4/strict.dtd">
<html>
  <head>
    <title>File Manager</title>
    <link rel="stylesheet" href="fileman.css">
  </head>
  <body>
    <h1>Drag a file to a folder</h1>

    <div id="folders">
      <ul>
        <li>
          <a href="/" path="/" class="target">/</a>
          <ul>
            <li>
              <a href="spike" path="/spike"
                 class="target">spike</a>
            </li>
            <li>
              <a href="sync" path="/sync" class="target">sync</a>
            </li>
            <li>
              <a href="zfs" path="/zfs" class="target">zfs</a>
            </li>
          </ul>
        </li>
      </ul>
    </div>

    <div id="files">
    </div>

  </body>
</html>
```

As you can see, for the purposes of this example I've included a static list of folders in the HTML file itself. In a practical application, you would likely generate this list on the fly to reflect the folder structure that existed on the server at that time, but for this discussion, our focus will be on client-side functionality. In the code archive, I've provided a collection of sample files (test_data.zip) that match this static directory structure; use these as you try out this script.

You might have noticed the nonstandard `path` attribute on the folder links. This attribute contains the full path relative to the root directory of each folder, and will make our script's job a lot easier. If you object to such attributes, feel free to modify the script to use a JavaScript array, or some other construct to hold these values.

The CSS code we'll use to lay out this page is nothing special, but I'll include it here for completeness:

File: **fileman.css (excerpt)**

```css
body {
  padding: 0;
  margin: 0;
}

li {
  width: 10em;
}

div#folders {
  float: left;
  width: 35%;
  border-right: 2px solid black;
  padding-left: 1em;
}

div#folders ul {
  padding: 0 0 0 10px;
  margin: 0;
}

div#folders li {
  padding: 0;
  margin: 0;
}

div#files {
  float: left;
  width: 60%;
  padding-left: 5px;
}

div#files ul {
  padding: 0;
  margin: 0;
```

```
}
div#files li {
  float: left;
  width: 7em;
  list-style: none;
  font-size: small;
  padding: 3px;
  margin: 0;
}
```

Let's turn our attention to the JavaScript. This is a complicated example, but there's no need to write all the code ourselves. As we go along, we'll see that there are at least three JavaScript libraries that we can reuse. Still, our own library will be sizeable:

File: **fileman.js (excerpt)**

```
var fM = {
  init: function() { ... },

  setUpDraggables: function() { ... },
  createProxyTargets: function() { ... },
  removeProxyTargets: function() { ... },
  targetOver: function(e) { ... },
  targetOut: function(e) { ... },
  elementDropped: function(draggedObj, x, y) { ... },

  moveFileHere: function (dragged) { ... },
  receiveMoveDetails: function(data, dragged) { ... },

  openFolder: function (e) { ... },
  loadFiles: function(path) { ... },
  receiveFilenames: function(xml, path) { ... },

  addEvent: function(elm, evType, fn, useCapture) { ... },
  findPosX: function(obj) { ... },
  findPosY: function(obj) { ... }
}

fM.addEvent(window, 'load', fM.init, false);
```

In the above object signature, the first nine methods look after the in-page drag-and-drop operations; the next three methods coordinate file operations between the browser and Web server, and update the page with new data. The methods whose names start with receive are callback methods. The last three methods are familiar: there's our old standby, addEvent, as well as findPosX and findPosY, which were last seen in Chapter 5.

Listing Files and Folders

We'll start the project with an easy task: the simple retrieval of the directory list. To retrieve a list of the files in a directory, or a list of folders, we send a request to the server and get back a stream of data. It's exactly the same process we used in Chapter 8.

The server script will be called like this:

http://www.example.com/getFiles.php?path=*path*

Here, *path* is the path of the chosen directory, relative to some predefined root path. The predefined root path is there to ensure that the file manager can only manage files within a certain directory; for security reasons, it should not be able to manage every file on the system. This root path is hard-coded into the script.[2]

When called, the script should return a list of all the files in the supplied directory path, as in this XML fragment:

```
<files>
  <file>FILENAME1</file>
  <file>FILENAME2</file>
  ...
</files>
```

A simple PHP script that lists all the files in a directory, and returns their names in XML, might look like this:

File: **getFiles.php**

```php
<?php
header('Content-Type: text/xml');

$ROOT = realpath($_SERVER['DOCUMENT_ROOT'] . '/test');

echo "<files>\n";
$pth = isset($_GET['path']) ? $_GET['path'] : '/';
$rp = realpath($ROOT . $pth);
```

---

[2]It's hardcoded for simplicity in this example, at least. In the context of a larger Website (if we were to offer file management capabilities to many users on an ISP-hosted Web server, for example), it would need to be smarter.

```
// Be paranoid; check that this is a subdir of ROOT
if (strpos($rp, $ROOT) === 0) {
  $dir = dir($rp);
  while ($entry = $dir->read()) {
    if (!is_dir($dir->path . '/' . $entry)) {
      echo '<file>' . htmlspecialchars($entry) . "</file>\n";
    }
  }
}
echo "</files>\n";
?>
```

We'll use this script to populate the right half of the file manager page.

The defined $ROOT variable is the root directory for the file manager. A useful application might make this the user's home directory. In any case, the file manager should not permit the user to see files outside this directory. Note that although the script is short and simple, it ensures that users can't exploit it to get file listings from outside the $ROOT directory. We don't want clever users gaining more access than they should have by typing something like this:

getFiles.php?path=./../../etc

Calling this script and parsing the returned data is another application of the techniques outlined in Chapter 8. To start, we'll take a look at the openFolder method. This will be set up by the init method as the click event listener for our folder links:

File: **fileman.js (excerpt)**

```
openFolder: function(e) {
  var t = window.event ? window.event.srcElement : e ? e.target
    : null;
  if (!t) return;
  fM.loadFiles(t.getAttribute('path'));
  if (window.event) {
    window.event.cancelBubble = true;
    window.event.returnValue = false;
  }
  if (e && e.stopPropagation && e.preventDefault) {
    e.stopPropagation();
    e.preventDefault();
  }
},
```

This method gets a reference to the folder link, and passes the value of its `path` attribute to the `loadFiles` method.

Here's the `loadFiles` method that calls `getFiles.php`:

File: **fileman.js** (excerpt)

```
loadFiles: function(path) {
  var files = document.getElementById('files');
  files.innerHTML = 'loading files...';
  var xmlhttp = Sarissa.getXmlHttpRequest();
  var url = 'getFiles.php?rnd=' +
      (new Date()).getTime() + '&path=' + escape(path);
  xmlhttp.open('GET', url, true);
  xmlhttp.onreadystatechange = function() {
    if (xmlhttp.readyState == 4) {
      fM.receiveFilenames(xmlhttp.responseXML, path);
    }
  };
  xmlhttp.send(null);
},
```

The `loadFiles` method is another example of the use of XMLHTTP to call a remote script. It uses Sarissa to do so; thus, we need to make sure Sarissa is loaded first by the HTML file:

File: **fileman.html** (excerpt)

```
<script type="text/javascript" src="sarissa.js"></script>
<script type="text/javascript" src="fileman.js"></script>
```

Sarissa is called with a path, constructs the URL getFiles.php?rnd=*random*&path=*path*, where *random* is a number based on the current time, to prevent the browser from caching the response, and *path* is the path for which a file listing is needed. The script then fetches the output of that URL. When the anonymous callback function reads the server output, it passes that output to the `receiveFilenames` method shown below.

File: **fileman.js** (excerpt)

```
receiveFilenames: function(dom, path) {
  var files = document.getElementById('files');
  files.innerHTML = '';

  var ul = document.createElement('ul');
  var fileNodes = dom.getElementsByTagName('file');
  for (var i = 0; i < fileNodes.length; i++) {
    var li = document.createElement('li');
```

```
      li.className = 'draggable';
      var s = '';
      for (var j = 0;
          j < fileNodes[i].firstChild.nodeValue.length; j += 5) {
        s += fileNodes[i].firstChild.nodeValue.substr(j, 5);
        s += '<wbr>';
      }
      li.setAttribute('path', path + '/' +
          fileNodes[i].firstChild.nodeValue);
      li.innerHTML = s;
      ul.appendChild(li);
    }
    files.appendChild(ul);
    setTimeout(fM.setUpDraggables, 100);
  },
```

receiveFilenames receives the XML returned by the server in the form of a
Sarissa DomDocument object (xmlhttp.responseXML in loadFiles), and constructs
from it a slice of HTML—a document fragment. Here's an example of that fragment, based on two retrieved files: file1.html and longfilename.html:

```
<ul>
  <li class="draggable"
      path="www.example.com/html/file1.html">file1<wbr>.html</li>
  <li class="draggable"
      path="www.example.com/html/file1.html"
      >longf<wbr>ilena<wbr>me.htm<wbr>l</li>
</ul>
```

Essentially, receiveFilenames creates an unordered list of filenames, and adds
to each list item a class of draggable (ensuring that our drag script, later, will
know that this is a draggable item). It also adds a custom path attribute with the
full path of the file (to make life easier on the drag script). Finally, it breaks the
filename into five-character chunks and inserts a <wbr> tag after each chunk. The
<wbr> tag indicates a point at which a word may be broken for wrapping at the
end of a line. This is used to ensure that the filename can be word-wrapped, so
that it doesn't break the layout.[3]

---

[3]<wbr> is a nonstandard tag, the use of which may well engender some guilty feelings. However,
there is no cross-browser way to say, "break up this word wherever you need to in order to get it to
fit into a box properly." The other possibilities are ­, the soft hyphen, which is unsupported
by Mozilla, and the official solution: zero-width space , which has patchy support. MSIE
also has the nonstandard CSS word-wrap property, but there is no cross-browser equivalent.

If you work through the method slowly, you'll see that three document hierarchies are at work: the page itself, the XML document fragment returned from the server, and the document fragment being built up for insertion into the page.

The method clears the contents of the document element that has the ID `files` (which is a container `div` that will be used to display the file list), and puts the newly-created list structure into it.

Finally, it calls `fM.setUpDraggables`, which we'll look at later, to make the new filename elements draggable.

Server Control Commands

Now that we've got a list of server files to work with, we'll need to be able to manipulate them: to tell the server what to do with the files. Control instructions will pass from browser to server. In this application, we have only one control instruction: "move file A to directory B."

Sending a command to the server can be achieved using `XMLHttpRequest` in exactly the same way as we'd use it to retrieve data. The mechanics of sending a communication to the server are the same, it's just that the focus has changed. Before, we were conceptually sending a request for data, and getting back some data; now, we send a command and retrieve a success or failure message. Here, the browser tells the server what to do, rather than asking the server for information.

The server code should achieve the following:

1. It should accept two query string parameters: `path` and `file`. The `file` parameter is the full path of the file that we want to move (again, relative to the root); the `path` parameter is the relative path to the directory to which the file should be moved.

2. It should be paranoid, and check that:

   ❏ the directory is under the root path

   ❏ the file is under the root path

   ❏ the directory is a directory and the file is a file.

3. It should move the file into the directory.

Here's the PHP server-side code:

File: **moveFiles.php**

```php
<?php
$ROOT = realpath($_SERVER['DOCUMENT_ROOT'] . '/test');

$path = isset($_GET['path']) ? $_GET['path'] : '/';
$rp = realpath($ROOT . $path);
// Be paranoid; check that this is a subdir of ROOT
if (strpos($rp, $ROOT) === 0) {
  $fname = isset($_GET['file']) ? $_GET['file'] : '';
  $fn = realpath($ROOT . $fname);
  if (strpos($fn, $ROOT) === 0) {
    if (is_dir($rp) && file_exists($fn)) {
      $fileonly = basename($fn);
      rename($fn, $rp . '/' . $fileonly)
        or die('Moving file failed');
      echo 'OK';
    } else {
      echo 'File or directory bad';
    }
  } else {
    echo 'Bad filename';
  }
} else {
  echo 'Bad directory';
}
?>
```

As with getFiles.php, this script is paranoid: it does not allow the user to exploit it in order to move files around outside the $ROOT directory. Since we know that our designed client-side code will only pass legitimate parameters to the server code, any non-legitimate parameters that are detected must have been sent by someone who's trying to exploit the script. Therefore, the error messages are intentionally not particularly helpful (but at least there are error messages; the script itself does not throw an error).

The client code that uses this server move script is the moveFileHere method. It is passed the element that was dragged (which will be an element describing a file, with a path attribute). It also has access to the folder that's the drag-n-drop target in the variable this (the current object).

File: **fileman.js (excerpt)**

```javascript
moveFileHere: function(dragged) {
  var file = dragged.getAttribute('path');
```

```
    var path = this.getAttribute('path');
    var xmlhttp = Sarissa.getXmlHttpRequest();
    var qs = '?path=' + escape(path) + '&file=' + escape(file);
    var url = 'moveFiles.php' + qs;
    xmlhttp.open('POST', url, true);
    xmlhttp.onreadystatechange = function() {
      if (xmlhttp.readyState == 4) {
        fM.receiveMoveDetails(xmlhttp.responseText, dragged);
      }
    };
    xmlhttp.send(null);
  },
```

This code extracts the source and destination locations in its first two lines, then tells the server what to do. Although we still use the URL query string to pass instructions to the server, we use a POST request, rather than a GET request, to indicate that we wish to perform some kind of action on the server—not just retrieve information. Again, the server response is sent to an anonymous callback function, which calls `receiveMoveDetails`:

File: **fileman.js (excerpt)**

```
receiveMoveDetails: function(data, dragged) {
  if (data == 'OK') {
    dragged.parentNode.removeChild(dragged);
  } else {
    alert('There was an error moving the file:\n' + data);
  }
},
```

This method deletes the dragged element from the HTML, so that it appears that the drag target beneath the dragged item has "swallowed" the dragged item. Now, let's see how the dragging is achieved.

Implementing Drag-and-Drop

We've now done all the required client-server interaction, but this time, unlike Chapter 8, the server requests are hidden under a thick layer of user interface: the collapsible menu, and the drag-n-drop system. Let's look at the latter of those two interface elements. Figure 9.2 shows the user interface halfway through a drag action.

Figure 9.2. Dragging a file to a folder.

Drag a file to a folder

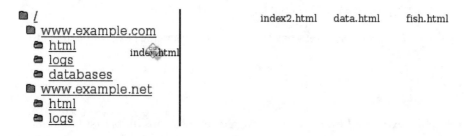

The user has left-clicked and held the mouse button down on the `index1.html` item; the user then dragged the mouse to the left, carrying the item with it. Since the item's not on top of any of the listed directories, none of them is highlighted as the current drag target.

Basic Drag-and-Drop with DOM-Drag

Making elements draggable is, in concept, a pretty simple thing to implement via DHTML. It works like this:

1. When the user holds the mouse button down over a draggable element, set variable `dragMode` to `true` and record which element fired the `mousedown` event.

2. When the user releases the mouse button, set `dragMode` to `false`.

3. If the mouse moves, and `dragMode` is `true`, change the position of the recorded element to the position of the mouse.

That's it, in concept. However, it can be a fiddly thing to get right. Fortunately, other people have already done the heavy lifting on this; unobtrusive JavaScript libraries are available that make the implementation of draggable elements easy. One of the best is Aaron Boodman's DOM-Drag[1].[4]

Usage of DOM-Drag is pretty simple, First, we include the library:

---

[1] http://www.youngpup.net/2001/domdrag
[4] Aaron says "DOM-Drag was written for you. Because I care about you." That's the spirit!

File: **fileman.html (excerpt)**

```
<script type="text/javascript" src="dom-drag.js"></script>
<script type="text/javascript" src="sarissa.js"></script>
<script type="text/javascript" src="fileman.js"></script>
```

Then, add initialization calls for each draggable element:

```
Drag.init(element);
```

Additionally, any element that you want to drag must use absolute or relative positioning in the style sheet:

File: **fileman.css (excerpt)**

```
.draggable {
  position: relative;
}
```

Once you've loaded the DOM-Drag library, you've succeeded in added basic dragging functionality to an element. We'll use this method in our script to make elements draggable.

That explains how we'll do the dragging, but what about the dropping?

Simple Drag Target Tactics

DOM-Drag provides no facility for knowing whether the user is currently dragging one element over another, so we'll need to build this ourselves. At first examination, it sounds simple:

1. Attach mouseover and mouseout listeners to all potential drop target elements. A **drop target** is an element on which the user can drop a dragged element. If a dragged element is dropped anywhere other than a drop target, it should "snap back" to its original position.

2. The mouseover listener on a drop target element must check if dragMode is true (i.e. if a dragging operation is in progress). If it is, then set a class hover on this target element (so that it can be highlighted with CSS).

3. The mouseout listener on a drop target element should remove the hover class.

4. When a dragged element is dropped (step 2 in the simple description of dragging above), check if any target has class hover. If one has, then the

dragged element must have been dropped on that target element, so call moveFileHere, from above, for that target.

This approach is fine in theory, but sadly, it's not quite as simple as that.

Smarter Drag Target Tactics

When an element is being dragged, mouseovers on any dragged-over drop target elements will not fire in Mozilla-based browsers. The reason for this is that the cursor isn't over the target element; it's over the dragged element. Figure 9.3 illustrates this point.

As shown in Figure 9.3, the cursor is on a plane of its own, on top of the dragged element. The cursor and the dragged element move together on top of the drop target element. The cursor is never over the drop target element itself, because the dragged element is in between the two. This means that the target's mouseover event never fires.

Figure 9.3. Mouse, element, and target layers.

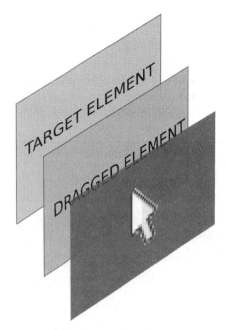

One way to solve this problem is with a **proxy element**. Imagine that every drop target element is actually two elements: the drop target itself, and an invisible a element that's the same size and position as the drop target, and exactly on top of it. This structural alteration would have no effect on the page's appearance.

With careful manipulation of the z-index of each element, we can create a situation where the invisible proxy element lies on top of the dragged element. To do this, leave the drop target's z-index unset (so it defaults to zero), set the dragged element's z-index to 999, and set the invisible proxy's z-index to 1000. The elements will then stack up as shown in Figure 9.4.

Now, the cursor is immediately on top of the invisible proxy element. That means the proxy element will receive mouse events. The dragged element, when moved, slides *underneath* the proxy (but you can't tell, because the proxy is invisible) and, hence, does not receive events. The proxy never moves. This use of proxy elements isn't restricted to DHTML; elsewhere in user interface development it's sometimes called a **hotspot**.

Figure 9.4. The transparent proxy element layer.

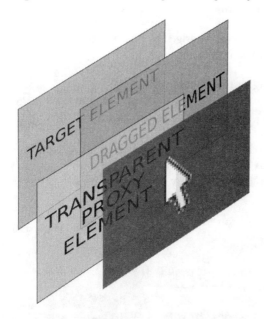

A better procedure for dragging an element, including the new proxy elements, might be:

1. When the user holds the mouse button down over a draggable element:

   ☐ Set a variable `dragMode` to `true`.

   ☐ Record which element fired the `mousedown` event.

   ☐ Create invisible proxy elements for each target element in the document (note that this is done every time a drag starts, not just once at document creation).

   ☐ Each proxy element should have a `mouseover` and `mouseout` event listener; the `mouseover` listener must apply the `hover` class to the real element corresponding to this proxy (not the proxy itself).

   ☐ The `mouseout` listener should remove the `hover` class from the real element corresponding to this proxy.

2. When the user releases the mouse button, set `dragMode` to `false`. Remove the transparent proxy targets. If a target is of class `hover`, call the `moveFileHere` method for that element.

3. If the cursor moves, and `dragMode` is `true`, change the position of the recorded element to reflect the position of the cursor.

That's the right recipe for highlighting drag targets.

Creating Proxy Drag Targets

The creation of proxy targets will be triggered whenever the user starts to drag a draggable element. We'll see how this is set up in a moment, but for now, let's look at the process itself, which is completed by the `createProxyTargets` method:

File: **fileman.js** (excerpt)

```
createProxyTargets: function() {
  fM.PROXY_TARGETS = [];
  var targets = document.getElementsByTagName('*');
  for (var i = 0; i < targets.length; i++) {
    var t = targets[i];
    if (t.className.search(/\btarget\b/) != -1) {
      var proxyTarget = document.createElement('a');
      proxyTarget.className = 'proxyTarget';
      proxyTarget.style.left = fM.findPosX(t) + 'px';
```

```
            proxyTarget.style.top = fM.findPosY(t) + 'px';
            proxyTarget.style.width = t.offsetWidth + 'px';
            proxyTarget.style.height = t.offsetHeight + 'px';
            proxyTarget.href = '#';
            proxyTarget.realElement = t;

            fM.PROXY_TARGETS[fM.PROXY_TARGETS.length] = proxyTarget;
            document.body.appendChild(proxyTarget);

            fM.addEvent(proxyTarget, 'mouseover', fM.targetOver,
                false);
            fM.addEvent(proxyTarget, 'mouseout', fM.targetOut, false);
        }
    }
},
```

This method iterates through each drop target element t, and dynamically creates a new a element with a CSS class of proxyTarget. We use this in our style sheet to style the proxy element as required:

File: **fileman.css** (excerpt)

```
.proxyTarget {
  cursor: crosshair;
  position: absolute;
  background-color: white;
  z-index: 1000;
  opacity: 0;
  filter: alpha(opacity=0);
}
```

In addition to changing the mouse cursor, our proxy objects are given a background color so that they occupy the entire rectangular area of the drop target. The z-index of 1000 ensures that they will float over the draggable elements. Finally, we render the proxy objects invisible by setting an opacity of zero (the filter property is required to do this in Internet Explorer).

The createProxyTargets method calculates the drop targets' sizes and positions, and copies them to this proxy element. A reference to the proxy's associated real target element is stored in proxyTarget.realElement, so that it can be retrieved later if the proxy is moused over. The proxy element is then added to fM.PROXY_TARGETS (a list of all proxy elements), as well as the document. Finally, the proxy gets its own listeners that will respond to the mouseover and mouseout events. They're discussed in the next section.

Once dragging is finished, the proxy elements need to be removed from the document. Again, we'll get around to discussing how this is triggered shortly, but here's the method that will do the job:

File: **fileman.js (excerpt)**

```
removeProxyTargets: function() {
  for (var i = 0; i < fM.PROXY_TARGETS.length; i++) {
    var tt = fM.PROXY_TARGETS[i].realElement;
    tt.className = tt.className.replace(/\bhover\b/, '');
    document.body.removeChild(fM.PROXY_TARGETS[i]);
  }
  fM.PROXY_TARGETS = [];
},
```

In addition to removing from the document all of the proxy elements that were stored in the fM.PROXY_TARGETS array, and emptying this array, this method also performs a little cleanup for the mouseover event listener. The method removes the hover CSS class (discussed in the previous section) if the event listener has set it on any of the drop target elements.

Highlighting a Drag Target

The specification says that dragging a file onto a folder should highlight the folder while the cursor is over it. In our planning, we decided that a moused-over target should have the hover CSS class applied to produce this effect. The createProxyTargets method above sets targetOver and targetOut as the mouseover and mouseout listeners for a proxy element. It's these proxy methods, combined with a little CSS, that do the highlighting work.

File: **fileman.js (excerpt)**

```
targetOver: function(e) {
  var t = window.event ? window.event.srcElement : e ?
      e.target : null;
  if (!t) return;
  var tt = t.realElement;
  tt.className += ' hover';
},

targetOut: function(e) {
  var t = window.event ? window.event.srcElement : e ?
      e.target : null;
  if (!t) return;
  var tt = t.realElement;
```

```
    tt.className = tt.className.replace(/\b ?hover\b/, '');
  },
```

Remember that the `mouseover` event is fired by the proxy element, but the `hover` class should be applied to the corresponding drop target element. So `targetOver` obtains the element that fired the event, which is the proxy, gets the proxy's corresponding real drop target element, and applies the `hover` class to that element. `targetOut`, similarly, removes the `hover` class from the drop target element.

Highlighting the target element is then a trivial application of CSS, since all targets have a class of `target`, and currently-hovered targets also have a class of `hover`:

File: **fileman.css (excerpt)**

```css
.target.hover {
  background-color: #999;
  color: red;
}
```

Note the combined class CSS selector: there is no space between `.target` and `.hover`, meaning that it selects any element that has both classes.

Dropping onto the Drag Target

Lovely highlighting effects aside, the primary reason why the proxy elements exist is so that when the user releases a draggable element over a drop target, that drop target will be tagged with the `hover` CSS class. We can now use that class to identify and process completed drag-and-drop operations.

Our library's `elementDropped` method will be called whenever the user releases a draggable element. As with `createProxyTargets` and `removeProxyTargets`, we won't worry about how this method is called just yet. Let's just look at the code:

File: **fileman.js (excerpt)**

```javascript
elementDropped: function(draggedObj, x, y) {
  var elements = document.getElementsByTagName('*');
  for (var i = 0; i < elements.length; i++) {
    var t = elements[i];
    if (t.className.search(/\btarget\b/) != -1 &&
        t.className.search(/\bhover\b/) != -1 && t.onDroppedOn)
    {
      t.onDroppedOn(draggedObj);
    }
```

```
    }
  },
```

This method receives a reference to the draggable element (as well as the mouse coordinates, which we won't use).

In our application, the action that is taken as a result of a drag-and-drop operation will be controlled by the drop target. Each drop target will store its action as a handler function stored in an onDroppedOn property. The elementDropped method, therefore, searches through all the elements in the document, looking for an element with both the target and hover CSS classes. That element will be the drop target over which the cursor was positioned when the draggable element was released, so elementDropped calls its onDroppedOn handler function, passing to it the reference to the draggable element.

It's up to the init method of our script to set up the onDroppedOn handlers for each of the drop targets in the document. Now's a good time to take a look at that method:

File: **fileman.js (excerpt)**

```
init: function() {
  if (!document.getElementById ||
      !document.getElementsByTagName || !Drag || !Drag.init)
    return;

  // Make the targets remove the element when dropped upon
  var elements = document.getElementsByTagName('*');
  for (var i = 0; i < elements.length; i++) {
    var t = elements[i];
    if (t.className.search(/\btarget\b/) != -1) {
      t.onDroppedOn = fM.moveFileHere;
    }
  }

  // Make folders clickable to list that folder's files
  var fs = document.getElementById('folders').
      getElementsByTagName('a');
  for (var i = 0; i < fs.length; i++) {
    fM.addEvent(fs[i], 'click', fM.openFolder, false);
    // Safari
    fs[i].onclick = function() { return false; };
  }

  // Load the initial fileset
```

```
    fM.loadFiles('/');
  },
```

After checking for the features required by the script, `init` loops through all elements in the document, looking for those with the CSS class `target`—the drop targets. To each of those, it assigns the `moveFileHere` method as its `onDroppedOn` handler function. Remember, this is not a standard DHTML property; it's just a convenient property name we've chosen for use by the `elementDropped` method.

The rest of the `init` method has to do with setting up the file listing. It adds the `openFolder` method as a click event listener to each of the folder names on the page; this will cause a click on a folder name to load the contents of the associated folder into the file list. Since this listener can't cancel the `click` event in Safari, we also assign an old-style event handler to do that.

Finally, the root directory (`'/'`) is loaded by calling `loadFiles` directly to create the initial file listing on the page.

Handling Drag-and-Drop Events

We've now written a slab of code that hinges on the dragging functionality provided by the DOM-Drag library. To make it all work, we need to hook that library into our script. We need to tell the library which elements should be draggable; we need it to do things when a drag operation begins (`createProxyTargets`), and we need it to do things when a drag operation ends (`elementDropped`, `removeProxyTargets`). We'll implement all of this with the last method in our script, `setUpDraggables`.

`setUpDraggables` is called by the `receiveFilenames` method after it has received the list of filenames from the server and added them to the document as `li` elements of class `draggable`:

File: **fileman.js** (excerpt)

```
receiveFilenames: function(xml, path) {
  ...
  files.appendChild(ul);
  setTimeout(fM.setUpDraggables, 100);
},
```

`setUpDraggables` starts by finding all such elements, and making them draggable using the DOM-Drag library:

File: **fileman.js (excerpt)**

```
setUpDraggables: function() {
  var elements = document.getElementsByTagName('*');
  for (var i = 0; i < elements.length; i++) {
    var draggable = elements[i];
    if (draggable.className.search(/\bdraggable\b/) != -1) {
      Drag.init(draggable);
```

Once an element has been made draggable using DOM-Drag, you can provide handler functions to be called whenever a drag operation starts or finishes. Do this simply by assigning functions to the draggable elements' `onDragStart` and `onDragEnd` properties. Again, these are special property names used by the DOM-Drag library, not standard DOM events.

Here's the `onDragStart` handler for this application:

File: **fileman.js (excerpt)**

```
draggable.onDragStart = function(x, y) {
  document.body.className += ' dragging';
  fM.createProxyTargets();
  this.ZINDEX = this.style.zIndex;
  this.style.zIndex = 999;
  this.SAVED_POSITION = [x, y];
};
```

First of all, this handler adds a CSS class of `dragging` to the `body` element. Our style sheet will use this to change the cursor while a drag-and-drop operation is in progress:

File: **fileman.css (excerpt)**

```
body.dragging {
  cursor: move;
}
```

Next, it calls `createProxyTargets`, which creates proxy objects for all of the drop targets on the page.

The draggable element's original `z-index` is stored into a `ZINDEX` property on the object, before a new value of 999 is applied, so that it floats just below the proxy objects. Finally, the draggable object's starting position—as provided by the `x` and `y` arguments to the handler function—is stored in a `SAVED_POSITION` property.

When the user releases the mouse button, completing the drag operation, DOM-Drag calls the onDragEnd handler:

File: **fileman.js** (excerpt)

```
draggable.onDragEnd = function(x, y) {
  this.style.left = this.SAVED_POSITION[0];
  this.style.top = this.SAVED_POSITION[1];
  this.style.zIndex = this.ZINDEX;
  fM.elementDropped(this, x, y);
  fM.removeProxyTargets();
  document.body.className =
      document.body.className.replace(/\b ?dragging\b/,
      '');
};
      }
    }
  }
},
```

This function starts by moving the draggable element back to its starting position and z-index, which were stored in the SAVED_POSITION and ZINDEX properties, respectively. This causes dragged filenames to "snap" back if they aren't dropped on a valid target.

Next, the function calls our elementDropped method, which checks if the element was dropped on a valid target, and, if so, triggers the file move operation.

It then cleans up the proxy elements by calling removeProxyTargets, and finally removes the dragging CSS class from the document body.

Expanding and Collapsing Lists

At this point, we have a working file manager, which allows the user to drag files to folders; the element showing the filename is removed from the HTML and a command is sent to the server to move the file on the server's file system. The remaining requirement is to allow the folder list to be expanded and collapsed.

Fortunately, this can be implemented with very little extra work, using my own aqtree3 script[2]. To make a set of nested, unordered lists expand and collapse, simply load the aqtree3 JavaScript and CSS files in the HTML:

---

[2] http://www.kryogenix.org/code/browser/aqlists/

File: **fileman.html** (excerpt)

```
<script type="text/javascript" src="aqtree3clickable.js">
</script>
<script type="text/javascript" src="dom-drag.js"></script>
<script type="text/javascript" src="sarissa.js"></script>
<script type="text/javascript" src="fileman.js"></script>
<link rel="stylesheet" href="aqtree3clickable.css">
<link rel="stylesheet" href="fileman.css">
```

Then, change the folder list `<ul>` tag to have class `aqtree3clickable`:

File: **fileman.html** (excerpt)

```
<ul class="aqtree3clickable">
```

As it turns out, this doesn't quite work. If you loaded the page at this stage, you'd find yourself unable to expand the folder list to view the subfolders. Can you guess why?

To ensure compatibility with Safari, I wrote the aqtree3 script using old-style event handlers instead of event listeners. In particular, the `onclick` event handler of each of the folder links is used to expand and collapse the folder tree. Our file manager script overwrites this event handler with its own `onclick` handler, designed to cancel the click event in Safari:

File: **fileman.js** (excerpt)

```
// Safari
fs[i].onclick = function() { return false; };
```

This is an example of clashing event handlers, which is the reason modern DOM event listeners were created. You can assign as many listeners as you want to an event, but only one event handler. In a more sophisticated script, we might detect the existing event handler and call it from our own event handler, but since the aqtree3 script does a fine job of cancelling the `click` event with its own event handler, we can simply not assign our event handler when an existing one is found:

File: **fileman.js** (excerpt)

```
if (!fs[i].onclick) {
  // Safari
  fs[i].onclick = function() { return false; };
}
```

The number of free, unobtrusive DHTML scripts designed to drop into place in your pages grows daily. Scripts like this file manager application are precisely the purpose for which they're designed. These scripts enhance functionality and are easy to implement, so save yourself sweat and toil and enjoy the convenience. Just be sure to watch out for clashes—until such time as all browsers fully implement the DOM standard for events, scripts written for maximum compatibility may not be strictly unobtrusive.

With all that code in place, the file manager is finished. Looking back on the specification, everything in it is complete. This is another good reason to have a clear specification up front: it lets you know when to stop coding!

Using XML-RPC

Some Web applications—front and back ends—are built as one unit, like the file manager example. In such cases, the developer can choose to implement the set of methods that are called in the back end, and the way in which those methods are called, using any approach that seems appropriate. This list of methods, combined with the ways in which they're called, forms the back end's API, or **application programming interface**.

Sometimes, instead of implementing both the front and back ends together, you may want to write an API for other developers to call via HTTP requests from their own applications. One way to write such an API is to use XML-RPC—a simple standard for Web-accessible APIs, commonly called **Web services**.

A service that provides (**exports**) an XML-RPC API, when used with an XML-RPC client library, can be called as if it were a local set of methods, even though it is not. The complexity of sending requests and receiving responses over HTTP is completely hidden.

For example, the Blogger[3] API is an XML-RPC API presented by the Blogger weblogging application, which provides the functionality to maintain a journal, or Weblog. It offers methods such as `editPost`, `newPost`, and `getUserBlogs`.

The data that you pass to a given method (such as `editPost`) is passed over HTTP to a remote server on which the method is executed. The return value is passed back by HTTP to your code. Your code does not have to concern itself with details of network connectivity; those and similar details are all taken care of by the XML-RPC client library. This gives the technology the second part of its name: RPC stands for **Remote Procedure Call**, the idea being that one can call a method that takes effect on a remote server *as if it were a local method*. **Pro-**

---

[3] http://www.blogger.com

cedure is an old name for function or subroutine. Figure 9.5 illustrates this arrangement.

Figure 9.5. Local methods vs. XML-RPC remote methods.

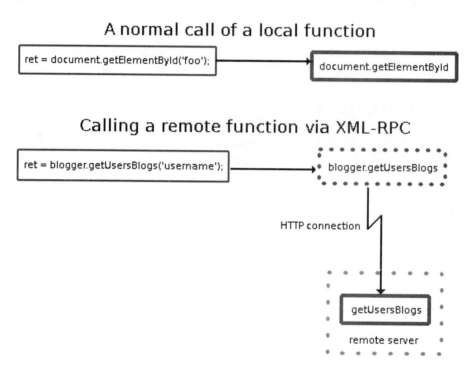

In Figure 9.5, the user code (in the boxes on the left) calls `document.getElementById` and `blogger.getUsersBlogs` in identical ways, as if both were local methods. The `blogger.getUsersBlogs` method, however, is actually provided by the JavaScript XML-RPC client library, because it is acting as a proxy for the `blogger.getUsersBlogs` method on a remote server. The two methods are called identically from user code.

The first part of XML-RPC's name comes from the method it uses to pass your function call over HTTP; it converts the method call and the passed parameters to XML. You do not need to know the detail of how this works in order to use it; in fact, the whole point of XML-RPC is that you can call remote methods without having to worry about how that call happens. Those who are curious, or don't have enough to do, can find more detail than they will ever need in the XML-RPC specification[4].

Calling XML-RPC APIs

Let's continue with the Blogger example. The Blogger API, as mentioned above, is an API that allows the editing and creation of posts on a Weblog, and it's a fully documented XML-RPC API[5]. This means that any program that can act as an XML-RPC client can use the API to edit posts on a Weblog. The relevant methods in the API are `blogger.getRecentPosts`, which returns a list of recent posts, `blogger.newPost`, which adds a new post to the Weblog, and `blogger.editPost`, which supplies new content for an existing post.

To use the API from JavaScript, a JavaScript XML-RPC client is needed. There are a few around; one of the best is the xmlrpc module of jsolait[6]. Using the client is simple. First, include the library in your code with a `<script>` tag:

File: **editblog.html (excerpt)**

```
<script type="text/javascript" src="jsolait/init.js"></script>
```

Everything else occurs in custom JavaScript that you must write for each page. Start by loading the xmlrpc module using jsolait's `importModule` function:

```
var xmlrpc = importModule('xmlrpc');
```

Next, create an object to represent the particular XML-RPC API you wish to call. You can either get jsolait to create the object for you, and auto-detect all the methods it makes available using the `ServerProxy` class:

```
var remoteAPI = new xmlrpc.ServerProxy(URL);
```

or you can create the object yourself and use the `XMLRPCMethod` class to create methods that call the XML-RPC API. The advantage here is that you can name your local methods whatever you like:

```
var remoteAPI = {
  getRecentPosts: new xmlrpc.XMLRPCMethod(URL,
      'blogger.getRecentPosts'),
  editPost: new xmlrpc.XMLRPCMethod(URL, 'blogger.editPost')
};
```

[4] http://www.xmlrpc.com/spec
[5] http://plant.blogger.com/api/1_docs
[6] http://www.jsolait.net/

279

In the above example, the XML-RPC API's method names contain a dot (.), so they won't work as JavaScript method names. We've therefore used the second technique to assign simpler method names.

In either case, we must specify the location of the XML-RPC API (this is sometimes called the **endpoint**, and is the URL of the script to which you pass the XML-RPC commands). The remote method becomes accessible as a method of the API object. What that actually means in plain English is that code can now call the remote `blogger.getRecentPosts` method transparently, by calling the following (for example):

```
var result = remoteAPI.getRecentPosts(arguments);
```

Pages that make these calls are normally retrieved from the same server that processes the calls. Security restrictions prevent you from loading a page from one server and making XML-RPC calls to a server that's located elsewhere. So, in JavaScript, the client and server form a consistent pair. This is not true of Web services in general.

Example: Weblog Post Editor

Armed with this knowledge of the Blogger API, and a trusty XML-RPC client library, we can very easily build a simple post editor for a Weblog. Only three actions are required:

1. Get a list of posts from the server.

2. Display the content of one of the fetched posts for editing.

3. Save the edited post back to the server.

Before we design our page, it makes sense to confirm that the Blogger API can do what we want it to. All APIs are different; there's no point committing to a big design project if the XML-RPC system won't support it.

Exploring the Blogger API

For all three of the required actions, start by turning to the Blogger API specification. That document states that the method signature for `blogger.getRecentPosts` requires five arguments: appkey, blog name, username, password, and number of posts. The first four are specific to the Weblog in use (appkey may be blank for non-Blogger Weblogs that support the Blogger API).

Retrieving the five most recent posts, then, given that `getRecentPosts` was "wrapped" above with a call to `add`, is this simple:

```
var posts = remoteAPI.getRecentPosts(appkey, blogname, username,
    password, 5);
```

The `posts` variable now contains a list of post objects that have `content` and `postid` properties (along with a few others). We can use that data to display one of the posts for editing.

Saving an edited post back to the server is similarly easy. According to the Blogger API specification, it's done this way:

```
remoteAPI.editPost(appkey, postid, username, password, content);
```

These arguments are quite self-explanatory.

Armed with those two methods, we have all we need to access the back end.

Setting up the Page Content

For this simple example, all we need is a little event handling to tie everything together, as well as some HTML to define the editing controls. We'll use a `textarea` and a couple of buttons, which give us this starting point:

File: **editblog.html**

```
<!DOCTYPE HTML PUBLIC "-//W3C//DTD HTML 4.01//EN"
    "http://www.w3.org/TR/html4/strict.dtd">
<html>
  <head>
    <title>editblog</title>
    <script type="text/javascript" src="jsolait/init.js"></script>
    <script type="text/javascript" src="editblog.js"></script>
  </head>
  <body>
    <button id="get">Get posts</button>
    <ul id="posts"></ul>
    <textarea id="post" cols="80" rows="16"></textarea>
    <button id="save" disabled="disabled">Save</button>
  </body>
</html>
```

The first script loaded by this page is the jsolait library; the second is our own code. The `ul` element will display the received posts. The buttons will, eventually, call the XML-RPC methods of the Blogger API.

We're not using styles for this simple example, but as usual, we'll build ourselves a JavaScript library object. Here's the object signature that we'll end up with:

File: **editblog.js** (excerpt)

```
var eB = {
  /* Change these bits */
  USERNAME: 'sil',
  PASSWORD: 'nowayjose!',
  API_URL: 'example_blogger.php',
  BLOG_NAME: '/main',

  /* Don't change anything below here */
  posts: null,

  init: function() { ... },
  addEvent: function(elm, evType, fn, useCapture) { ... },

  getPosts: function() { ... },
  addItem: function(para, post) { ... },
  clickLink: function() { ... },
  sendPost: function() { ... }
}

eB.addEvent(window, 'load', eB.init, false);
```

init and addEvent have their usual roles. clickLink is an event listener; getPosts and sendPosts wrap up the two required XML-RPC calls; addItem is a utility method that updates the page.

We've also declared a property named posts, which holds no initial value, but which is used later to store the posts retrieved from the server. While handy, this approach does mean that we can only have one blog editor per page.

The init method that sets up the necessary event listeners, as well as the XML-RPC service, looks like this:

File: **editblog.js** (excerpt)

```
init: function() {
  if (!jsolait) return;
  if (!document.getElementById) return;

  var xmlrpc = importModule('xmlrpc');
  eB.api = {
    getRecentPosts: new xmlrpc.XMLRPCMethod(eB.API_URL,
        'blogger.getRecentPosts'),
```

```
    editPost: new xmlrpc.XMLRPCMethod(eB.API_URL,
        'blogger.editPost')
  };

  var element;
  element = document.getElementById('get');
  eB.addEvent(element, 'click', eB.getPosts, false);
  element = document.getElementById('save');
  eB.addEvent(element, 'click', eB.sendPost, false);
},
```

XMLRPCMethod is a method of the jsolait library's xmlrpc module; it takes the URL of the XML-RPC service as a parameter, as well as the method name you wish to be able to call, and creates a method that will call that remote method. Since it is creating a JavaScript object, it must be called as a **constructor** using JavaScript's new operator. In this case, we create XMLRPCMethod objects for the blogger.getRecentPosts and blogger.editPost methods of the Blogger API.

As you've come to expect by now, the init method finishes off by setting up the event listeners required by our application. A click on the get button will call getPosts, while a click on the save button will call sendPost.

Coordinating Page and Server

The Blogger API describes the exact data that moves back and forth between client and server. The jsolait library wraps that API up in a JavaScript library, and allows us, via init, to expose the XML-RPC calls to direct use. As such, there's no server side work to do, except for installing a server-side script that supports the Blogger API. Once that's done, all we have to do is hook up the API to the page by filling in our library object. Let's go through the required methods one at a time.

The getPosts method fetches the posts from the server (using eB.api.getRecentPosts, as above):

File: **editblog.js (excerpt)**

```
getPosts: function() {
  try {
    eB.posts = eB.api.getRecentPosts(
        '', eB.BLOG_NAME, eB.USERNAME, eB.PASSWORD, 5);
  } catch(e) {
    alert('There was an error fetching posts.');
    return;
  }
```

```
    var p = document.getElementById('posts');
    p.innerHTML = '';
    for (var i = 0; i < eB.posts.length; i++) {
      eB.addItem(p, eB.posts[i]);
    }
  },
```

This is the first example we've seen of JavaScript **exception handling** (not event handling or error handling). There are two parts to exception handling: the so-called **try block** (the keyword `try` and its following curly brackets) and the **catch block** (the keyword `catch` and its curly brackets). Adding a try block to a piece of ordinary JavaScript does *absolutely nothing*, unless that code creates an exception. An **exception** is a special kind of object that interrupts the code immediately it's created. If an exception occurs, then the try block prevents the exception from turning into an error message. Instead, the code in the catch block is executed. In our case, that means showing an alert that contains some user-readable text.

`getPosts` uses `try` and `catch` because the jsolait library sometimes throws exceptions. When the `getRecentsPosts` method is called, it might send back an exception if something goes wrong. Our code has to be ready for that possibility, so we wrap the call in a try block. If nothing goes wrong, `getPosts` will get back an array of posts. It then creates a clickable link for each post in the returned array by calling `addItem` repeatedly. Here's `addItem`:

File: **editblog.js** (excerpt)

```
  addItem: function(para, post) {
    var text = document.createTextNode(post.postid);

    var a = document.createElement('a');
    a.href = '#';
    a.postID = post.postid;
    eB.addEvent(a, 'click', eB.clickLink, false);
    a.appendChild(text);

    var li = document.createElement('li');
    li.appendChild(a);

    para.appendChild(li);
  },
```

This method takes a container element (para) and the post information, and creates extra HTML content. First, it creates a plain text node. Next, it creates a link, which it decorates with an event listener and a property containing the post ID. Then, it puts the text node inside the link. It then creates a list item, and puts the link inside it. Finally, it places the whole list item—link, text, and listener—inside the container element. That's when it appears on the page.

Here's the `clickLink` listener that's dynamically added to the links created by `addItem`:

File: **editblog.js** (excerpt)

```
clickLink: function(e) {
  var t = window.event ? window.event.srcElement : e ?
      e.target : null;
  if (!t) return;
  while (t.nodeName.toLowerCase() != 'a' &&
      t.nodeName.toLowerCase() != 'body')
    t = t.parentNode;
  var postid = t.postID;
  for (var i = 0; i < eB.posts.length; i++) {
    if (eB.posts[i].postid == postid) {
      eB.CURRENT_POST = postid;
      document.getElementById('post').value =
          eB.posts[i].content;
      document.getElementById('save').disabled = '';
      return;
    }
  }
},
```

All this does is copy the post ID from the property on the current link, scan all the posts for a match, make this post the current one, and place the post's content in the visible text box, where the user can edit it. Here's the final step, `sendPosts`, which submits the edited post:

File: **editblog.js** (excerpt)

```
sendPost: function() {
  try {
    eB.api.editPost(
        '', eB.CURRENT_POST, eB.USERNAME, eB.PASSWORD,
        document.getElementById('post').value, true);
    alert('Post saved OK!');
    document.getElementById('post').value = '';
    eB.CURRENT_POST = null;
    document.getElementById('save').disabled = 'disabled';
  } catch(e) {
    alert('There was an error saving your post.\n(' +
        e.message + ')');
    return;
```

```
    }
  },
```

This is very similar to `getPosts`: again we have to be sure to catch any exceptions that might occur. Otherwise, it's quite straightforward: send the data to the server, and tell the user what happened.

Summary

Any sufficiently complex Web application will involve a great deal of back-and-forth data exchange with the server. As we saw in Chapter 8, the nature of the DOM and the `XMLHttpRequest` class lets the browser perform these data exchanges without interruptions or page refreshes. You can go further than just reading data from a server; you can control the server from the client.

Techniques used in larger applications can also be put to good use when adding extra functionality to Websites. There's no need to write everything yourself when many standard libraries are available for free.

Dynamically requesting extra data, or running commands on the server based on user actions, makes it possible to add an extra degree of interactivity to your sites. Running commands remotely is made even easier with the advent of XML-RPC, which makes the remote methods available as local methods and removes the complexity of passing the commands across the network yourself. These techniques help DOM scripting take a step towards a whole new world of application richness

10

DOM Alternatives: XPath

The path of precept is long, that of example short and effectual.
—Seneca

So far, this book has concentrated on manipulating HTML documents using DOM interfaces and scripts. In this final chapter, we'll examine an alternative: XPath syntax. XPath is a handy tool for extracting elements from documents. It is also a vital starting point for XSLT, which we won't have time to cover here.

Previously, we looked at the HTML DOM in detail. Most of the DOM features we have explored also apply to pure XML documents. For example, an XML DOM object provided by the Sarissa library offers the same methods as the `window.document` object: `getElementById`, and `getElementsByTagName`. Similarly, if you load an XHTML or plain XML document into a modern browser, these methods appear on the document object there as well.

These DOM methods are simple and obvious to use, but they're also quite wordy. When complex manipulation is required, it can take a lot of JavaScript code to string these methods together in the right order. That's less than ideal.

XPath is a significantly more powerful method than the DOM for accessing the parts of an XML document. In simple cases, it's also more compact. Let's see how it's done.

Introducing XPath

XPath is a W3C standard, like HTML, but it contains no elements or tags. Instead, it provides syntax for special strings.

An XPath string identifies nodes in an XML document, similar to the way in which file paths identify files in a file system. Just as file paths can have wildcards (patterns) that match more than one file, so too can XPath strings match more than one node.

Imagine we have this simple XML document:

```
<day>
  <activity type="fun" time="1300" duration="1h">
    Drink beer
    <activity type="fun work">
      <purchase type="book">Modern DOM Scripting</purchase>
    </activity>
  </activity>
  <activity type="work" time="0900" duration="9h">
    Write code
  </activity>
  <activity type="fun" time="2200" duration="2h">
    Write code
  </activity>
  <activity>
    sleep
  </activity>
</day>
```

Suppose also that we have a DOM document object, dom, which contains this XML. To select the day element using the standard DOM methods, we would use:

```
var day = dom.getElementsByTagName('day')[0];
```

By comparison, an XPath string (henceforth, simply an XPath) that identifies this node[1] is as follows:

```
/day
```

---

[1] Technically, it actually identifies a list of matching nodes, and that list has only one item in it.

As for a file system path, an XPath string starting with a slash represents an **absolute** path, from the root of the document. Selecting all the top-level activity nodes (of which there are four) is achieved with the following string:

```
/day/activity
```

This path identifies a list of nodes in the same way that `dom.getElementsByTagName` will return a list. But this particular XPath does not select every single `activity` element! It selects only those four `activity` elements that are immediate children of the day element.

There's no equivalent for that selective behavior in the DOM. To get the same list, you'd have to look at all the `childNodes` of the day element, and loop through them, tossing out any that aren't `activity` elements. Here's how it would be done in JavaScript:

```
function get_some_activities(dom) {
  var result = [];
  var kids = dom.getElementById('day').childNodes;
  for (var i = 0; i < kids.length; i++) {
    if (kids[i].tagName == 'activity')
      result.push(kids[i]);
  }
  return result;
}
```

That's a lot of code, compared to the XPath alternative.

The additional, nested `activity` element (`type="fun work"`) can be identified by this path:

```
/day/activity/activity
```

Here's another example. An XPath that begins with a double slash will select all nodes in the document that have the specified name. Here's an example:

```
//activity
```

This identifies all `activity` elements, including the nested element. This is nothing like a file path, because it looks all the way through the DOM tree. Nor is it anything like a Windows network share (e.g. `\\server\docs`). Instead, it is exactly equivalent to this DOM call, which also looks throughout the DOM tree for elements with the specified name:

```
dom.getElementsByTagName('activity');
```

An XPath path can also select nodes based on attribute values.

```
//activity[@time="0900"]
```

The above path would select all `activity` elements with a time attribute of "0900" (in this example, one element only). We can also specify an index to select one node from a group of nodes.

```
/day/activity[2]
```

The above XPath selects the second `activity` that is a child of the `day` (in this case, writing code at work from 0900). Notice how XPath numbering starts at 1 (one) not 0 (zero)—another difference between XPath and JavaScript arrays.

Applying XPath to XML

The two major browsers provide access to XPath searches on XML documents in different ways. Mozilla-based browsers implement the W3C DOM Level 3 specification for XPath[1], while Internet Explorer implements a proprietary set of methods. Fortunately, the Sarissa library comes to the rescue, providing a cross-browser set of methods. Unfortunately, there is no solution that also works on Opera or Safari. Nevertheless, we recommend using Sarissa if you can get away with it.

To enable Sarissa's cross-browser XPath support, you need to load the `sarissa_ieemu_xpath.js` file in addition to the usual `sarissa.js` file:

File: **xpath-example.html (excerpt)**

```
<script type="text/javascript" src="sarissa.js"></script>
<script type="text/javascript" src="sarissa_ieemu_xpath.js">
</script>
<script type="text/javascript" src="xpath-example.js">
</script>
```

Here's an example of XPath use with Sarissa:

File: **xpath-example.js**

```
var xml = '<?xml version="1.0" encoding="UTF-8"?>' +
    '<day>' +
```

---

[1] http://www.w3.org/TR/DOM-Level-3-XPath/

```
    '  <activity type="fun" time="1300" duration="1h">' +
    '    Drink beer' +
    '    <activity type="fun work">' +
    '      <purchase type="book">Modern DOM Scripting</purchase>'+
    '    </activity>' +
    '  </activity>' +
    '  <activity type="work" time="0900" duration="9h">' +
    '    Write code' +
    '  </activity>' +
    '  <activity type="fun" time="2200" duration="2h">' +
    '    Write code' +
    '  </activity>' +
    '  <activity>sleep</activity>' +
    '</day>';

var dom = Sarissa.getDomDocument();
dom.loadXML(xml);

/* Commands to make the XPath selections work in IE */
dom.setProperty('SelectionNamespaces',
    'xmlns:xsl="http://www.w3.org/1999/XSL/Transform"');
dom.setProperty('SelectionLanguage', 'Xpath');

var xpaths = [
    '//day',
    '/day',
    '/day/activity',
    '/day/activity/activity',
    '//activity',
    '//activity[@time="0900"]',
    '/day/activity[2]'];

function queries() {
  for (var i = 0; i < xpaths.length; i++) {
    var nodes = dom.selectNodes(xpaths[i]);
    var results = xpaths[i] + '\n';
    for (var j = 0; j < nodes.length; j++) {
      results += nodes[j].nodeName + '\n';
    }
    alert(results);
  }
}

window.onload = queries;
```

We set up a Sarissa DOM document object (in production code, this would be retrieved from the server), then use the document object's `selectNodes` method to return nodes. `dom.selectNodes(xpath)` returns the list of nodes that are identified by the XPath string *xpath*.

Document objects also have a `selectSingleNode` method; this should be used when only one node will be identified by the XPath. Be careful with this: if the XPath actually identifies more than one node, the results are unpredictable (in Mozilla, it returns only the first matched node; in IE it may throw an error). The best approach is to always use `selectNodes` and extract the first node out of the results in cases in which there is any doubt at all.

The returned nodes are still part of the document from which they came. If you change them once they've been retrieved, the document from which they came will also be changed. You must copy them, or detach them from the document if you want to work on them in isolation.

XPath Learning Resources

The methods described here are part of the DOM specification for XPath; you should be aware, however, that there is a lot more to explore.

The full XPath specification[2] is an outstandingly long and complex document, though it contains a lot of power. A better introductory guide is the XPath tutorial at zvon.org[3], which walks through increasingly complex XPath expressions. It's worth your time if you are likely to work with XML in any depth. The W3Schools Website also has an introductory guide to XPath[4] that compliments the Zvon guide.

Example: Parsing RSS Feeds

A good proportion of Weblogs have a blogroll: a list of other recommended Weblogs that the discriminating user might like to read. Most Weblogs also offer RSS feeds: an alternative version of the Weblog's content in XML. That being the case, a useful enhancement might be to display alongside a link to another Weblog, links to specific posts in that Weblog.

---

[2] http://www.w3.org/TR/xpath
[3] http://www.zvon.org/xxl/XPathTutorial/General/examples.html
[4] http://www.w3schools.com/xpath/default.asp

Getting the names of, and links to, the posts from the XML of the RSS feed is a task that's well-suited to XPath.

About RSS 1.0

RSS is complicated, and offers many different and mutually incompatible versions.[2] For the sake of simplicity during this example, it will be assumed (a vast and horrible oversimplification!) that all RSS feeds are actually RSS 1.0. An RSS 1.0 feed looks something like this:

File: **rss-example.rdf**

```
<?xml version="1.0" encoding="utf-8"?>
<?xml-stylesheet href="/rss.xsl" type="text/xsl"?>
<rdf:RDF xmlns:rdf="http://www.w3.org/1999/02/22-rdf-syntax-ns#"
    xmlns="http://purl.org/rss/1.0/"
    xmlns:dc="http://purl.org/dc/elements/1.1/">
  <channel
      rdf:about="http://www.sitepoint.com/blog-view.php?blogid=5">
    <title>SitePoint's DHTML &amp; CSS Blog: Stylish
      Scripting</title>
    <link>http://www.sitepoint.com/blog-view.php?blogid=5</link>
    <description>The latest posts in SitePoint's DHTML &amp; CSS
      blog, 'Stylish Scripting'.</description>
    <image rdf:resource=
        "http://www.sitepoint.com/images/sitepoint-logo.gif"/>
    <items>
      <rdf:Seq>
        <rdf:li rdf:resource=
            "http://www.sitepoint.com/blog-post-view.php?id=197199"
        />
        <rdf:li rdf:resource=
            "http://www.sitepoint.com/blog-post-view.php?id=196678"
        />
      </rdf:Seq>
    </items>
  </channel>

  <image rdf:about=
      "http://www.sitepoint.com/images/sitepoint-logo.gif">
    <title>SitePoint's DHTML &amp; CSS Blog: Stylish
      Scripting</title>
    <link>http://www.sitepoint.com/blog-view.php?blogid=5</link>
```

---

[2]Those readers who already know about this will be nodding ruefully at this point: http://diveintomark.org/archives/2004/02/04/incompatible-rss has more details.

```
    <url>http://www.sitepoint.com/images/sitepoint-logo.gif</url>
  </image>

<item rdf:about=
    "http://www.sitepoint.com/blog-post-view.php?id=197199">
  <title>CSS tricks in both dimensions</title>
  <link>
    http://www.sitepoint.com/blog-post-view.php?id=197199</link>
  <description>Cameron Adams and Dave Shea both came through
    recently with some smart new CSS techniques. Cameron's
    trick, entitled Resolution dependent layout, provides a
    welcome new angle to the long running debate over liquid vs.
    fixed width designs. The standard dilemma is that fixed...
  </description>
  <dc:date>2004-09-22T06:10:41Z</dc:date>
</item>

<item rdf:about=
    "http://www.sitepoint.com/blog-post-view.php?id=196678">
  <title>A9 and Google Local</title>
  <link>
    http://www.sitepoint.com/blog-post-view.php?id=196678</link>
  <description>If you want proof that remote scripting has hit
    the mainstream, look no further than the recent launches of
    both Amazon's A9.com search engine and Google's new Google
    Local service. Both make extensive use of remote scripting,
    a technique whereby JavaScript is used to refresh...
  </description>
  <dc:date>2004-09-20T05:41:45Z</dc:date>
</item>
</rdf:RDF>
```

This listing is an abridged snapshot from the RSS 1.0 feed for SitePoint's DHTML and CSS Weblog[6].

There are three sections to this document: channel, image, and item elements. Each <rdf:li> tag in the channel section points to a single <item> tag—that's how the items are collected together. Don't be confused by the use of RDF syntax (RDF is another W3C XML standard); though complex, this file is still just plain XML.

---

[6] http://www.sitepoint.com/blog.rdf?blogid=5

Constructing Simple XPaths

The interesting parts of this feed, for our purposes, are the `item` elements that describe Weblog posts, and the `title`, `link`, and `description` elements inside them, which contain actual details. These elements are shown in bold above. You can see that there is more than one `item` on the Weblog. In this case, there are two posts. A list of these `items` can be obtained by applying the following XPath expression to the document:

```
/rdf:RDF/item
```

Similarly, we can retrieve the `title` for an `item` by applying the following XPath to the `item`'s node:

```
title
```

Without a leading forward-slash, this XPath is **relative** to the thing it's applied to—in this case, it's relative to the `item` element. XPath has an idea of the current node just as file system shells have an idea of the current directory.

Given all this, parsing the `item` elements and their associated data out of the RSS 1.0 feed with XPath appears to be easy. Let's parse the RSS into a JavaScript object first. That can be done as follows, assuming that `xml_content` contains the full text of the feed:

```
var dom = Sarissa.getDomDocument();
dom.loadXML(xml_content);
```

Having turned the document text into a DOM document fragment, we can apply XPath expressions to it. Here's some simple code to do just that:

```
var items = dom.documentElement.selectNodes('/rdf:RDF/item');
if (items.length > 0) {
  for (var j = 0; j < items.length; j++) {
    var i = items[j];
    var link =
        i.selectSingleNode('link').firstChild.nodeValue;
    var title =
        i.selectSingleNode('title').firstChild.nodeValue;
    var desc =
        i.selectSingleNode('description').firstChild.nodeValue;
    alert(link + ' ' + title + ' ' + desc);
  }
}
```

This code should produce an alert for every feed post. While it's good in principle, in practice, it doesn't work, because the feed document isn't a simple example of XML. Our code is not sophisticated enough to handle complex XML. Let's address that shortcoming.

Adding XML Namespaces

In order to understand why this simple code doesn't work, you'll need to understand the concept of **XML namespaces**. This is another wide-ranging and horribly confused topic, but fortunately, we don't need to know it all—just select sections. [3] In fact, if people were to stop shouting about it, you'd see in a second that namespaces are really quite trivial.

A namespace in XML is a way of categorizing the elements in an XML document. An element name may be a word, like `item`, or may include a namespace before a colon, such as `example:item`, or `rdf:RDF`. In the second example, `rdf` is the namespace, and `RDF` is an element name that occurs in that namespace. [4]

If an element has a namespace, that namespace has to be specified in the XPath, and Sarissa has to be told about the namespace. The namespace for our RSS document is described in the `<rdf:RDF>` tag in the XML. The `xmlns` attribute holds the namespace declaration:

```
xmlns:rdf="http://www.w3.org/1999/02/22-rdf-syntax-ns#"
```

This means, "the XML namespace `rdf` is associated with the URL `http://www.w3.org/1999/02/22-rdf-syntax-ns#`." Actually, namespaces need only be assigned a plain string, but developers nearly always use a URL in accordance to convention, regardless of whether it points to an actual Website or not.

Our code teaches Sarissa about this namespace with the following line:

```
Sarissa.setXpathNamespaces(dom,
    'xmlns:rdf="http://www.w3.org/1999/02/22-rdf-syntax-ns#"');
```

This fix is not sufficient to solve the problem, because the RSS feed content also has a **default namespace** on the `<rdf:RDF>` tag. That default namespace is declared with this attribute:

---

[3] The formal specification is at http://www.w3.org/TR/REC-xml-names/, and a useful FAQ and summary document is available at http://www.rpbourret.com/xml/NamespacesFAQ.htm if you'd like to know more.

[4] Think of the namespace as *qualifying* the element. For example, a title element in HTML has a different meaning from title in RSS. The namespace indicates which *sort* of title this is.

```
xmlns="http://purl.org/rss/1.0/"
```

Notice there's no colon or name to the left of the equals sign. There's no namespace name (unlike the earlier case, where xmlns:rdf specified the namespace name rdf). So in this example, as in most RSS 1.0 feeds, the default namespace is associated with the URL http://purl.org/rss/1.0/.

The default namespace is assigned to every element for which a namespace is not specified explicitly. In particular, the item elements in which we're interested don't have specified namespaces, so they're in the default namespace.

Sarissa doesn't deal well with default namespaces, so we have to pretend that it's an explicit namespace, and use it as such. As such, we tell Sarissa that the default namespace URL is actually associated with a real namespace, my, then use that namespace in the XPaths.

```
Sarissa.setXpathNamespaces(dom,
    'xmlns:my="http://purl.org/rss/1.0/" ' +
    'xmlns:rdf="http://www.w3.org/1999/02/22-rdf-syntax-ns#"');
var items = dom.documentElement.selectNodes('/rdf:RDF/my:item');
if (items.length > 0) {
  for (var j = 0; j < items.length; j++) {
    var i = items[j];
    var link =
        i.selectSingleNode('my:link').firstChild.nodeValue;
    var title =
        i.selectSingleNode('my:title').firstChild.nodeValue;
    var desc =
        i.selectSingleNode('my:description').firstChild.nodeValue;
    alert(link + ' ' + title + ' ' + desc);
  }
}
```

The XPath is now /rdf:RDF/my:item, rather than /rdf:RDF/item. We're explicitly specifying the default namespace instead of leaving it out.

Designing the Blogroll

Having determined what works on the XPath side, let's now develop the content of the blogroll page.

Designing the HTML

A simple blogroll might look like this:

```
<h1>Weblogs</h1>
<ul id="blogs">
  <li>
    <a href=http://www.sitepoint.com/blog-view.php?blogid=5
       >SitePoint: DHTML &amp; CSS Blog: Stylish Scripting</a>
  </li>
  <li>
    <a href=http://www.sitepoint.com/blog-view.php?blogid=6
       >SitePoint: Open Source Blog: Open Sourcery</a>
  </li>
</ul>
```

With a little CSS, this fragment will display as shown in Figure 10.1.

Figure 10.1. A simple blogroll with styles.

Weblogs

SitePoint: DHTML & CSS Blog: Stylish Scripting
SitePoint: Open Source Blog: Open Sourcery

To make the associated RSS feeds accessible to our script, we'll add a new attribute to each blogroll link. This new attribute,[5] rss, will point to a locally cached copy[6] of the appropriate RSS feed for each Weblog.

File: **read-rss.html (excerpt)**

```
<h1>Weblogs</h1>
<ul id="blogs">
  <li>
    <a href="http://www.sitepoint.com/blog-view.php?blogid=5"
       rss="sitepoint-dhtmlcss.rdf"
       >SitePoint: DHTML &amp; CSS Blog: Stylish Scripting</a>
```

---

[5] Note that this new attribute will cause the pages to not validate as HTML.

[6] Remember that Sarissa, and all JavaScript, can retrieve data only from the server from which the page was served. It would be possible to have a server-side program that grabbed the remote RSS feed when requested, but this would mean that the blogroll wouldn't work properly if the remote site was down; it would also generate one hit to the remote RSS feed for every hit on your site—a bad abuse of other people's bandwidth. So, we assume that the RSS feeds are fetched on a regular basis by some process on the server, which is left as an exercise for the reader; thus our client-side JavaScript can simply access them.

```
    </li>
    <li>
      <a href="http://www.sitepoint.com/blog-view.php?blogid=6"
         rss="sitepoint-opensource.rdf"
         >SitePoint: Open Source Blog: Open Sourcery</a>
    </li>
  </ul>
```

Specifying Script Actions

Now we can implement a JavaScript library that unobtrusively finds all blogroll links with RSS feeds attached, fetches the appropriate RSS feed, parses it, and alters the DOM of the page to contain links to each item in the feed. One way of doing all that is as follows:

1. On page load, find all **a** elements with an **rss** attribute inside a **ul** that has the ID **blogs**.

2. For each link, fetch the RSS feed identified by **rss**. Make sure the fetch is asynchronous, so that it happens in the background and doesn't hold up page rendering.

3. If a list of **item** elements can be parsed out of it, then do so. Add to the page a new **ul** containing those items, so that the HTML is altered like so:

```
<h1>Weblogs</h1>
<ul id="blogs">
  <li>
    <a href=http://www.sitepoint.com/blog-view.php?blogid=5
       >SitePoint: DHTML &amp; CSS Blog: Stylish
    Scripting</a>
    <ul>
      <li>
        <a href="http://link/to/item">Title of item</a>
        <p>Summary of item</p>
      </li>
      <li>
        <a href="http://link/to/item">Title of item</a>
        <p>Summary of item</p>
      </li>
    </ul>
  </li>
  <li><a
        href="http://www.sitepoint.com/blog-view.php?blogid=6"
        >SitePoint: Open Source Blog: Open Sourcery</a>
```

```
    ...
  </li>
</ul>
```

These new ul elements should be hidden by default.

4. Finally, alter the main link to the remote Weblog, so that instead of navigating to that Weblog, it shows and hides the nested ul.

Figure 10.2. The blogroll, showing retrieved items for the first blog.

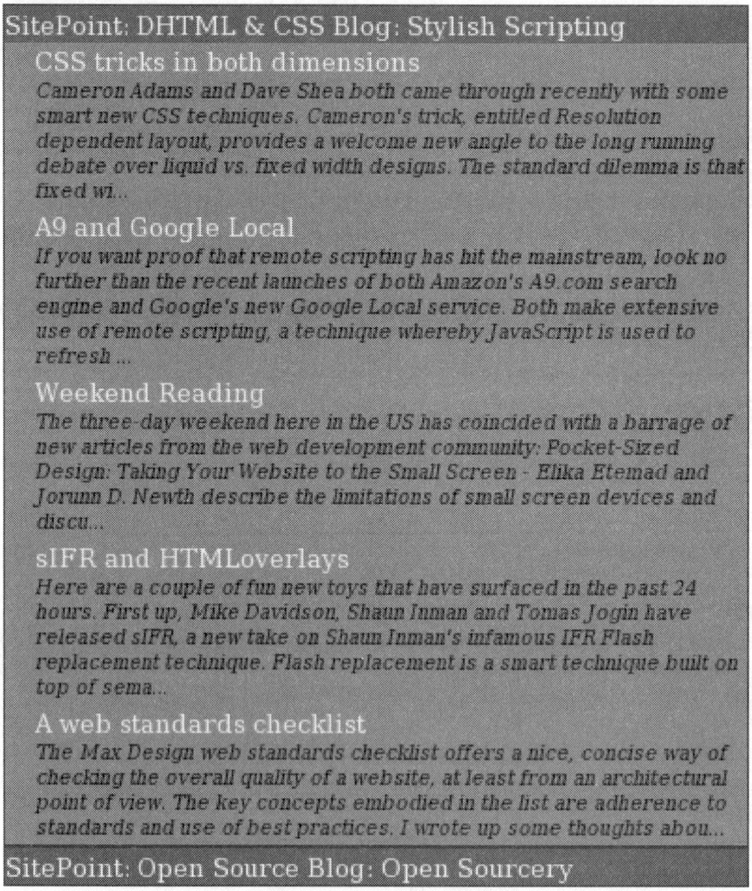

SitePoint: DHTML & CSS Blog: Stylish Scripting

CSS tricks in both dimensions

Cameron Adams and Dave Shea both came through recently with some smart new CSS techniques. Cameron's trick, entitled Resolution dependent layout, provides a welcome new angle to the long running debate over liquid vs. fixed width designs. The standard dilemma is that fixed wi...

A9 and Google Local

If you want proof that remote scripting has hit the mainstream, look no further than the recent launches of both Amazon's A9.com search engine and Google's new Google Local service. Both make extensive use of remote scripting, a technique whereby JavaScript is used to refresh ...

Weekend Reading

The three-day weekend here in the US has coincided with a barrage of new articles from the web development community: Pocket-Sized Design: Taking Your Website to the Small Screen - Elika Etemad and Jorunn D. Newth describe the limitations of small screen devices and discu...

sIFR and HTMLoverlays

Here are a couple of fun new toys that have surfaced in the past 24 hours. First up, Mike Davidson, Shaun Inman and Tomas Jogin have released sIFR, a new take on Shaun Inman's infamous IFR Flash replacement technique. Flash replacement is a smart technique built on top of sema...

A web standards checklist

The Max Design web standards checklist offers a nice, concise way of checking the overall quality of a website, at least from an architectural point of view. The key concepts embodied in the list are adherence to standards and use of best practices. I wrote up some thoughts abou...

SitePoint: Open Source Blog: Open Sourcery

Once all this has happened, clicking a link to a Weblog should not take you there; instead, it will show the retrieved items, as in Figure 10.2.

Building the Scripts

Like most good DOM page scripting enhancements, there isn't anything revolutionary here; in fact, it's all glued together from bits of scripts that we've used before. It's a familiar process: start up on page load; walk through the DOM of the page to find particular elements; load some content from a URL and parse it into an XML DOM; manipulate the DOM of the page to add new content; later on, show and hide an element on click.

Here's the library object's signature:

File: **read-rss.js (excerpt)**

```
var rR = {
  init: function() { ... },
  loadRssData: function(rssURL, liTag, aTag) { ... },
  showAndHide: function(e) { ... },
  addEvent: function(elm, evType, fn, useCapture) { ... }
}

rR.addEvent(window, 'load', rR.init, false);
```

We have three methods to create: `init` to complete initialization, `loadRssData` to pull in the feed content via Sarissa, and `showAndHide` to expand and collapse the blogroll. Firstly, here's the `init` method:

File: **read-rss.js (excerpt)**

```
init: function() {
  if (!document.getElementById || !document.createElement ||
      !document.getElementsByTagName || !Sarissa) return;
  // Find all <a> elements with an "rss" attribute that are
  // inside <ul> elements with id "blogs"
  var blogs = document.getElementById('blogs');
  var as = blogs.getElementsByTagName('a');
  for (var i = 0; i < as.length; i++) {
    var rssURL = as[i].getAttribute('rss');
    if (rssURL) {
      rR.loadRssData(rssURL, as[i].parentNode, as[i]);
    }
  }
},
```

All this does is scan through the content and load matching RSS feeds wherever one is specified.

Here's that `loadRSSData` method, with the XPath processing shown in bold:

File: **read-rss.js (excerpt)**

```
loadRssData: function(rssURL, liTag, aTag) {
  // Asynchronously request the data from the appropriate RSS
  // file, and insert it into the document
  var xmlhttp = Sarissa.getXmlHttpRequest();
  xmlhttp.open('GET', rssURL, true);

  xmlhttp.onreadystatechange = function() {
    if (xmlhttp.readyState == 4) {
      var dom = Sarissa.getDomDocument();
      dom.loadXML(xmlhttp.responseText);
      dom.setProperty('SelectionLanguage', 'XPath');
      dom.setProperty('SelectionNamespaces',
        'xmlns:xhtml="http://www.w3.org/1999/xhtml"');
      Sarissa.setXpathNamespaces(dom,
        'xmlns:my="http://purl.org/rss/1.0/" ' +
      'xmlns:rdf="http://www.w3.org/1999/02/22-rdf-syntax-ns#"'
      );
      var items =
        dom.documentElement.selectNodes('/rdf:RDF/my:item');
      if (items.length > 0) {
        var ul = document.createElement('ul');
        for (var j = 0; j < items.length && j < 5; j++) {
          var i = items[j];
          var li, a, p, tn, dn; // new elements
          var title, desc;      // existing elements

          li = document.createElement('li');
          a = document.createElement('a');
          p = document.createElement('p');

          a.href = i.selectSingleNode('my:link').firstChild.
            nodeValue;
          title = i.selectSingleNode('my:title').firstChild.
            nodeValue;
          desc = i.selectSingleNode('my:description').
            firstChild.nodeValue;
          tn = document.createTextNode(title);
          dn = document.createTextNode(desc);

          a.appendChild(tn);
```

```
                p.appendChild(dn);
                li.appendChild(a);
                li.appendChild(p);
                ul.appendChild(li);
              }
            liTag.appendChild(ul);

            // and since there are some items to show, change the
            // link in the main list to show and hide these items
            rR.addEvent(aTag, 'click', rR.showAndHide, false);
          }
        }
      }
    xmlhttp.send(null);
  },
```

Nearly all of this method comprises the anonymous callback used to receive the RSS content. Once the document is retrieved, we use XPath to put all the items we want into the array named `items`. Four steps are required to prepare the XPath processor inside the browser, yet just one line (that which calls `selectNodes`) actually does the work. The rest of the code simply inserts the retrieved content into the page. It's standard DOM manipulation stuff.

Finally, the event listener is added to the blogroll item that makes the item expandable and collapsible:

File: **read-rss.js (excerpt)**

```
showAndHide: function(e) {
  var el = window.event ? window.event.srcElement :
      e ? e.target : null;
  if (!el) return;

  // ascend the DOM tree until we get to our parent LI
  while (el.nodeName.toLowerCase() != 'li' &&
         el.nodeName.toLowerCase() != 'html') {
    el = el.parentNode;
  }
  if (el.nodeName.toLowerCase() == 'html') return;

  if (el.className.search(/\bshow\b/) == -1) {
    el.className += ' show';
  } else {
    el.className = el.className.replace(/\b ?show\b/, '');
  }
  if (e && e.stopPropagation && e.preventDefault) {
```

```
      e.stopPropagation();
      e.preventDefault();
   } else {
      e.returnValue = false;
      e.cancelBubble = true;
   }
 },
```

The logic merely steps up through the DOM from the node on which the event fired, and flips on or off a CSS class called show on the first li element it finds. This also requires some appropriate style rules to facilitate the show and hide functionality:

File: **read-rss.html** (excerpt)

```
#blogs li ul {
  display: none;
}
#blogs li.show ul {
  display: block;
}
```

That's all that's required to turn the page's blogroll from a simple list of links into a dynamic and up-to-date directory of what's being published on your favorite sites.

Summary

If you need to perform advanced processing on the DOM of a document, or a DOM document fragment, there are alternatives to coding long scripts that manipulate DOM nodes directly. XPath is one such alternative. It provides a powerful query system for extracting complex sets of elements into a JavaScript array, and from there, the world's your oyster!

This quick look at XPath also brings this DHTML book to a close. DHTML techniques are both interesting and useful additions to Web pages, especially with the increasing use of modern browsers. Professional Web developers should never be scared of using quality DHTML techniques. Furthermore, skill with DHTML prepares you well for a host of other XML-based scripting activities—but that's another book! Good luck with your DHTML.

Index

Books for Web Developers from SitePoint

Visit http://www.sitepoint.com/books/
for sample chapters or to order!

3rd Edition
Covers PHP5, MySQL4
and Mac OS X

Build Your Own

Database Driven Website
Using PHP & MySQL

By Kevin Yank

A Practical Step-by-Step Guide

HTML Utopia:

Designing Without Tables
Using CSS

By Dan Shafer

A Practical Step-by-Step Guide

The CSS Anthology

101 Essential Tips, Tricks & Hacks

By Rachel Andrew

Practical Solutions to Common Problems

The PHP Anthology

Object Oriented PHP Solutions
Volume I

By Harry Fuecks

Practical Solutions to Common Problems

PHP 5 Ready

sitepoint

The PHP Anthology

Object Oriented PHP Solutions

Volume II

By Harry Fuecks

Practical Solutions to Common Problems

Build Your Own

ASP.NET Website

Using C# & VB.NET

By Zak Ruvalcaba

A Practical Step-by-Step Guide

Flash
MX 2004

 sitepoint

The Flash Anthology

Cool Effects &
Practical ActionScript

By Steven Grosvenor

Practical Solutions to Common Problems

Kits for Web Professionals from SitePoint

Available exclusively from
http://www.sitepoint.com/

Dreaming of running your own successful Web Design or Development business?

This kit contains everything you need to know!

The Web Design Business Kit

Whether you are thinking of establishing your own Web Design or Development business or are already running one, this kit will teach you everything you need to know to be successful…

Two ring-bound folders and a CD-ROM jam packed with expert advice and proven ready-to-use business documents that will help you establish yourself, gain clients, and grow a profitable freelance business!

Folder 1:
Covers advice on every aspect of running your business:

- *How to sell yourself*
- *How to land bigger jobs*
- *What to charge*
- *How to keep clients for life*
- *How to manage budgets*
- *How to hire & fire employees*
- *And much more*

Folder 2:
Contains 64 essential, ready-to-use business documents:

- *Business Plan*
- *Sample Proposal & Contract*
- *Client Needs Analysis Form*
- *Marketing Surveys*
- *Employment Documents*
- *Financial Documents*
- *And much more*

CD-ROM:
Contains electronic copies of all the business documents in Folder 2, so you can apply them instantly to your business!

- *Ready to apply*
- *Easily customizable*
- *MS Word & Excel format*

The Web Design Business Kit is available exclusively through sitepoint.com. To order, get more information, or to download the free sample chapters, visit:

www.sitepoint.com/books/freelance1/

What our customers have to say about the Web Design Business Kit:

"The Web Design Business Kit (Documents & Manual) is the best marketing tool that I have found! It has changed my business strategies, and my income."

Barb Brown
www.barbbrown.com

"We've already closed 2 deals by following the suggested steps in the kit! I feel like I shouldn't pass the word about this kit to others or risk a lot of good competition!"

Jeneen McDonald
www.artpoststudios.com

"Of everything I have purchase on the Internet, related to bus ness and not, this is (withou question) the most value fc the money spent. Thank you.

Thom Parki
www.twice21.cor